ALIVE
ON THE
INSIDE

ALIVE
ON THE
INSIDE
CULTIVATING
YOUR INNER LIFE

JOHN MYER

PUBLICATIONS

Fort Washington, PA 19034

Alive on the Inside

Published by CLC Publications

USA: P.O. Box 1449, Fort Washington, PA 19034
www.clcpublications.com

UK: Kingsway CLC Trust
Unit 5, Glendale Avenue, Sandycroft, Flintshire, CH5 2QP
www.equippingthechurch.com

Printed in the United States of America

ISBN-13 (paperback): 978-1-61958-336-8
ISBN-13 (e-book): 978-1-61958-337-5

Contents

Acknowledgments

THE EARLIEST FORM of this book first appeared in 2004, when I presented it as a collection of spoken messages to a group of students at the Ohio State University. Some of that audience remains with me today at Hilliard Christian Assembly. The steadfast support of this fellowship down through the years has been an ark to me in the midst of dark waters. For this, I am deeply thankful.

My gratitude also goes to Jeff Friess, and Thad Townsend, church leaders who believed in me and in this book enough to provide a mini-sabbatical for its writing. During that time I was able to finish earlier manuscript drafts while on the banks of Cane River, in my native Louisiana.

Of course I also have to thank my dear wife, Aleisha, who in the final five months of this project gave me the adequate space I needed to complete it. She was willing to lower her expectations of me in the evenings and on week-ends, but never lowered her quota of kindness. This book is not our first rodeo in the publishing world, and I have many other times asked her for such inconvenient grace. She has always given it to me.

Thanks as well must go to the enthusiastic folks at CLC Publications, who responded to the content of this book without being perturbed over the fact that I am relatively unknown in the big, wide, Christian world.

And finally, I must credit the quiet multitude of saints who have left this world, and speak now only through the pages of their books. I owe their ministries a great debt. Theirs is a fraternity I would be honored to one day join, if the Lord delays His coming.

1

The Christian Dilemma of Inward Decay

No one ever reached the climax of vice at one step.

— Juvenale, *Satires*

YOU NEVER FORGET the lessons you learn the hard way. One morning in 1977, I ditched my freshman high school English class and went fishing at Flagon Bayou—a local favorite for kids cutting class. The place was deserted. I had my pick of any spot, so I chose a massive silver maple that had fallen across a narrow part of the creek. The trunk was lying in a way that created a natural platform. I edged out on it, adjusting balance every half-foot. The trick was not to fall in while wearing my school clothes. I steadied myself and launched the lure out in a perfect cast.

That's all I remember.

A nano-second later, I was in six feet of water. Several frenzied moments followed, while I thrashed around in the bayou, then crawled out onto the muddy bank. I glanced over my shoulder, bewildered. The maple was no longer there, only a cloud of wood particles. It had exploded out from under me. That trustworthy-looking trunk had been filled with nothing more than rotten pulp. It had appeared sturdy, but when tested, collapsed under the weight of one skinny, fifteen-year-old boy.

Failure Within the Camp

The object lesson that day so long ago has stayed with me ever since—*things that look strong on the outside are not necessarily strong on the inside.* I've been reminded of this maxim many times over the years. Sadly, some of those reminders have come from the "oaks" and "redwoods" that abound within Christian circles—impressive people who run ministry enterprises, write award-winning, best-selling books, and exercise a considerable amount of influence. Yet religious celebrities fall with disturbing regularity, and when they do, they fall hard—right into material greed, no-fault divorces, tax evasion, fraud, bullying, and varied forms of illicit sexual activity.

Attainment to some sort of standing in the church or in a ministry organization, grants no one immunity. Jesus warned the highly accomplished religious people of his day, "Woe to you, scribes and Pharisees, hypocrites! For you are like whitewashed tombs, which outwardly appear beautiful, but within are full of dead people's bones and all uncleanness. So you also outwardly appear righteous to others, but within you are full of hypocrisy and lawlessness" (Matt. 23:27–28). In teaching this, Jesus exposed the serious contradiction between the inward reality and the outward expression so routinely tolerated by some talented religious people.

Nor do moral collapses happen out of the blue. Healthy trees don't suddenly disintegrate. Catastrophic failures come from long-term interior decay. Jesus said, "Out of the *heart* come evil thoughts, murder, adultery, sexual immorality, theft, false witness, slander. These are what defile a person" (Matt. 15:19–20).

> **WHEN INWARD CORRUPTION GOES UNCHALLENGED, IT WILL FINALLY LEVEL EVEN THE LARGEST TREE.**

Hidden thoughts and desires defile and corrupt a person from within, slowly compromising him or her—yes, even while they might be leading Christian organizations, autographing books, and delivering motivational sermons. When inward corruption goes unchallenged, it will finally level even the largest tree.

A popular youth pastor described the night it happened to him. He had stepped away for a little while, looking for a reprieve from the confines of holy living. He found it with a young woman at a club where he thought no one knew him. After an evening of indiscretion, her eyes welled up with tears and she said, "I thought you were different." It was only then that he realized he knew the woman. She had recently begun attending the large campus Bible study that he led.

He wrote, "Obviously she was having trouble reconciling the Jesus in me at our Wednesday night gatherings, and the Jesus in me she had just slept with."[1] He continues: "It was not like I woke up one day and decided to live a life of duplicity. . . . Time had produced a widening gap between my external profession and my internal character. Those things I claimed to believe and do were far exceeding my reality."[2]

Great trees are not exempt from the incremental process of decay. Sometimes their size only guarantees a louder crash when they fall, to the disillusionment of the hundreds, or even thousands, who follow them.

But the problem is certainly not limited to those who are more visible in the faith community. As we're shaking our heads at the bad behavior of others, here's a memo from the apostle Paul: "You have no excuse, O man, every one of you who judges. For in passing judgment on another, you condemn yourself, because, you, the judge, practice the very same things" (Rom. 2:1). The sins we loathe in others are often present in our own lives, except packaged differently. Beef is beef, whether you find it in hamburgers, meatloaf, or chili.

For some reason, we think we're better because our sins don't make it into the headlines. Yet the lives of typical Christians are studded with things they wouldn't want their church to know, or their spouses, their mothers, their schools, their bosses, the IRS, and sometimes even the police. Tom Davis, author of *Confessions of a Good Christian Guy*, candidly writes, "I go to church, I read my Bible. . . . I've also slept with countless women, spent time in jail . . . *after* I became a Christian."[3] Davis isn't bragging here—far from it! He merely points out what happens when a believer's non-involvement with active faith allows decomposition to spread throughout his or her life.

I think of myself, a man dynamically saved, with over thirty years in the faith. I still deal with numerous petty insecurities, lusts that can scarcely be tamed, anxieties that can't be warded off except with a whip and a chair. The devil seems to treat my life like a drive-through, checking to see if I'm ready to give in to him, since it has been a week since I've last told him, "No." While we lament the failures of our leaders and other poster children of the faith, we seem to be a collection of all their faults in miniature. Big trees succumb to decay, falling with noise and drama, but be warned that little trees fall in far greater numbers, except without the fanfare.

A Problem Camouflaged

We may hardly be aware of the spiritual crises riddling our churches. Even as neat, well-oiled congregations busy themselves with numerical growth, facilities, programs, efficiency, and pragmatism, trouble is typically brewing at another level.

A husband teeters on the precipice of leaving his wife for another woman, even as he sits with his family on Sunday morning, mouthing the words to "Amazing Grace." In the same church service, a young man seethes with rage against a colleague at work, and makes plans to vandalize that person's car after dark. A teenage girl who plays guitar in the worship band has begun sending indecent photos of herself to her boyfriend's cell phone. A woman who works the church reception desk has a shopping addiction that is bringing her family to the brink of bankruptcy. An older man, dragged to church yet again by his spouse, sits almost comatose, wishing for the service, and his boredom, to end. An older woman glares across the room at a girl wearing too much makeup, and rehearses the complaint she will make about it to the church youth leader.

None of these dark, internal states are unusual for sinners. The real problem, rather, lies in the fact that we have learned to accept them as normal. Our religious pop culture either camouflages them, or draws a blank when it comes to confronting them.

The Difficulty of Self-Diagnosis

How is *your* Christian life doing? In order to answer that question, right now you're probably assessing your church attendance. Maybe you'll factor in mission work, Bible reading plans, bad habits you've successfully kicked, and your faithfulness to charities. In other words, you might gauge the condition of your Christian life based on religiously defined externals. But this book is firstly about the *interior* Christian life—the private, secret, inward, first-person life—and yes, sometimes the felt, inner experience made possible by the Holy Spirit living in you.

How is *that* dimension of your Christian life doing?

Not everyone can give a clear answer to that question. In fact, many of us aren't even comfortable talking about it. The Christian inner life experience strikes us as nebulous. We think of goosebumps, cold chills, or bursts of euphoria. How can anyone measure something so hopelessly subjective?

We've also heard people talk about "impressions," "still small voices," God "telling" them to do this or that, and since we don't seem to have these experiences, we wonder if there's something wrong with us. Or with the people who say they have them.

The Tricks and Traps of Spiritual Experience

I can sympathize with these less than favorable feelings. After thirty years of ministry work, I've witnessed my fair share of questionable spirituality. I'm speaking of folks who made reckless decisions to buy or sell, start or quit, do or not do, based on alleged religious feelings from beyond. They gave God the glory, so to speak, but it's hard to say God wanted it. Some abandoned healthy spiritual pursuits in favor of flamboyant, miraculous phenomena. Others allowed their "spirituality" to overrule biblical doctrine and morals. In the name of obeying sensations they thought were from God, they disobeyed His clearly written word. Most of these situations left me dealing with fallout which usually included damage to the church.

In view of all this, why would I write a book that explores and encourages spiritual experience when it can be so easily misunderstood and misapplied? Because the opposite extreme is just as unacceptable. An arid, stale Christian heart can do as much damage to us as a heart deceived by subjective fantasy. But in our zeal to avoid mystical excess, we err on the side of caution. We assure ourselves that a handful of baseline behaviors are all that's needed for a fulfilling Christian life.

WHAT HAPPENS WHEN THE CORRECT BUTTONS GET PUSHED AND THE DIFFICULTIES STILL REMAIN?

Consider the advice we give one another when trying to remedy spiritual troubles. We say, "Read your Bible" or "Go to church more," "Tithe faithfully," "Get involved in ministry," or simply, "Behave!" It's as though no problem could possibly appear that these things couldn't handle.

Sometimes such basic advice is needed, but what happens when the correct buttons get pushed and the difficulties still remain? Even more humiliating, what happens when, after you prescribe these things for others, you eventually find yourself in a crisis of your own, and the advice you previously gave out doesn't work for you?

It reminds me of a Christian I knew who had begun backsliding. When friends tried to help her, she said, "Don't tell me to do things I've told everybody else to do!" The dirty little secret she seemed to know was that most religious admonitions won't work as advertised—at least not with the mechanical certainty we claim.

Our faith cannot be limited to a holding pattern of applied principles and taught behaviors. If you suspect that being a Christian must be more than a go-to panel of worn-out switches and levers, you're correct. A large part of this book's emphasis therefore, will clarify how the Holy Spirit has primed you for a rich inner life and all its associated experiences of tasting, enjoying, and participating in salvation.

Alive on the Inside

We will begin at the starting point of every true experience of inner life for a Christian—the momentous occasion of the second birth. Without a doubt, the term "born again" has made it into the dictionary of mainstream culture. It is hard to say, though, how much those using or abusing the term know what it actually means. We can only move closer to defining it after clearing away the political, cultural, and religious, baggage wrongly attached to it. Broken into component parts, "born again" simply signifies "born," referring to life conceived and generated, and "again," meaning a repeat. Thus, born again means a *re*generation.

Jesus coined "born again" and He did not intend it to become a metaphor borrowed for use at business seminars. The new birth occurs through an authentic transmission of spiritual life. When we heard and believed the gospel of Jesus, the Holy Spirit entered us as "the Spirit of life" (Rom.

8:2), and enlivened our previously dead spiritual condition. We were born anew, that is, "born of the Spirit" (John 3:8). Eternal life became our current possession, and although it is too grand to completely apprehend until the next age, we can at least begin to taste it now, from within. All the thoughts in this book rest upon that premise.

Religion often encourages a certain amount of fudge factor when it comes to emotion, zeal, solemnity, and power—a "fake it 'til you make it" approach. But, as I have heard it said, a Christian life of manufactured sentiments will begin to feel as though we are pushing a wet noodle uphill. It simply isn't us. Such "help" isn't needed, though. Without coercion, real spiritual affections spring out of a believer's inner life. Just as a newborn baby does not need to be taught to cry, or to spit out sour things, eternal life needs no instruction. It produces in us sensations, impulses, and responses, like every other life.

One of those immediate experiences relates to an enlivened conscience. This territory of the human interior had been mostly sleepy, numbed by sin, and in the main, only responsive when we offended human standards of conduct. Men consider their conscience an annoyance, if not an enemy. Washed by the blood of Christ, and touched by eternal life, though, conscience becomes a witness capable of agreeing with the Holy Spirit. It turns into a window through which we can perceive the glory of God.

And the first revelatory flash of divine brilliance inspired in us a range of impulses, though not all equally occurring in every person. Some of us cried, others praised. Many were provoked into stumbling, happy prayers, while others sunk into quiet, awestruck humility. There were silly songs, marathon Bible readings, and unusual generosity. These purely knee-jerk reactions to the beauty of Christ made it apparent that we were in possession of a newly enlivened ability to worship. It was worlds away from the stifling thing we once labeled as worship.

> WE OFTEN FALL SHORT OF THE TRUTH, OR LEAP BEYOND IT—EXAGGERATE OR NEGLECT ASPECTS OF SPIRITUAL LIFE.

Furthermore, bound up with our new inward reality was not only a budding distaste for sin, but a disinclination toward even the possibility of getting involved with darkness. We began to intuitively sense being "warned away" from certain courses of action once so welcome to us. Alternatively, we seemed encouraged into another, less recognizable way, that included goodness, holiness, and self-sacrifice. These directive impressions alerted us to the fact that we possessed a fresh, enlivened awareness of the mind of God.

You could call this description of conscience, worship, and intuition a composite snapshot of the inner life. Unfortunately, though, we aren't always the picture of spiritual health. We have often either fallen short of the truth, or leapt beyond it—exaggerated aspects of spiritual life, or neglected them. Course corrections will be needed from a stout diet of Scripture, and a discipline of prayer, for in order to flourish, every life must be fed.

Nor is this new adventure a solitary enterprise. Rugged individualism might have become the rallying cry of many believers today, but a cursory reading of Scripture will show God is calling in a different direction. A new birth has taken place in the depths of our being, but it equally finds home in the native soil of the church. The faith community is a family where we give and receive, where our bond is not flesh and blood, but eternal life. In fact, a person born of the Spirit orients toward relational normalcy. This happens not only between church members, but in all our ethical relationships, from marital to parental to the workplace, as Paul and Peter consistently mention in their epistles. When we rightly experience the new birth, it saves us from becoming self-centered relational misfits, making others miserable with our company, and vice-versa.

Surprisingly perhaps, the final barometer of our inward condition lies not in feelings, but in deeds of kindness and mercy, generosity, and love. Some Christians disdain referring to works as spiritual, yet we all know there's something wrong when a believer claims transcendent spirituality while being stingy, vindictive, lustful, crude, self-absorbed, or numb to the needs of others. As those who learn the life within, and thus "learn Christ" (Eph. 4:20, NASB), we should never neglect the fruit of Christ-like character and good works. After all, behavior always functions as an indicator of what has privately gained ascendancy within us.

How's your Christian life doing?

By the end of this book, I hope you can respond in a new way. Rather than consulting the religious culture, or your own self-defined standard, or comparing yourself to that other person who seems to have it all together, you'd reflect upon what is emanating out of your new birth. You'd consider the clarity of your conscience. You'd think of the glories of Christ you've been enjoying in your worship, your obedience to the new things you're learning of God, your blessed fellowship in the community of believers, and the overflow of all those splendid things into good works.

And all because you're alive on the inside.

2

The New Life—Real, or Religious Delusion?

*Doubt, indulged and cherished, is in danger of becoming
denial; but if honest, and bent on through investigation,
it may soon lead to full establishment in the truth.*

—Tyron Edwards, *A Dictionary of Thoughts*

A ND THAT'S WHY I dropped out of church and
stopped believing in God . . ."

Too many internet videos have recently closed with this
sort of statement. "Deconversions," as they are called, often
follow on the heels of other people's failures: the moral collapse of a church leader; a beloved minister whose dastardly
secret life is only discovered after death; a church planter who
bears more resemblance to Herod than to Christ; a Christian
celebrity who constantly tweets uncharitable remarks.

The list goes on—excessive earthly riches, coverups,
political tantrums. Based on these things erupting from
the flesh of others, some people, shocked and disillusioned,
will make the worst decision of their lives, and walk away
from Jesus.

Regardless of how much it is their own poor decision, however, we cannot dodge their parting question: "If the Christian faith is truly supernatural, why is it not more evident in the lives of so many Christians?" Where is the spiritual power we talk about so much?

A lot of the faithful secretly wonder, as well. In the face of failures great and small, perhaps we've begun to think the gospel over-sells and under-delivers.

In fact, more than a few of us have stopped short of the life of God, thinking we've found it in low-powered forms of Christian culture. Because we champion family values, stand on the correct side of moral issues, vote the right way, and homeschool, we think we've found what Jesus is all about. We assume we've struck oil. Is it any surprise when we're *under*-whelmed with our own discovery? If anemic religious products are all there is to being a Christian, God is not in any sense the ultimate, but only a way to help us find the ultimate.

Could it be there is no "new life" at all—at least nothing more potent than simple self-generated enthusiasm? Duty on steroids, perhaps? A generation of young evangelicals suspect as much. Worse, many view their cynicism as somehow fashionable, a fact easily seen in online forums. Dallas Willard writes,

> For centuries now, our culture has cultivated the idea that the *skeptical* person is always smarter than one who believes. You can be almost as stupid as a cabbage as long as you *doubt*. . . . Therefore only a very hardy individualist or social rebel—or one desperate for another life—stands a chance of discovering the substantiality of the spiritual life today. Today it is the skeptics who are the social conformists, though because of powerful intellectual propaganda they continue to enjoy thinking of themselves as wildly individualistic and unbearably bright.[1]

What Exactly Did Jesus Come to Bring?

Against this tide of skepticism Jesus Christ has a message: "I came that they might have life and have it abundantly" (John 10:10). His reason for coming—being born, dying on a cross, rising from the dead—was for us to have an abundance of the life that is uniquely His. Jesus refers to life as an actual bequest from Him, something you were not born with, nor could you ever appropriate on your own. It is a life larger than the physical, created life the Bible designates with the Greek word *bios*. It is also different from the soulish life of the mind, emotion, and will, that Scripture defines with Greek words like *nous* and *psyche*. The exact word Jesus used when speaking of the life He brought was *zoe*.

> ## ETERNAL LIFE—*ZOE*—IS INCOMPARABLE, INDESTRUCTIBLE, AND INCORRUPTIBLE. IT BELONGS IN A CATEGORY OF ITS OWN.

Though *zoe* could comprehensively describe the whole of life in general (hence, the use of it in our word zoology), Jesus elevated, restructured, and radicalized the term by further defining it as "eternal" in John 10:28. Of course, the added thought of being eternal, makes *zoe* incomparable, indestructible, and incorruptible. It clearly belongs in a category of its own.

And as Scripture unfurls, this fact only becomes clearer:

- **Eternal *zoe* is Christ Himself.** Jesus said, "I am the resurrection and the *life*" (John 11:25). He also said, "I am the way, the truth, and the *life*. No one comes to the Father except through me" (14:6).

- **Eternal *zoe* is the Holy Spirit.** He is called "the Spirit of *life*" (Rom. 8:2).

- **Eternal *zoe* causes us to know the Father and the Son.** Jesus prayed to God, saying, "And this is eternal *life*, that they know you, the only true God, and Jesus Christ whom you have sent" (John 17:3).

- **Eternal *zoe* frees us from spiritual death.** "For the law of the Spirit of *life* has set you free in Christ Jesus from the law of sin and death" (Rom. 8:2). It also delivers us from the second death—"This is the second death, the lake of fire. And if anyone's name was not found written in the book of *life*, he was thrown into the lake of fire" (Rev. 20:14–15).

- **Eternal *zoe* is the domain of God's ongoing work of salvation within us.** "For if while we were enemies we were reconciled to God by the death of his Son, much more, now that we are reconciled, shall we be saved by his *life*" (Rom. 5:10).

Obviously, then, the "abundant life" Jesus brought is not the equivalent of Cadillacs and cash, much to the contrary of grossly misguided, materialistic preaching. Yes, God blesses us with creature comforts, and grants gifts related to our physical existence. We are grateful for these, because each day brings a need for daily bread, in some form or another. But the immeasurably valuable sacrifice of Christ must grant an immeasurably valuable outcome—like for like. It would be a perverse mismatch if Christ died so we could accumulate worldly trinkets. "God so loved the world that He gave His only begotten Son, that whoever believes in Him should not perish, but have everlasting life" (John 3:16, NKJV). He yielded up what He loved most, His only Son. In turn, His Son yielded up His life. These are two great facts. Great plus great cannot equal less. The climactic note of John 3:16 does not end with private jets, tailored suits, successful businesses, fulfilled personal dreams, or even flourishing ministries. No, not even heaven itself. The sacrifice of Calvary must result in nothing less than the unsearchably rich life of God found only in Christ, for "In Him was life, and the life was the light of men" (John 1:4). Jesus came to give us this kind of life, not to endlessly spruce up our old one.

If you find yourself thinking of eternal life as boring, puzzling spiritual stuff, and conclude there's nothing to be found in it, please let the voice of truth check you. The Father didn't give the Son, and the Son didn't give His life as a mirage. The pivotal moments of Calvary and the emptied tomb actually gave something—eternal life, which is supposed to be a high-definition reality for us all. It is "that which is truly life" (1 Tim. 6:19).

The People of Scripture Have Their Say

When we read the Bible and study the people recorded within it, we see them experiencing the very life we're talking about. Old Testament saints extensively prefigure it as they enjoy a foretaste of coming New Testament realities. Later, New Testament believers enjoy it as a foretaste of eternity. All of them borrow metaphors and similes from the sensory world, like seeing, tasting, hearing, smelling, to somehow describe what they are coming into contact with.

David sets the tone for the Old Testament faithful: "As a deer pants for flowing streams, so pants my soul for you, O God" (Ps. 42:1); "Oh, *taste* and *see* that the LORD is good!" (34:8); "With you is the fountain of life; in your light do we *see* light" (36:9); "How sweet are your words to my *taste*, sweeter than honey to my mouth!" (119:103). Solomon, as well, penned an entire book—Song of Solomon—that transcends mere romance, and manages to become a foreshadowing of a believer's relationship with Christ.

This theme continues among the prophets, such as Jeremiah, who said, "Your words were found, and I ate them, and your words became to me a joy and the delight of my heart" (Jer. 15:16). Although the Old Testament revelation was incomplete, it was not without some measure of reality (see Heb. 11:13, 39–40). Its principal voices rise up in agreement that spiritual life is not imaginary.

And what about those portrayed in the New Testament? Luke Timothy Johnson declares, "It is literally impossible to read the New Testament at any length without encountering claims that something is happening to these people, and it is happening *now*."[2]

The New Testament also borrows examples from the physical world to portray what *zoe* life is like. Jesus said, "My sheep *hear* my voice" (John 10:27). Paul said that "we are the *aroma* of Christ . . . a *fragrance* from life to life," and that "we all, with unveiled face, [are] *beholding* the glory of the Lord" (2 Cor. 2:15–16; 3:18). Peter speaks of those who "have *tasted* that the Lord is good" (1 Pet. 2:3). The book of Revelation repeatedly calls out to all believers, "He who has an ear, let him *hear* what the Spirit says to the churches" (Rev. 2:7, 11, 17, 29; 3:6, 13, 22).

Johnson comments, "The experience expressed by these texts involve power, but power of a peculiar sort."[3] It is the language of "intense intimacy and communication."[4]

Looking at the redeemed people of Scripture, we find a flow of "Excessive love, flagrant mercy, radical affection, exorbitant charity, immoderate faith, intemperate hope, inordinate love,"[5] as Barry L. Callen describes it. The reason? *Zoe* life touched them. Now their united testimony resounds from Scripture, insisting that "This life is real!"

A Flawed Church with a Perfect Life

The sheer weight of biblical witness alone ought to settle any doubts about the current relevance of eternal life. But we Christians often respond to our scriptural counterparts in a nicely dismissive manner, saying, "Oh, those folks were *biblical.*" We think the life that the apostles and prophets experienced has already played out during the golden oldies of godliness. They were special. Whatever they once had is no longer available to mere mortals who now have kids in soccer, or work mundane jobs.

Yet that same wonderful life documented in the Bible has burst off the page into the very flow of time. We now have the record of church history—the flesh and blood accounts of believers not unlike ourselves, who have lived in every imaginable context, and under every conceivable circumstance. They testify to sharing a commonly held, peculiar inward vitality that for two thousand years has translated into unquenchable joy, lovely virtue, and phenomenal endurance.

We read of Polycarp, who, before being burned at the stake, prepared dinner for his Roman persecutors when they came to seize him. They later ordered him to curse Christ, and he replied, "Eighty and six years have I served Him, and He hath done me no wrong; how then can I blaspheme my King who saved me?"[6] These are not the words of a contrarian, of an obstinate, stubborn religious personality! Polycarp's response smells of a long, cultivated affection for Christ made possible through the presence of a superior inward life.

Likewise, when the furnace of suffering appeared, believers often found indomitable joy. A young mother named Perpetua wrote, after standing trial and being sentenced to face the lions in the arena, "We were condemned to the beasts, and we returned to prison in high spirits."[7] Frequently, their endurance confounded those who persecuted them. One such believer, Blandina, "was filled with such power, that those who by turns kept torturing her in every way from dawn until evening were worn out and exhausted, and themselves confessed defeat from lack of aught else to do to her; they marveled that breath still remained in a body all mangled and covered with gaping wounds."[8]

> **MORE BELIEVERS MAY HAVE DIED FOR CHRIST IN THE TWENTIETH CENTURY THAN IN ALL THE PREVIOUS CENTURIES COMBINED.**

The enduring reality of *zoe* life stretches from those early times all the way into our contemporary moment. It has not abated in the least. Though it is impossible to say with certainty, records suggest that perhaps more believers died for Christ in the twentieth century than in all the previous centuries combined.[9] If that statement is true, then the one-hundred-year landmark we passed scarcely twenty years ago was the bloodiest in the history of the church.

The files of Christian relief organizations like Voice of the Martyrs bristle with the accounts of both the horrendous sufferings and the remarkable responses of the believers who bore them:

- Christians in North Korea were made to lay down in a row, while a bulldozer was driven across their bodies. As they arranged themselves for death, they managed to sing the words of a final hymn—"More Love to Thee, O Christ."[10]

- A Christian in a Soviet prison was finally released after a long internment in a freezing cell, and many beatings. However, the police raided his tiny apartment soon after, confiscating, and destroying a unique collection of devotional hymns he had spent years crafting. Following this, he quickly composed another. "I worship You with gratitude for all You ever gave me, but also for everything, Beloved, You took from me. You do all things well, and I will trust in You."[11]

- Under threat of death, a pastor denounced two young Chinese women he himself had once led to believe the gospel. They refused to reject Christ, and before being shot, thanked the pastor for having introduced them to Jesus. They also begged him not to be swallowed up in grief later on over what he had done, as Judas Iscariot had, but to repent like Peter.[12]

This tiny sample of anecdotes confirms that over the course of twenty centuries, eternal life has never stopped manifesting itself in devotion to Christ. Neither genocides, slavery, tyrants, or hostile, ideologically driven governments have ever been able to extinguish it.

The endurance of this abundant life is impressive, if not shocking. However, its virtues are also noteworthy down through the stream of history. Justin Martyr, one of the first church apologists, wrote this now-famous description of early Christians:

> Those who once delighted in fornication now embrace chastity alone . . . we who once took most pleasure in accumulating wealth and property now . . . share with

everyone who needs; we who hated and killed one another and would not associate with men of different
tribes because of their different customs now, since the
coming of Christ, live familiarly with them and pray for
our enemies.[13]

Tertullian, another second century luminary, wrote of
what pagans said about Christians at that time: "'See,' say
they, 'how they love each other! . . . how ready they are to
die for each other!'"[14] Clearly, the Romans didn't know what
to make of this. One of them, a notorious opponent of the
Christian faith, a Roman emperor named Julian the Apostate, complained that the Christians "feed not only their own
poor, but ours also."[15]

These observations have rightly become part of the
historical record because they document humans behav-
ing under the influence of eternal life. Over time, such
virtuous spirituality yielded practical outcomes that shaped
this world. For instance, the Christian love of knowledge
and truth birthed institutions of higher learning, such as
Harvard, Yale, Princeton, Oxford, and Cambridge. Their
love of service and charity spawned the concept of modern
hospitals. Their love of righteousness elevated standards
of justice in legal codes throughout the world. Their love
of holiness condemned various perversions and vices that
tended to destroy human dignity. Their love of creativity
produced some of the greatest art ever seen and music ever
heard. And yet these were only the by-products of men and
women alive in Christ.

For twenty centuries, the Word of life has swept the
globe, igniting movements great and small, and bringing the
knowledge of Jesus Christ. The results have typically fallen

outside the unity of any particular denomination, sometimes traveling so far apart from other traditions, that believers must consciously practice the Pauline instruction to "keep the unity of the faith." Some of the founders of these various streams have written of their beginning, or triggering stimuli. John Wesley (1703–1791) testified that his heart had been "strangely warmed" after listening to an exposition of Martin Luther's preface to the Book of Romans. This inward experience of God's presence supplied an early impetus for his ministry, and he would go on to phenomenal fruitfulness as a key figure in the Great Awakening.

D.L. Moody (1837–1899) said,

> I was crying all the time that God would fill me with His Spirit. Well, one day, in the city of New York—oh, what a day!—I cannot describe it, I seldom refer to it; it is almost too sacred an experience to name. Paul had an experience of which he never spoke for fourteen years. I can only say that God revealed Himself to me, and I had such an experience of His love that I had to ask Him to stay His hand. I went to preaching again. The sermons were not different; I did not present any new truths; and yet hundreds were converted. I would not now be placed back where I was before that blessed experience if you should give me all the world—it would be as the small dust of the balance.[16]

Moody went on to reach millions of souls, and shape contemporary evangelism.

Nor were these kinds of experiences a fleeting impulse, only felt at the start of a great ministry work. Charles Spurgeon (1834–1892), one of the most prolific preachers in church history, said,

As for myself, my consciousness of being a new man in Christ Jesus is often as sharp and crisp as my consciousness of being in existence. I know that I am not solely what I was by my first birth. I feel within myself another life—a second and a higher vitality—that often has to contend with my lower self, and by that very contention makes me conscious of its existence.[17]

These few quotes are only representative of millions who have realized new life in Christ. As this life flowed from the Savior's wounded side, it reached a tremendous array of times, countries, and people groups, redeeming and reclaiming them. They have variously described this inward reality as "filled with the Spirit," "baptized in the Spirit," "walking by faith," "sanctified," "enlivened," "revived," "illuminated," and "entering union."

These terms, and the way they are used, may vary, more or less, in their theological accuracy. The explanation of the experience may also differ as to whether it is only crisis-related, or a continuum we are to some degree aware of daily. The effort to name and describe it, however, serves to remind us that a diverse group of people throughout history have encountered a life power held inside the saving faith of Christ.

Sadly, whenever Christians deviated from the *zoe* life within them, shameful things occurred. We strayed into the tar pits of political power, violence, hatred between races, sexual vice, insularity, materialism, and miscellaneous social evils. Believers have unfortunately often understood their faith in the lowest possible way, as though they were in possession of something whose ends could be achieved through coercion, or worse, oppression.

However, down through church history, the Holy Spirit has always worked to open closed Bibles, and clear calcified hearts, so *zoe* life could be fully realized once again. As the church at large, we must humbly admit our story is too often that of deeply flawed people who are easily distracted. Still, the great chorus of the redeemed tells of a far superior life contained within us—the same life that now belongs to you.

Participation in the Now

Even in the face of so many praiseworthy examples, again there's the contemporary dismissal—"Oh, those folks were *historical.*" In other words, we shouldn't take them seriously because they were outstanding. They made history. Most of us will never even see our names in a news piece, let alone an encyclopedia. Spiritual life and experience seems to be the domain of those destined for greatness, so the average Joe can probably forget about it.

Yet we must never give in to spiritual mediocrity. David Goetz, author of *Death by Suburb*, assures us the life is there, waiting even for those mired in the modern daily grind:

> The outward physical world of SUVs and minivans, drearily earth-toned subdivisions, golden retrievers and chocolate labs, and endless Saturday morning soccer games is only one dimension. There's another dimension or two. This much thicker world is a world in which I am alive to God and alive to others, a world in which what I don't yet own defines me. It's a higher existence, a plane where I am not the sum total of my house size, SUV, vacations, kids' report cards—and that which I still need to acquire.[18]

All of the biblical and extra-biblical testimonies put together are like Joshua and Caleb bringing back an enthusiastic report of the good land. They have a gigantic cluster of grapes slung between them as proof of its richness. "Let us go up at once and occupy it," they say (Num. 13:30). Yet we are trapped in skepticism, not able to see over that horizon, and imagine that even if we could, we would not be able to enter. For all the wonderful things said about it, *zoe* life tends to sound like nothing more than a lovely rumor, forever someone else's but never yours.

And yet as a believer in Jesus, it is yours, and you are supposed to experience it right now! John wrote, "Whoever has the Son, *has* life" (1 John 5:12). That means if you have Jesus now, you have eternal life now. It would be terrible to possess something so incredible, and not be able to enjoy it.

It's like an odd piece of pop art I saw featured in a magazine—a slice of chocolate cream pie, cast in solid aluminum. It was perfect in every detail, down to the ripples of the cream. You couldn't taste it, savor it, or swallow it. All you could do was look at it. Eternal life is not this way. It is accessible for us in the here and now, even before we go on to fully enjoy it in eternity.

> WE WEREN'T SUPPOSED TO RECEIVE
> A CARGO FULL OF DIVINE TREASURE,
> ONLY TO DRY-DOCK IT UNTIL WE DIE.

Perhaps the difficulty lies in the reductionist way we view the gospel—as though the forgiveness of sins is the only real bequest of salvation, with nothing to follow. None of the apostles believed in that kind of truncated message. Paul celebrated the fact that the Ephesian believers had received so much from God, including predestination, adoption, forgiveness, and the sealing of the Holy Spirit. Then he prayed for them in chapter 3, asking God to grant them the *experience* of all the things they'd gotten. Paul knew we weren't supposed to receive a cargo full of divine treasure, only to dry-dock it until we die.

This was also the point of John 15, when Jesus said, "Abide in me and I in you. . . . I am the vine; you are the branches" (15:4–5). It makes sense that Jesus chose the example of vine and branches to illustrate our relationship with Him, because it is impossible to portray a closer or more ongoing and life-giving relationship than that of branch and vine. He was telling the disciples, *Now that you've been hooked up to Me in a life union, stay there. In the daily sense, keep your head and your heart there.* If we want the ongoing experience of salvation, and not just an invisible positional truth, we must abide in Him. That is how the reality of God in us continues.

The quality of our Christian experience, rich or poor, directly corresponds to how much we remain in this inner life flow. Not long ago, I packed some grapes in a bag with my lunch. I had not plucked them individually, but broke off an entire branch of them. A week later, I reached into the bag to empty out the contents, and grabbed something that felt like a bundle of toothpicks. It was the branch, now dried into brittle wood. The few grapes remaining on it were mushy and unappealing, like frog eyeballs in an anatomy class—something you would never want to pop into your mouth.

We would never say that the condition of those grapes proved that the inner life of the vine was fictitious, superstitious, or imaginary—worse yet, that the grapes hadn't tried hard enough. Similarly, when defeats afflict the Christian population, we often assume that the individuals concerned were never saved to begin with, or they lost their salvation.

However, some of us find those explanations unsatisfactory, and cynicism creeps in. We begin to wonder if anything of faith is real, including the much-celebrated new life in Christ.

Returning to the blighted little cluster of grapes in my lunch bag, a better explanation would be that, though the branch had been green and flexible with appealing fruit attached to it, separation from the "experience" of the vine— even for a few days—had diminished its freshness. As Jesus said, "Apart from me, you can do nothing" (John 15:5).

Conversely, every triumph we experience demonstrates the ability of "vine" life. The apostle John wrote, "whoever says he abides in him ought to walk in the same way in which he walked" (1 John 2:6). Genuine abiding literally reproduces the walk of Jesus in this world—not an obscure copy made by religious efforts. And so, if we learn to abide in Him, we also will enjoy, in the freshest sense possible, the life showcased on the pages of Scripture, and exemplified by others in church history.

Believers never need to settle for a religious charade. New life exists, a life above anything in this mortal sphere. Based on the fact that "the free gift of God is eternal life in Christ Jesus our Lord" (Rom. 6:23), and that the Lord Jesus gave up everything so we could have it, we should "bet the farm" on it. It is worth any hardship, can make up for any loss, and can uphold any burden. It is our hope, our future, our enablement, and our *now*.

3

The Miracle Within

Christ alone, of all the philosophers, magicians, etc., has affirmed eternal life as the most important certainty, the infinity of time, the futility of death, the necessity and purpose of serenity and devotion. He lived serenely, as an artist greater than all other artists, scorning marble and clay and paint, working in the living flesh. In other words, this peerless artist, scarcely conceivable with the blunt instrument of our modern, nervous and obtuse brains, made neither statues nor paintings nor books. He maintained in no uncertain terms that he made . . . living men, immortals.

— Vincent Van Gogh

IN 1995, JEAN-DOMINIQUE BAUBY, editor of the French magazine *Elle*, had a stroke and fell into a coma. He eventually awoke, and was mentally aware, but physically paralyzed—a condition called locked-in syndrome. He couldn't speak, so using his one good eye (the other had to be sewn shut), Bauby blinked out in alphabetic code a manuscript that later became the book *The Diving Bell and the Butterfly*. It went on to sell more than a million copies. Shortly after he wrote it, he died of pneumonia.

Bauby experienced something we would find unimaginable—complete loss of connectivity, a claustrophobic existence closed off from the world, with distorted hearing at best, and only the memories of taste and smell. The scenario is nightmarish, for we often measure the quality of human experience by our ability to access it with our senses. In a situation where nothing goes in, and nothing goes out, we would feel buried alive, entombed in a smothering static state.

Bauby's condition is actually a prime example of fallen humanity, except the paralysis humankind suffers is not outward and physical, but internal and spiritual, toward God. Few Christians understand how significant this really is. According to us, salvation was remarkable because we escaped bad attitudes, and evil behavior. According to the book of Romans, this is correct. It tells us "all have sinned" (3:23). However, the book of Ephesians tells us all were *dead* (see 2:1). Being dead is far more serious than being bad.

> **YOU. WERE. DEAD. YOU MUST COME TO TERMS WITH THIS BEFORE YOU CAN APPRECIATE BEING ALIVE.**

We get a typological window into this thought by looking at Mosaic law. There, more strenuous ceremonial cleansing and wait times are commanded over the pollution resulting from contact with death, than over lawbreaking deeds, which could be cleansed immediately through sacrificial blood (see Lev. 11, 21; Num. 5–6).

You. Were. Dead. You must come to terms with this before you can appreciate being alive. Your story does not start with doing evil, but with interior death. And it all originated

with Adam. "Sin came into the world through one man, and
death through sin" (Rom. 5:12).

We understand the sin part of that equation. The role of
death, however, is harder to grasp. If it weren't for the testimony of scripture, we would have little idea of what death meant,
and the sheer strangeness of it. After Adam "died," his heart
continued beating. On a psychological level, he was still able
to think. But in his deepest recesses, his spirit withered and
darkened. Though he had previously walked with God, suddenly he sensed a profound disconnection from his Creator.

> And they heard the sound of the LORD God walking in the
> garden in the cool of the day, and the man and his wife hid
> themselves from the presence of the LORD God among the

THE BODY
*Biologically alive,
but fragile and dying*

**THE SOUL
(MIND/EMOTIONS/WILL)**

**THE
HUMAN SPIRIT**
Dead to God

*Active, but estranged
from God*

The Deadened Human Condition

trees of the garden. But the LORD God called to the man and said to him, "Where are you?" And he said, "I heard the sound of you in the garden, and I was afraid, because I was naked, and I hid myself." (Gen. 3:8–10)

Just that quickly, the prior friendship the couple had enjoyed with God, had been replaced with estrangement, awkwardness, shame, and avoidance.

If the situation were not tragic enough, this spiritually dead man went on to have children, passing down his broken state to all of us. "Death spread to *all* men because all sinned" (Rom. 5:12). And rather than this corruption diluting as it proliferated throughout our race, it intensified. Victor Kuligin says, "We have taken this original sin which was simple disobedience, and underscored it millions of times; we have eaten the fruit until our bellies are gorged."[1] Full of death, we were affected in myriad ways by an existential vacuum within, where there was no spiritual sight, no sound, no feeling.

Death cannot be solved by being forgiven. It needs something to occur fundamentally miraculous. Jesus referred to this as being "born again," a radical transformation involving a new beginning with a new life.

False Gods, False Life

Never confuse spiritual death with inactivity. In the days before the miracle of new birth, we were all busy. In fact, when spiritual death is paired with an active intellectual life, men are alive to *everything else* except God.[2] Your pre-Jesus history, as well as mine, was full of clawing at anyone, or anything, in the hopes it could give you life.

In the meantime, our human spirit, abused, neglected, and mummified, silently mourned the absence of the God for whom we were made. We were unable to sense, and experience Him. We could not find Him, and in a bizarre twist of logic, we would have preferred it to stay that way. Humans have little awareness of their own darkened state. We fancy ourselves seekers of God until we are in danger of actually finding Him. C.S. Lewis, a man who had once harbored a certain moral dread of the biblical God, wrote, "Amiable agnostics will talk cheerfully about man's search for God. To me, as I then was, they might as well have talked about the mouse's search for the cat."[3]

We have feeble, innate registrations of desire for God, but our wayward minds deliberately misinterpret them as a need for other things. Even while we yearn for Him, we do not want to admit it, like a child who is exhausted, but becomes enraged when her mother suggests taking a nap. Emotional resistance to God is woven throughout our inner being.[4] As Clifford Williams puts it, God is a threat to "the supremacy of self,"[5] so we carefully side-step our obvious need for God, because we want to retain control.

It is no coincidence that the first of the Ten Commandments prohibits idolatry. In our fallen condition, we instinctively, by sinful impulse, handpick alternate gods. For a while these substitutes seem to help us transcend the monotony, and grayness of human life, delivering short term doses of joy. They help us *feel* alive, even if, in the most profound way, we are not.

Each of these choices offers a fleeting taste of life wished for, but they cannot ultimately deliver. Idols, after all, are nothing more than crude imitations of God, and His life.

As a lonely, insecure teen, Louie chose bourbon to be his crutch. During his tumultuous young adult years, it seemed to grant him superpowers. The more he drank, the more funny, confident, and relaxed he became. But then slowly, the bourbon chose him. At some point, it began taking from him more than it gave. By then, it was too late for Louie to simply quit and walk away.

And so his addiction-recovery cycle continues to this day, with him achieving ninety days sober, then giving in to the bottle, lying about the amount of alcohol consumed, lamenting his alienation of loved ones, losing jobs, borrowing money, getting sick, and finally, checking in to yet another dry-out clinic. He tells himself and others the answer to his problem has nothing to do with God, because he was raised in an evangelical home, and found the scene severely off-putting.

In the meantime, he continues his love-hate relationship with alcohol, both trying to get away from it, and leaning on it to get him through life. It won't. In fact, it will end his life. Louie had started off wanting a connection with something—a power that could soothe him, calm him, bring him into a more fully alive version of himself. Instead, it has prematurely aged him and poisoned his liver. As a god, alcohol has failed him, miserably.

> **WHEN WE USE THE GIFTS FROM A GRACIOUS CREATOR TO ANSWER A DEADENED SPIRIT, THEY QUICKLY PROVE UNABLE TO DELIVER.**

There are plenty of other candidates vying for the role of God in this world, though, including things considered legitimate and essential. When the spiritually dead lay hold of them, they see them as not only necessary for life, but begin looking to them *as* life. This attitude quickly changes true human needs into idolatry. For instance, eating, required for survival, becomes spoiled, thankless gluttony—"their god is their belly" (Phil. 3:19). Sleep, needed for refreshment, becomes dull, unproductive laziness—"How long will you lie there, O sluggard? When will you arise from your sleep?" (Prov. 6:9). Sex, a gift for pleasure and procreation, becomes an insane itch to be scratched any way one desires—"God will judge the sexually immoral and adulterous" (Heb. 13:4).

Human life is full of gifts from a gracious Creator, and "nothing is to be rejected if it is received with thanksgiving" (1 Tim. 4:4). However, when we use these gifts to answer a deadened spirit, and solve our deepest needs, they quickly prove unable to deliver.

Idols are also frequently hidden in more noble pursuits. These lure even the most intelligent, self-disciplined people. They offer purpose to the dead in spirit who wish for a larger, fuller life. God has created us in such a way that we're compelled to look for meaning and productivity. But as a god of its own, the Protestant work ethic, so universally admired, inflicts great harm. Tim Keller writes, "What many call psychological problems are simple issues of idolatry. Perfectionism, workaholism . . . these stem from making good things into idols that then drive us into the ground."[6] A preoccupation with being useful distracted Martha from Jesus, and generally made her unhappy, anxious, and troubled (see Luke 10:40–41). With us too, quests for achievement give way to obsessive comparisons, criticism of others, and dissatisfaction with self. After heavily investing in them, we find the life they deliver is not what we saw advertised in the window.

And yet when lofty goals are actually attained, they disappoint relentlessly. People who are driven to scale the mountain discover only the briefest gust of euphoria once arriving at the top, followed by long, deep disillusionment, and sometimes even suicidal impulses. Olympic champions themselves frequently suffer from post-game depression. "So focused on winning gold medals, they often fail to prepare themselves for the rest of their lives and are left with a sense of hopelessness."[7] In 2012, Michael Phelps won fifteen gold medals and was considered the greatest swimmer of all time. Yet his lowest point was after his triumph. Phelps said, "I didn't want to be in the sport anymore. . . . I didn't want to be alive anymore."[8]

Though physiological problems can trigger such feelings, spiritual needs also certainly compound them. The glory of the world is fleeting. Solomon captured its anticlimactic nature when he wrote, "I became great and surpassed all who were before me in Jerusalem. . . . Then I considered all that my hands had done and the toil I had expended in doing it, and behold, all was vanity and a striving after wind, and there was nothing to be gained under the sun" (Eccl. 2:9, 11). Achievement-worship promises that with enough trophies, certificates, and bragging rights, we will finally experience a certain supremacy of life. And we do—for five minutes.

When spiritually dead people finally, grudgingly, admit their need for God, never underestimate their warped ability to still find something other than Him. Unwilling to submit to the Bible, they wander off to sample the buffet of world religion. The appeal, this time, lies in the promise of some exotic truth that will illuminate one's life, while allowing their sinful behavior to continue undisturbed. This religious stubbornness, perhaps more than anything else, explains the enduring popularity of weird cults, space aliens, crystals,

New-Age ceremonies, and religious figures who abuse and fleece their followers. "For the time is coming when people will not endure sound teaching, but having itching ears, they will accumulate for themselves teachers to suit their own passions, and will turn away from listening to the truth and wander off into myths" (2 Tim. 4:3–4). The spiritually dead find no life in the maze of these darkened alleys. Ironically, while the painful void within them drives their search for God, their sinful prejudices will not allow them to find Him. Almost anything else is acceptable, though.

We could continue ad nauseum with examples of how people look for love with all the wrong people, search for validation in the shallow waters of social media, or try to create intimacy with pornographic materials. It would only demonstrate what we have already shown, that humankind obviously craves a connection with the life of God, and spends a tremendous amount of time combing dumpsters for it.

The Miracle Worker Explains

One day I was browsing in a souvenir shop southwest of Columbus, Ohio. I picked up a crudely carved wooden head. It was savage looking, with a mouth full of sharp teeth. It seemed to be old. A sticker was attached to it that said, "Certified Altar Piece." Someone had apparently gotten the thing from a faraway jungle tribe.

It struck me that what I held in my hand had at some point been used in pagan religious rituals. Perhaps the head itself had been trusted in, prayed to, worshiped. Now here it was, next to a Cessna Cub plastic model kit, vintage Timex watches, and a chipped plate with a fish painted on it. This god was on sale for eighty bucks. I can say with confidence that it never gave anything to anybody, yet at some time in the past, a group of people believed it would.

Of all the idols we could ever find or create, none of them have ever worked, because none of them *could* work. Psalms says,

> They have ears, but do not hear;
>   noses, but do not smell.
> They have hands, but do not feel;
>   feet, but do not walk;
>   and they do not make a sound in their throat.
>
> (115:6–7)

If substitute gods can't do these simple things, they certainly can't do miracles. And a miracle is exactly what the spiritually dead need—a miracle not done upon them, but *within* them. Even those of us who have already received this amazing work have difficulty understanding how it happened, and what it involved.

No one ever gave a clearer explanation of the new birth than Jesus did in the Gospel of John chapter 3, where He outlined the details of it. When He said to Nicodemus, "You must be born again," it perplexed the elderly Jewish man. Though today "born again" is often borrowed as a motivational idea for personal growth seminars, Nicodemus rightly understood it to be a miracle of unusual order, peculiar in all the chronicles of God's other works. He was "the teacher of Israel" (3:10), but was having a hard time wrapping his mind around this difficult concept. He asked Jesus, "How can a man be born when he is old? Can he enter a second time into his mother's womb and be born?" (John 3:4). In his struggle for understanding, he had perceived the second birth in a concrete, physical sense.

Jesus clarified, "Truly, truly I say to you, unless one is born of water and the Spirit, he cannot enter the kingdom of God" (John 3:5).[9] This response indicated that new birth is neither mere metaphor, nor blunt physicality. It is spiritual— of the Holy Spirit, and by the Holy Spirit.

Even if Nicodemus had been able to go back into his mother's womb, and be physically born again, it wouldn't have helped him. Jesus said, "That which is born of the flesh is flesh, and that which is born of the Spirit is spirit" (3:6). Flesh can only birth more flesh, more skin, more bone. More sin. Being reborn of your mother a thousand times would only yield the same result a thousand times over—a human being who is inwardly dead. Only the Holy Spirit can reach our dark core, give it life, birth it—"that which is born of the Spirit is spirit."

The second birth is beyond scrutiny, and invisible. It occurs on the inside, without spectacle or theater. This miraculous operation, stranger by far than the dramatic parting of the Red Sea or the walls of Jericho falling, happens in a gentle, sublime way. Nicodemus must have registered astonishment at this, so Jesus further told him, "Do not marvel that I said to you, 'You must be born again.' The wind blows where it wishes, and you hear its sound, but you do not know where it comes from or where it goes" (John 3:7–8). Thus Jesus reminded the man that every day we believe in things unseen; indeed, we casually assume their existence. When leaves rustle or tree limbs shake, we take for granted that an invisible agency—a huge, swirling sea of air—caused it. "So it is with everyone who is born of the Spirit," Jesus said (3:8).

There was one thing left for Nicodemus to ask: "How can these things be?" (3:9). What clears the path for the Holy

Spirit to enter a person and bring the miracle of new birth? What enables the Spirit to do this kind of work in a man or woman?

Jesus answered by describing His being "lifted up" on the cross (John 3:14). His death would need to facilitate the second birth, because sin had blocked our access to eternal life, as surely as Adam's sin had blocked him from partaking of the tree of life (see Gen. 3:22–24). The holy, righteous, glorious life of God would not come to anyone until sin had been adequately judged. The cross of Christ was that judgment.

> **WITHOUT THE CROSS, NO ONE CAN BE BORN AGAIN. THE SPIRIT WILL NOT COME. PEOPLE REMAIN DEAD IN THEIR SINS.**

And so when Jesus was lifted up, John 19:34 says, "one of the soldiers pierced his side with a spear, and at once there came out blood and water." The day His redemptive blood was shed, the water of life flowed freely. Without the cross, no one can receive this life, and be born again. The Spirit will not come. People remain dead in their sins.

But as it stands, Christ has died for our sins, "that whoever believes in Him may have eternal life" (3:15–16). With sin out of the way, nothing can forbid the Holy Spirit from entering you and causing you to come alive. Truly, Christ *enabled* the new birth, but the Spirit *activates* it, directly causing it to happen.

Through the Spirit's ministry, we enter a solidarity, a union with Christ in which we benefit from His accomplishments. The crucifixion and resurrection of Christ, which are objective historical facts, and eternal realities into which we are positioned, become available to us for our subjective inward reality. As Jesus said of the Spirit, "He will take what is mine and declare it to you" (John 16:14).

And so the Bible describes how we share His accomplishments, and the effects they have upon us. It says you were

> . . . buried with him in baptism, in which you were also raised with him through faith in the powerful working of God, who raised him from the dead. And you, who were dead in your trespasses and the uncircumcision of your flesh, God made alive together with him, having forgiven us all our trespasses. (Col. 2:12–13)

THE BODY
Biologically alive, but fragile and dying—yet

THE SOUL
(MIND/EMOTIONS/WILL)

THE HUMAN SPIRIT
Alive to God

Imperfect, but influenced by transformative new life

sometimes affected by new life, and anticipates resurrection

The Enlivened Human Condition

Never dismiss these statements as mere doctrine. They expound what happened to you, and their miraculous reality is present with you in the depths of your being.

Nothing Less than Resurrection

Years back, I stood in front of an audience in Africa and told them I had been resurrected from the dead. I heard a gasp ripple through the crowd. Then I went on to explain my resurrection not from the physical, but the spiritual standpoint. The listeners settled down then, as though my story was not so spectacular after all. I had only been dead in spirit. No big deal. The thought of an interior resurrection had seemed to them a play on words. My friends that day hadn't known how dead I was before my second birth—the dark intentions of my heart, the weird ideas, the upside-down hopes and dreams, the rampant idolatry, not to mention my gross insubordination toward anything of the real God.

Not only so, they had perhaps briefly forgotten an ancient terrorist named Saul of Tarsus, who, possessed by rage, had pursued and persecuted Christians. But then, having met Christ and received new life, he had gone on to live and die for the gospel, and write half the New Testament.

Perhaps they didn't know the stories of modern-day jihadists who have been born again, like Bashir Mohammad, who admitted the gross unlikelihood of his ever coming to Christ. "Frankly," he said, "I would have slaughtered anyone who suggested it."[10] He now leads Christian worship in his home.

Or maybe they had not heard of such dramatic stories as hostile lesbian activist and lecturer Rosaria Butterfield, whose new birth was so transformative she has now become an influential voice for repentance and faith.[11]

Maybe my listeners that day had forgotten for the moment their own stories, each of which possessed its own set of impossibilities. But there they sat, like the calyx of a flower, enclosing the priceless jewel of eternal life.

Lastly, I am certain they didn't know your saga, of the countless things you did, and the things others did to you—sometimes allegedly in the name of Christ and the church—that made you swear you would never turn to Jesus. Yet here you are, reading this book with the intention (hopefully) of developing your Christian life.

At any rate, the new birth is a miracle. It does not bestow instant behavioral perfection, but it does awaken new experiences of what we call "inner life." Certain metaphysical and New-Age spokespersons have taken possession of this term for use in their teachings. They make it synonymous with non-Christian concepts like self-actualization, Christ-consciousness, and various undefined forces of the universe. Others generically portray inner life as anything that occurs on the psychological spectrum. But authentic spiritual life as defined in the Bible cannot become subjective, inner life for you without the cross of Jesus Christ and the Holy Spirit.

If by faith in Christ, you have received it, then the life you have longed for has begun. The outward marvels that Jesus performed so long ago on paralytics, lepers, demoniacs, the blind, the deaf, and the dead become yours as an internal reality. Having been born into a different kingdom, you will begin to taste, to see, to hear, to feel—and all because this grace "has been manifested through the appearing of our Savior Christ Jesus, who abolished death and brought life and immortality to light through the gospel" (2 Tim. 1:10).

4

The Fully Functional You

*Through the indwelling Spirit the human spirit is brought
into immediate contact with higher spiritual reality. It
looks upon, tastes, feels, and sees the powers of the world to
come and has a conscious encounter with God invisible.*

— A. W. Tozer

IF YOU'RE A LITTLE older, you remember living
through the remarkable time of information and com-
munication breakthroughs in the 1990s and early 2000s.
Technology inflicted quite a learning curve on some of us.
Personally, I hoped the whole thing would blow over. I had
already made huge concessions in getting a flip phone that
I wore on my belt. Anything else seemed a waste of money.
How much technology did a person need to make a call?

Frankly, I wouldn't have minded if the world had gone
back to rotary dial wall phones, six-foot cords and all. But
after my wife and daughter made comments about my need
to leave "dumb" technology behind, I finally agreed to get
a smartphone. The first six months I had the gadget, I only

made calls with it. There wasn't much else I liked about it except the larger screen, which was good for use as a flashlight, so I could navigate to the bathroom in the middle of the night. I was overpaying for a device I was underusing.

But then I found out I could read Kindle books on my phone, and my attitude began to change. In short order, I also realized I could use it to get directions on the fly, watch videos, and check the weather, Facebook, and emails. When I began dictating notes (some of which went into this book), it suddenly hit me: *Hey, this thing is a handheld computer!* That was a big revelation, especially since I had been treating my phone as nothing more than a glorified walkie-talkie.

We know more about our phones than ourselves. The Western world has plunged hip deep into psychological and social research, hoping to solve the puzzle of humanity and its many issues. We haven't been good at getting answers, but we're great at finding questions. Some of them are downright bedeviling. For instance, why do we have inside our skulls three hundred times more neural connections than stars in the galaxy? This seems like rigging for something a lot more serious than simple hunting/gathering, and much more than is needed for mere reproduction and survival. Why are we so over-engineered for existence in this world?

Naturalism states that human beings have no purpose other than the random purposes we invent for ourselves. However, with the wiring we've got inside, that would be an incredible example of underuse. It would mean that we, such complex beings, exist for the sake of hobbies, appetites, and various diversions—things far inferior to us.

The biblical worldview offers something superior—that you are not an accident of nature, but a deliberate product of God's creation. And even better, we can say that through faith in Christ, we have been born again, with a new life. However, many of us expect nothing more from our new status than for it to deliver pleasures and meaning within this worldly horizontal plane. We hope too low. When I came to Christ, I was down to seven dollars in my bank account. I had also lost a fiancée. Had I hoped to go through life using my new birth to fix only these kinds of things, or even just get through them, again, it would have been an *under*use of what God had given me. I would have been settling for less. Living less. *Jesus, please, just this once, give me that thing. Lord, take away the pain. God, bless this business/trip/date, etc. Change this. Fix that.*

Like thousands of other born-again Christians, I have benefited from being able to "let your requests be made known to God" (Phil. 4:6). But is there anything more our new life can do than manage the crises and affairs of this world? Apparently so, for Paul himself wrote, ". . . much more, now that we are reconciled, shall we be saved by his life" (Rom. 5:10). As believers, we should aspire to discover that kind of salvation, living at a capacity fully employing God's gift of divine life. According to the biblical record, this means containing Him, experiencing Him, enjoying Him, fellowshiping with Him, and glorifying Him.

A View from the Drawing Board

When we reflect upon the highest potential of the Christian life, few of us think about looking backwards. Yet, the Genesis creation account is a treasure trove of clues. We find there declarations of intent that will blossom as the Scriptures unfold, making sense of what we ought to be, and, with the enablement of God's own life, what we will become. Consider the divine pause in Genesis 1:26, as our Creator premeditated His last and crowning work of the created order.

"God said, 'Let us make man in our image, after our likeness. And let them have dominion over the fish of the sea and over the birds of the heavens and over the livestock and over all the earth and over every creeping thing that creeps on the earth'" (Gen. 1:26).

Embedded within His thought, like gems, lie the words "image," "likeness," and "dominion." To begin with, we look like God. That statement is jarring at first, because we wonder what use God has for actual nostrils, ears, eyes, and limbs. The Bible tells us God is Spirit (see John 4:24), which would hardly require Him to have such equipment.[1]

How much "image" and "likeness" refers to physical attributes, we can't say with hard certainty. It is more probable that we are shaped like God in His moral dimensions—His love, righteousness, goodness, and perhaps transcendence, rationality, self-awareness, creativity, and aesthetic sensibilities. In essence, we were intended to be wallet-sized photographs of deity—like God, without actually being Him.

WE WERE MADE TO CONTAIN OUR MAKER. GOD FITS US AND WE FIT HIM.

But that's not all. Paul brought to bear his penetrating apostolic revelation to the Genesis account, by mentioning one further detail—that human beings are "vessels," or containers (see Rom. 9:20–21). We were deliberately made incomplete, and although functional on the worldly wavelength, we were born hollow. That is why, from our earliest moments, we begin receiving and internalizing everything around us. The drive to fill ourselves never ends.

The facts of creation combine to tell us we are vessels shaped like God. The wisdom of this design is simple, indeed as simple as asking why a glove was fashioned as a hollow fabric container in the image and likeness of a hand. It was obviously meant to contain a hand. In a profoundly similar way, we were made to contain our Maker. God fits us and we fit Him. His life was to animate ours, and bring us into full functioning capacity, expressing God ("image" and "likeness"), while we inhabited this world as benevolent servant-lords ("dominion"). Before this could happen, though, our interests took us in an entirely different direction (as seen in the previous chapter). Blinded by temptation, we saw nothing lovely or promising in the Tree of Life (see Gen. 2:9).

Ultimately, nothing will run right for us, until we and God unite like hand in glove, content in container, His life in ours. That's why the New Testament expresses the hope "that you may be filled with all the fullness of God" (Eph. 3:19).

Blaise Pascal, French mathematician and theologian, once said, "There is a God-shaped vacuum in the heart of each man which cannot be satisfied by any created thing but only by God the Creator, made known through Jesus Christ."

This is an amazing truth of great, explanatory proportions, and yet given time, it can slip past even those of us who have been in the faith for a while. I recall one day going with another Christian, Ronnie, to visit a college student who was in our campus ministry. The student wasn't in any great trouble, but had become scarce of late, which is to say even when he showed up for church, he "wasn't there." On our way into his house, I desperately searched my heart for something, anything that might encourage a floundering Christian life. I tried sharing high thoughts, practical admonitions, and various applications. The best I can say about the encounter was that the student tolerated it. I got the impression he was happy we came, and even happier that we were leaving. Apparently our fellowship had been for him like a twenty-minute meal of boiled Brussels sprouts—something you know is good for you, but you're thrilled when it's over. A cloud of disappointment settled over me.

As soon as we got in the car, Ronnie turned to me and said with a low voice, "You didn't know it back there, but while you were talking to that guy, you were speaking to me the whole time." He went on to summarize how his Christian life, while exemplary to the naked eye, had been sputtering and wheezing along for a while. I was shocked. Ronnie was one of those guys church leaders loved. He could be counted on to volunteer, to give rides, to help at events—all good things, yet in the midst of doing them, he had allowed his identity (in his own eyes) to change from vessel of glory to religious tool. And if such a positive person could forget, *any* of us could, and many of us have.

I suppose sitting there in the car that day, I could have tried to encourage Ronnie by coddling him, as though he were a victim of religion. Misguided evangelicals often do this, launching into a rant against "the system," but that only creates a straw man to beat up. Bad religion is not merely a thing outside of us; it is an internal state of befuddlement and underuse.

Ronnie didn't need to renounce reading the Bible and attending church. Nor did he need to swear off his good works toward others. Instead, he needed to remember his identity as a vessel of glory. And then, rather than continue to run on the low-octane fuel of Mr. Nice Guy, he needed to rediscover the life that was his in Christ. This is the way it works for any born-again believer who wants to begin—or recover—a fully functional inner life.

A Floor Plan of the Vessel

The introductory phase of our new birth does not require advanced theological understanding. We need only do what infants do—eat, sleep, breathe, and eliminate waste. However, when we begin to long for the considerable blessings of spiritual maturity, the benefits and assistance of advanced knowledge will become clear. A fair amount of this instruction will have to do with understanding *yourself*—that is, your inward arrangement.

Suppose you were interested in buying a particular home, and asked a real estate dealer for information on it. You would expect to hear more than, "It was built in the image and likeness of a two-story colonial, with a large empty space inside—for a resident, of course."

"How many bedrooms? How many baths?" you ask. "Refinished basement? Sunroom?"

The real estate agent shrugs and says, "That's anyone's guess. Real estate dealers argue about it all the time. I suppose it's up to your own interpretation."

If this conversation ever happens, you can be sure of two things: 1) You need a new real estate agent; 2) With so little information available, you will never learn anything about the potential functionality of that house.

In the same sense, the Bible must tell us more about the inner structure, the floor plan, of our human vessel. And it does. Observe the engineering that went into the first human: "The LORD God formed the man of dust from the ground and breathed into his nostrils the breath of life, and the man became a living creature [soul, KJV]" (Gen. 2:7).

This description specifies three distinct spheres, or rooms, of humanity—"dust," referring to the physical body; "the breath of life," referring to our created human spirit (the Hebrew word translated "breath" is *ruach*, meaning spirit), and "soul" (*psyche*), referring to the psychological dimension of a human being.

Although this early stage of the scriptural narrative lacks expanded commentary, the precision of New Testament teaching eventually makes our internal makeup much clearer. We are explicitly taught that we have an "inner man" and an "outer man," but Paul also writes, "Now may the God of peace himself sanctify you completely, and may your whole *spirit* and *soul* and *body* be kept blameless at the coming of our Lord Jesus Christ" (1 Thess. 5:23). The complete human being is not merely a two-part soul and body, but three parts—*spirit* and soul and body.

Most of us routinely think of the soul as synonymous with the spirit. Strictly speaking though, there is a difference. The soul refers to an individual's mind (thoughts—Ps. 139:14; Ps. 13:2; Lam. 3:20), emotion (feelings—1 Sam. 18:1; Song 1:7; 2 Sam. 5:8), and will (volition—Job 7:15, 6:7; 1 Chron. 22:19, NASB). In other words, your soul is your personality. Occasionally the Bible even uses the word "soul" to refer to your entire being (Acts 2:43, 3:23).

Theologians argue about the distinctions and differences of human makeup, because the Scriptures do not always seek to teach a systematic internal map of man. Sometimes the

Bible speaks holistically of your inward parts as your "heart." At other times, it treats them as interchangeable, because they can overlap each other in certain particulars. For instance, your conscience is part of your spirit as well as part of your heart. Also, you can think and feel with your heart as well as your soul. And yes, the Bible can talk about human beings as though they were only body and soul; at other times, as body, soul, and spirit. Lewis Chafer comments,

> The Bible supports both. . . . The distinction between both soul and spirit is as incomprehensible as life itself, and the efforts to frame such definitions must always be unsatisfactory. . . . Many have assumed that the Bible only teaches [a two-part man]. . . . Over against this is the truth that oftentimes these terms [soul and spirit] *cannot* be used interchangeably.[2]

In the book *Man as Spirit, Soul, and Body*, Woodward comments on the way the Bible speaks of "spirit" and "soul":

> There is variation in Scriptural testimony, but not contradiction. Since the spirit is not separated from the soul, a summary statement that only mentions two parts of a person does not contradict one that clarifies the third part. Passages that distinguish spirit from soul are presenting further detail and precision.[3]

Some have disparaged this teaching by saying it is a Greek invention rather than a product of biblical revelation. Yet, the ancient Greeks, as exemplified by Plato, said that human beings are a composite of body, soul, and *reason*. They got it wrong. It would have been amazing if they had said body, soul, and *spirit*, because such spiritual matters can only be made known through the Holy Spirit (see 1 Cor.

2:13). The subtle distinctions between soul and spirit are only discerned through the dividing power of the Word of God (see Heb. 4:12).

We have distinct areas of influence within us, and even though we might use terms like "wiring," "parts," and "engineering" we shouldn't think of ourselves as actual machines built with various components. Sometimes flip charts of the three-part man do exactly that—leave us with the impression that there are hard starts and stops to every place in our being, as with an automobile or a computer. Our daily experience is far more organic and nuanced than that.

BODY-SOUL-SPIRIT—YOU ARE A SINGLE BEING, NOT THREE.

We live and move as a unified composite of body, soul, and spirit, not a collection of separate, independent compartments. For instance, at the gym, our bodies take center stage. When reading an instructional manual, our minds play the dominant role. Yet these two are never completely disconnected from one another. At other times, quite apart from any conscious effort to be spiritual, more winsome desires tug at us, evidence that our human spirit is present with our bodies and minds. You are a single being, not three of them. Otherwise, we would need to artificially belabor our own lives, figuring out what bucket to live in from hour to hour, rather than existing on a normal continuum.

This three-part pattern is immensely practical for maximum daily living in this world. God has created a body for us with five senses so we can occupy this physical world, and connect to it. He has given us a soul, so we can navigate the deeper realm of intelligent thought, feelings, and volition. And most profoundly, He has formed in us a spirit with the potential to relate to Him. You could say the body supplies world-awareness, the soul self-awareness, and the spirit God-awareness. This indeed, is preparation of a high order. God obviously had no interest in creating and indwelling simple, dumb receptacles. He wanted to interact with a being that was triple-tuned for full functionality.

A Closer Look at Our Epicenter

Having considered our floor plan, let's visit the basement. Down the steps of that nicely refinished space, we'll find a fusebox, the power central of the entire house. Think of it as your human spirit. Of the three main divisions of our human makeup, the human spirit is the part of us we are the least accustomed to hearing about.

We clearly understand the use of our bodies. And we are also aware of our souls, that busy place of thought and feeling. But whenever we've been exposed to the term "human spirit," it has typically been used synonymously with the ideas of fortitude or determination. *A moving tribute to the human spirit!* says an enthusiastic review of a film whose main character triumphs over adversity. *We've got spirit!* chants a team of high school cheerleaders.

And yet, these usages are far afield of what the Bible had in mind. Our spirit is the region of our inner being that acts as a connection point for the Holy Spirit. It is a created zone that, under the Holy Spirit's life-giving power, makes inner spiritual experience possible.

God ranked this central connection place among His highest priorities: "Thus declares the LORD, who stretched out the *heavens* and founded the *earth* and formed the *spirit of man* within him" (Zech. 12:1).

In the plan of salvation, the human spirit is needed to worship God (see John 4:24). It is the place Christ joins to us (see 1 Cor. 6:17), and is where the Holy Spirit witnesses within us that we are children of God (see Rom. 8:16). Apparently without a human spirit, we and God would be like two ships passing in the night. Humans were originally intended not only to be physical, thinking beings, but spiritual as well. From our very depths, we've been hardwired to want God, even though prior to salvation, we made a mess of our own hearts.

Our spirit cannot be visibly observed, nor isolated through clinical trials, but there are existential reasons to believe its presence. Although not a committed Bible student, famed psychologist William James (1842–1910), argued that "It is as if there were in the human consciousness a sense of reality, a feeling of objective presence, a perception of what we may call 'something there,' more deep and more general than any of the special and particular 'senses' by which the current psychology supposes existent realities to be originally revealed."[4] This description sounds suspiciously like the dynamic Paul describes when he asks the rhetorical question, "For what man knows the things of a man except the spirit of the man which is in him?" (1 Cor. 2:11, NKJV).

In his book *Existential Reasons for Belief in God*, Clifford Williams further laid out a fairly extensive list of commonly held needs that drive us to faith:

- A desire for a life well-led, filled with virtues and peace.

- An inclination toward a larger, more expansive existence, of color and awe, of fascination and variety.

- A need to be loved unconditionally.

- A longing to be truly forgiven.

- A yearning for cosmic security and protection, no matter what threatens.

- A wish for life beyond the grave, where we continue consciousness in eternal bliss, free from the ravages of time.[5]

These needs differ somewhat between individuals, based on their personalities and histories, but they represent a fair overall snapshot of the entire human condition. Williams goes on to explain that we will not feel all of these at once, nor will every person feel them with equal intensity. We may find it difficult to even verbalize them. That is because they emanate from the basement of our being.

In addition, we don't immediately associate these feelings with a need for God. I remember hanging around the hallway of my high school with a buddy of mine named Marcel. We were always trying to outdo each other for sheer sarcastic wit. One afternoon at lunch break, we were making fun of the cafeteria food, bad hair cuts, cheap sneakers, and locker doors that wouldn't shut. At the height of our comedy fest, I was suddenly struck with a sense of waste. I can only describe it as the world seeming to pass away, and taking me with it. "We'll never get these moments back," I said to Marcel.

It was a burst of uncharacteristic insight which, in the context of our super-shallow friendship, wasn't welcome. Marcel said, "Stop talking like that," and added a few other colorful words to make sure I got the point.

I instantly regretted having said it, because the comment did sound pretentiously grown-up, like a line straight out of *The Waltons*.[6] But it was *real*—a moment of melancholy had passed over me. I could only explain it as wishing to capture time and keep myself and everyone else from being reduced to a memory in a class yearbook. In effect, I wanted something eternal and timeless, though neither I, and especially not Marcel, realized what it meant. Neither of us knew what Solomon had written thousands of years before: "He [God] has put eternity into man's heart" (Eccl. 3:11). I had for a second brushed up against that reality. It was just powerful enough to create an exclamation mark on my life, lasting all the way down to the writing of this book, in 2021.

> ## WE'VE ALL UNFORTUNATELY RESPONDED TO SPIRITUAL PININGS WITH AN ENDLESS PARADE OF POOR SUBSTITUTES.

Everyone has reflective moods like these. On hearing them described, we recognize and relate, because from one human being to the next, we have a piece of equipment as standard as a liver—the human spirit. As we saw in the last chapter, we've all unfortunately responded to spiritual pinings with an endless parade of poor substitutes. Only the mercy of God was able to eventually sanctify our focus, and allow us to perceive Christ as our goal.

C.S. Lewis noted that the things we seek every day reveal a secret longing for something else.[7] We don't typically identify this as coming from "the human spirit"; in fact, we routinely dismiss it as psychological, but we *all* become dimly aware of its needs and desires at different times and in different ways.

Ultimately our three-part vessel shares a similar blueprint with the tabernacle (and later, the temple) of the Old Testament. Those ancient dwelling places of God contained three regions of worship—the outer court, the Holy Place, and the Holy of Holies. When "the cloud covered the tent of meeting, and the glory of the LORD filled the tabernacle" (Exod. 40:34), that three-part structure became the convergence point between heaven and earth, the locus of spiritual experience.

John Heard tells us that as it happened then, it also happens in us today: "We pass through the outer court of the senses and even through the inner court of reason to reach this sanctuary where God makes Himself known in silence and in stillness."[8] God has intentionally designed us as mobile places of worship, packaged for glorious interaction with Him—"Do you not know that your body is a temple of the Holy Spirit within you, whom you have from God?" (1 Cor. 6:19).

Intentionality

Jesus said, "That which is born of the Spirit is spirit" (John 3:6). But what exactly comes to life when our deadened spirit is made alive? As we launch into the main section of this book, we will see that our new inner life includes our conscience, defines our worship, and intuitively enables us to know and be led by God. This is our spirit in full function. It equips us to "seek the things that are above, where Christ is, seated at the right hand of God" (Col. 3:1), and to apprehend them from within.

For obvious reasons, then, neglect of our conscience-worship-intuition is unthinkable. I do not subscribe to the notion that born-again Christians can lose their salvation,[9] but it is possible to find some who, ignoring their inner life, have lost almost all positive spiritual inclination. Heard writes about our spirit, and the necessity of its regular use.

The organ disappears when the function ceases. Like the eyeless fish in the mammoth cave of Kentucky, we lose the spiritual faculty in proportion as we disuse it. . . . Where there is little sense of God's presence, there the *Pneuma* [spirit] is scarcely, if at all, developed.[10]

If we want to fully realize our function as vessels of glory, there is no way around it—we must become intentional about our new inner life. It is to this that we now turn our full consideration.

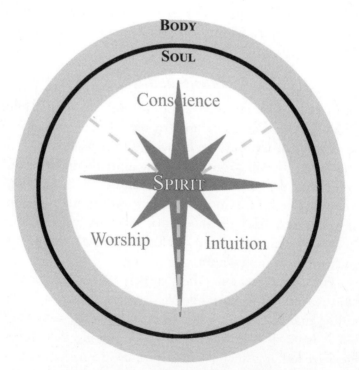

Functions of the Human Spirit

5

Conscience— the Truth-Teller

Let us give ourselves indiscriminately to everything our passions suggest, and we will always be happy. . . . Conscience is not the voice of Nature but only the voice of prejudice.

—Marquis de Sade

I don't believe in guilt, I believe in living on impulse as long as you never intentionally hurt another person, and don't judge people in your life. I think you should live completely free.

— Angelina Jolie

How pitiful is an intelligence used only to make excuses to quieten the conscience.

— Ignazio Silone, *Bread and Wine*

SOMETIMES HOLLYWOOD gets it right. The antagonist of a film is not always a serial killer, or a supervillain with metal teeth, or an invader from space. It can come from within—a part of us that tends toward truth-telling. Movies like *A Simple Plan* (1998), *The Machinist* (2004), M. Night Shyalaman's *Devil* (2010), and the Stephen King novella-based

69

film *1922* (2017), pits man against conscience. In each we immediately identify with the nature of the drama because it is so common to the human experience.

The conscience typically finds a home in children's church curriculum, where youngsters relate it to wrongdoing such as not sharing their toys, or lying about how something got broken. But it has hardly been treated as central to serious Christian spirituality. While conducting a workshop on inner life, a church leader approached me between sessions. "I don't understand what the fuss is all about," he said. "You taught on the conscience as though it were some special issue, but I've had a conscience since I was a boy. When I was ten years old, some kids playing in a sandlot hit a fly ball that landed nearby me in the woods. I took it home, but was so bothered that I returned it. You see, it's simple."

The man's point was that such an elementary item needn't be taught in adult settings, related to adult spiritual experience. Yet the apostle Paul testified, "I *always take pains* to have a clear conscience toward both God and man" (Acts 24:16). How often was he concerned for his conscience? *Always*. How intense was he about it? He *took pains*—that is, deliberate exercise that often involved discomfort. If we want to know the inner life that Paul experienced, pay attention to his testimony. Conscience cannot be ignored. We must deal with it, but we will not be able to "take pains" to do so, while knowing almost nothing about it.

We all hold vague abstractions about conscience that we have picked up from various sources, but what exactly is it? Can we label it psychological, a part of us educated by the forces of our family, current society, religion, and culture? Or is it a spiritual experience, approximating the voice of

God? The answer will require some sorting through, and it is a labor well worth the effort. If you can identify your conscience with some degree of understanding, it will spare you unnecessary angst, while on the other hand, opening floodgates of inward blessing.

An Internal Courtroom

Before its specific function in a Christian, conscience has a universal function inside all men. It is hardly a religious innovation. Paul Strohm notes that it "has outlasted epochs and empires, credos and creeds . . . is embraced with equal conviction by non-religious and religious alike . . . [with] a capacity for constant self-modification and adaption."[1] This is how Paul could write concerning the Gentiles, the non-people of God,

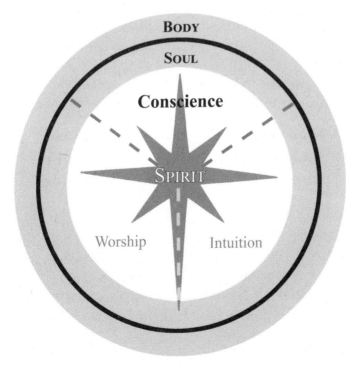

saying, "They show that the work of the law is written on their hearts, while their conscience also bears witness, and their conflicting thoughts accuse or even excuse them" (Rom. 2:15).

The same God who wrote the righteous law of the Ten Commandments, also created us. You could say He left His fingerprints on the soft clay of our hearts. There are impressions of His own goodness and morality—His *image*—within us. It is a reality enduring enough for Paul to refer to it as a law upon our hearts, a standard principle.

This natural law, though, does not teach precise theological concepts or standards of absolute good. Instead, it roughly approximates God's righteousness, a primal "oughtness" that we all gravitate toward. This is why evil things like murder, theft, or dishonesty are never considered virtuous in any global society, while truth, courage, loyalty, and generosity tend to be appreciated and emulated everywhere. With little experimentation, we seem to know some behavior is good, and some is evil. Therein lies our point: if we run afoul of this good natural law within us, conscience protests. It bears witness to right and wrong; it accuses or excuses.

> No MATTER HOW WE SWEAR OTHERWISE,
> WE ARE AWARE THAT SOMETHING ABOUT
> OURSELVES IS EITHER RIGHT OR WRONG.

When human beings do things against the law written on their hearts, their inward situation turns into a mini-courtroom. The conscience becomes the star witness, telling the truth as it is honestly known. This results in thoughts that either "accuse or excuse them." Conscience thus represents an inescapable interior knowledge. In fact, the very word *con* ("with") plus *science* ("knowledge") means no matter how we swear otherwise, we possess an awareness that something about ourselves is either right or wrong. That's why when people say, "I *knew* I shouldn't have done that," or, "I *knew* it was the right thing to do," or "You *know* you're wrong," they may not be using the word conscience, but that's exactly what they mean.

In fact, not only does conscience operate after a deed, but prior to it, granting knowledge of right or wrong in advance. Many people can testify that as they merely contemplated committing an unrighteous act, they already felt uneasy.

And yet a great many of these same people pretend, even try hard, not to know. They have apparently managed to normalize evil in their lives. For instance, the murderous Nazi regime was filled with sycophants whose "conscience" was actually an artificial construct forged by radical ideology. It was an attempted *override* of the law written in their hearts. During exit interviews after World War II, Rudolf Höss admitted as much. He spoke of his particular determination to suppress compassion for the Jews he saw brutally beaten, and as a reward, was promoted to commandant of Auschwitz. Heinrich Himmler also described Jewish liquidation as a "difficult task," and even Hitler mentioned his own resolve to grow "ice cold" for the sake of his genocidal mission.[2] Each of these tidbit quotes portend a hidden struggle within the individual, a tenacious resistance against what they knew was right.

And this knowledge is so significant, it has the power to exert felt effects upon a human being. The short-term consequences of guilt can trigger emotional reactions and behaviors that casual onlookers might find mystifying—things like unexplainable anger or relentless self-justification. Recall the hypersensitivity of Herod after he had John the Baptist decapitated.

It seemed wherever he turned he saw the man, and upon hearing about the miracles of Jesus, said, "This is John the Baptist. He has been raised from the dead; that is why these miraculous powers are at work in him" (Matt. 14:1–2).

Failure to satisfactorily address a troubled conscience in the long term can lead to psychological conflicts that may include a nervous breakdown or depression. In extreme cases it can turn suicidal, as with Judas Iscariot who said, "I have sinned by betraying innocent blood," and then hanged himself (see Matt. 27:3–5). Even mild levels of guilt create physiological registrations, such as shifting eyes, tell-tale twitches, and Pontius Pilate's infamous washing of hands at the sentencing of Jesus (see Matt. 27:24). Technology has also capitalized on the predictability of conscience. Today's lie detector machines measure breathing, and heart rates, both of which can be affected by guilt.

Ultimately, an unsettling sense of wrong suggests that I am somehow in conflict with God. As Thomas Baird says, "I am conscious that I have sinned, and another is conscious of my sin, and that other is no other than God. . . . *I* know and *God* knows. I *know* that God *knows*; and God *knows* that I *know* that He *knows*."[3] Arriving at this point, we can conclude, along with Martin Luther, "I am under the just judgment of God."[4] Such interior knowledge makes certain that even the *secrets* of men will be judged (see Rom 2:16; Luke 8:17, 12:1–2). The conscience, after all, occupies the ultimate secret place—our human spirit. It is intensely part of us, and yet disloyal to us, at the same time. It will always tell the simple truth, even if we attempt to lie with thousands of words, pie chart data, and a chorus of other lying voices to back us up. Conscience trumps all noise with two words: "You *know*."

Under this plain, but insistent declaration, even the strongest sinner can falter, as in the chilling story of a woman selling alcohol door to door in nineteenth-century Germany. She came to the home of a godly man named Johann Georg Boley.

> Boley . . . looked her firmly in the face. The woman, it appeared, could not help returning his look. became visibly uneasy under his searching gaze. . . . Thus they remained for a few minutes in silence, their eyes fixed upon one another. At length the woman gave signs of uneasiness. . . .
>
> "For God's sake," cried the woman, "do tell me why you look at me so!"
>
> Boley remained silent.
>
> "Lord Jesus help me!" the woman cried, wringing her hands; "I really have done nothing wrong, sir."
>
> Boley still continued to look at her.
>
> "For God's sake, take your eyes off me!" she cried, almost convulsively; "you pierce my heart. I see, I see," she then said, "you know all about me. I will confess, sir. I had one, sir, only one, sir."
>
> "*Only* one?" Boley asked, not knowing, however, what she meant.
>
> "O Lord! I see you know it!" she cried, bursting into tears. "Yes, I have had two illegitimate children, but I did them no harm."
>
> "No harm?" Boley repeated, still looking her in the face.
>
> "O Lord, have mercy upon me!" cried she; "Yes, I drowned one of them."
>
> "What!" Boley cried, now starting up.
>
> But away went the woman. She got out of the room with a leap, and he never saw her again.[5]

If such a small prod can dislodge an avalanche of awful, associated secrets, who knows what horrors and depths of depravity will finally and honestly be revealed on the great Day of Judgment—things that would make angels weep, and stir the just wrath of the Almighty? Scripture records no man or woman arguing at that time, defending themselves as they do today with a multitude of excuses. Their own conscience will witness to the truth of God's judgment. Even as they say, "I didn't know," conscience will testify "Yes. You did." Or, "No you didn't. You didn't want to know and deliberately kept yourself from finding out." For a person to prevail in this court, he must not only convince the judge (God), and triumph over the prosecutor (the law of God), but invalidate the most damning witness of all, his own conscience.

This Means War

With so many unpleasant verdicts delivered in the court of conscience, it is no surprise if the sinner begins to feel that his conscience is his enemy. Today, a person's willingness to violate even the most basic forms of morality is met with cheers of approval, calling it "courage." A conscience that witnesses to conservative forms of behavior is to them something to be defeated, overcome, or completely overhauled.

Philosophers have long flirted with the supposed paradise that might exist without compunctions of conscience. Nietzsche thought it would free a man to be the "beautiful beast" nature had intended him to be. B.F. Skinner theorized the conscience away as nothing more than the outcome of behavioral conditioning.[6] Sigmund Freud attempted to vanquish the conscience by naming it a psychological illusion.[7] Karl Marx saw it as an enemy of the state that needed to be eliminated.[8] A friend of mine who selected an unbiblical lifestyle, saw conscience as brainwashing. "If only we would stop telling people this behavior is wrong, then it wouldn't be wrong anymore." All of these views in some way understand conscience as a dilemma to be solved, and each suggest some form of makeover, if not eradication.[9]

And yet those who temporarily succeed in banishing their "inward foe" will find themselves in worse straits. The epistle to the Romans speaks of those who "by their unrighteousness suppress the truth" (1:18). They found a way to discredit the law in their hearts and suspend the protests of conscience. However, this is certainly not a victory for them. Their goal lies in defeating truth, something defined by the Person of God Himself. Therefore they must reject Him, His uncomfortable holiness, His inconvenient righteousness. Where could such a pathway take them, except into baldfaced idolatry? They "exchanged the glory of the immortal God for images resembling mortal man and birds and animals and creeping things" (1:23).

This absurd swap makes perfect sense to the darkened mind. For in that state, which has lost all healthy orientation, even the lowest things are more attractive than the real God. Eventually, freed from its prison of truth, sexual perversion appears, behavior that previously might have been labeled as deviant or even mentally defective, but now solidifies into a new normal. "Therefore God gave them up in the lusts of their hearts to impurity, to the dishonoring of their bodies among themselves, because they exchanged the truth about God for a lie and worshiped and served the creature rather than the Creator, who is blessed forever! Amen" (1:24–25).

The downward spiral of Romans chapter 1 continues into a host of other behaviors that branch out like the tendrils of some foul root system, reaching ever further into darkness. Some are so absurd in their error, and so backward in logic, that the entire scene can only be described as, in the words of John MacArthur, "the death of common sense."[10]

Truly, the most expensive war is the one waged on the conscience. Those who excel at living without it pay the highest price. Experts tend to label these people as sociopathic.

> [They] visit pain upon their families and communities, but in the end, they tend to self-destruct. . . . [They] never feel comfortable in their own skins . . . [and are] loveless, amoral, and chronically bored. . . . The absolute self-involvement of sociopathy creates an individual consciousness that is aware of every ache and twitch in the body.[11]

Our rush to diagnosis favors words like "mentally ill" to describe them. Indeed, in the aftermath of the Columbine school shootings, analysts described the shooters as "psychopathic," "troubled," "homicidal maniacs," but having dissected their personal writings, experts began to include in their list of other notations "a lack of conscience."[12]

Plenty of us who avoid the extreme clinical diagnosis of "sociopathic" may well find ourselves somewhere on the spectrum, anyway. Basic self-centeredness, of which we are all guilty, requires ignoring the conscience to benefit oneself. The more we do this, the more adept we become at doing it. Not only will our morality deteriorate, but our committed relationships will suffer.

The conscience is a vital part of what preserves our humanity, yet human beings themselves attack it with every weapon at their disposal. We will stop at nothing to halt its relentless advance, drawing on an arsenal of deception, anecdotes, statistics, stories, reports, research, opinions, or polls. This conflict resembles the first armored warfare in history. On September 15, 1916, the British sent the tank into action against Germany. Within an hour it became clear that no known weapon could stop the lumbering vehicle, although every enemy soldier on the battlefield tried. At the end of the day, when machine gun, rifle, and pistol bullets had pinged off its armor-plated sides, there was nothing left for the Germans to do but run.

And just like those tanks, though embattled, the conscience is in us to stay.

Imperfections

If we were to complete the picture of what happened on that opening day of World War I armored combat, we'd find that a lot of tanks didn't make it. Those that didn't, failed not because of the enemy's efforts, but due to mechanical breakdowns and getting stuck in the mud.

And the conscience, though it resists efforts to blast it into oblivion, is far from perfect. It is both psychological and spiritual, a connective tissue with one attachment point in the spirit, and the other in the soul. The spiritual aspect of it lies silent and dark until the Holy Spirit awakens it from its death slumber. Meanwhile, the psychological part of it feebly witnesses according to created goodness, home training, and various cultural norms and mores. This makes it vulnerable to imperfection. It not only can be overridden, but is capable of registering guilt when guilt is irrational, and of affirming things that are wrong.

For example, the Roman Emperor Aurelius famously boasted a good conscience, yet happily ordered Christians thrown into the arena to their deaths.[13] The Nazis were passionate conservationists, protecting their rivers and forests while gassing millions of Jews,[14] and Hitler himself was a vegetarian, considering it cruel to kill animals! Humans are nothing if not inconsistent, and often harbor serious internal contradictions.

Of course, not only politicians and social activists fall into this trap, but legions of religious folk, who fixate on minutiae to the exclusion of higher level concerns. To them, Jesus said, "Woe to you, scribes and Pharisees, hypocrites! For you tithe mint and dill and cumin, and have neglected the weightier matters of the law: justice and mercy and faithfulness. These you ought to have done, without neglecting the others" (Matt. 23:23). A lopsided conscience creates almost as many issues as it prevents. As Heard points out, it "is not real spiritual life though it wears the appearance of it, and sometimes deceives the inexperienced."[15]

Furthermore, conscience is not something molded in isolation. Forces outside of us also educate and shape it. That can be a good thing if we're talking about godly parents and peers, and most importantly as we'll see later, the Bible. But public consensus now ranks as the most influential power of all, and creates a herd morality that is frequently wrong concerning things of God—indeed, dramatically so. One only needs to remember the group enthusiasm for worship of the golden calf (see Exod. 32), the lynch mob that cried out for the crucifixion of Jesus (see Mark 15:13–14), and the last rebellion, when entire nations gather to try to overthrow Christ in the book of Revelation (see 20:7–8). In each case, sinful group opinions co-opted and refashioned personal conscience, with catastrophic results.

Our inward parts, even while attempting to tell the truth, can be maladjusted by our own wayward inclinations, and coerced by the seductive logic of others. Conscience, therefore, is not infallible. As Bonaventure says, it "can be damaged but not destroyed; it is and is not the voice of God."[16]

The Conscience Revived

Most of what we have seen thus far, has to do with conscience as held among human beings in general. Though we dislike its obstinate objections to the sins we love, we still celebrate those who stand up for what they believe is right (mostly when it has to do with social and political concerns with which we agree). We make much of human conscientiousness, canonizing new heroes with each passing day.

Yet the Bible has a much less rosy view of our internal condition and alleged sensitivities to what is right. It tells us that the people of this world "are darkened in their understanding, alienated from the life of God because of the ignorance that is in them, due to their hardness of heart. They have become callous and have given themselves up to sensuality, greedy to practice every kind of impurity" (Eph. 4:18–19).

We grossly overestimate our goodness, compassion, and decency. The real situation, of which we are mostly unaware, is that estrangement from God's life creates an insensitive condition in a person. Yes, though apathy saturates a sinner, our conscience, as we saw earlier, retains some limited function.[17] It is like a sickly oak tree that barely remains upright, whose spindly branches still somehow manage to produce a smattering of shriveled leaves every year. We thank God even for this anemic function, for without it, our world would descend into unlivable anarchy.

But the God-provided conscience not only saves us from the brutality of animal rule, it will hopefully become instrumental in the salvation of the soul. For when the gospel crosses a sinner's path, it will testify "of repentance toward God, and of faith in our Lord Jesus Christ" (Acts 20:21). At that point, the conscience is the part of a person that would register, *I have been wrong*, and, *This message is right*.

Still, in order for a meagerly functioning conscience to bear witness to such a heavenly message, it needs an open-chest heart massage by the Holy Spirit. "The world masquerades as righteous and suppresses any evidence to the contrary, and such behavior requires the Spirit to expose its guilt."[18] Heard writes that the Word of God "pierces not only into the soul, the seat of the emotions and mere intellectual notions, but down into the spirit, where the conscience lies sleeping and unalarmed."[19] It then awakens as "a guilty thing surprised."[20]

This certainly seemed to have been the case on the Day of Pentecost, when Peter preached the gospel to the gathered crowd, saying, "'know for certain that God has made him both Lord and Christ, this Jesus whom you crucified.' Now when they heard this they were cut to the heart" (Acts 2:36–37).

Peter's word, accompanied by the Holy Spirit, worked like a scalpel, cutting away the callus from their hearts. The result was a sudden pained response, as their mostly nocturnal consciences were bathed in a light alien to them. But rather than argue, or run, they accepted the sharp reproach from within: *You are complicit in killing the Christ of God.*

That day, those formerly proud, religious men, "said to Peter and the rest of the apostles, 'Brothers, what shall we do?' And Peter said to them, 'Repent and be baptized every one of you in the name of Jesus Christ for the forgiveness of your sins, and you will receive the gift of the Holy Spirit'" (Acts 2:37–38).

Jesus had promised this dynamic would take place whenever and wherever the Spirit worked.

> And when he comes, he will convict the world concerning sin and righteousness and judgment: concerning sin, because they do not believe in me; concerning righteousness, because I go to the Father, and you will see me no longer; concerning judgment, because the ruler of this world is judged. (John 16:8–11)

Conviction is the particular aspect of the Spirit's ministry that affects the conscience, and as these verses show, it occurs in multiple aspects. The first, Jesus says, concerns sin, "because they do not believe in me." Refusal to believe in Christ is the chief sin of all, because without receiving Him and His cross, then by default, all our other sins remain unforgiven, resulting in eternal destruction. Men delude themselves into thinking that their casual disregard of Christ is no big deal. But the Holy Spirit convicts the conscience otherwise, with warnings about the danger of unpaid sins.

The world has little or no idea of what sin is, and even less so about what is right. Therefore, the Spirit also convicts the conscience "concerning righteousness." People often believe they are justified by championing social positions, tradition, personally manufactured standards, and cherry-picked morality. However, in John 16:10, righteousness has nothing to do with one's attainments, but everything to do with Jesus going to the Father. When He sat down at God's right hand after crucifixion and resurrection, His redemptive work was finished. The Spirit thus preaches to the conscience that "all our righteous deeds are like a polluted garment" (Isa. 64:6), and that only Christ crucified and resurrected counts for righteousness in the eyes of God.

Finally, the Spirit convicts "concerning judgment, because the ruler of this world is judged" (John 16:11). The human race has long assumed that the god of this world is a benevolent, non-intrusive deity of their choice. Reality, however, is another story, where we find a dark angelic overlord sitting atop a pile of subjugated humanity. Jesus said as His cross drew near, "now is the judgment of this world; now will the ruler of this world be cast out" (John 12:31). Thus, the warning whispered to the conscience says that the devil, his world system, and all who are in it, lie under God's condemnation.

In other words, the Spirit delivers to the sinner the judgment of the court, appealing to his conscience and notifying it of great wrong, a wrong which if left unaddressed, will result in incalculable harm. Yet, this ministry does not convict merely to fill a human heart with dread. The Spirit's great object is to sanctify, or set apart a person "for obedience to Jesus Christ" (1 Pet. 1:2)—not in all particulars of behavior at this initial point, but for the "obedience of faith" (Rom. 1:5). This results in "sprinkling with his blood" (1 Pet. 1:2). Once our conscience is awakened by the agency of the Holy Spirit, nothing we can present to it will bring it peace. We will not settle for sin "made up for" by "good" deeds (as we once did), or sin excused, or sin overlooked, but only sin adequately paid for and washed away. Then the troubled conscience will find rest.

This is peace on God's terms. It does not lie to the sinner, telling him or her there is nothing wrong, that guilt is a psychological phantom. Truly, we felt guilty because we *were* guilty.[21] Truly, as well, we are at peace, because Christ's blood is effective.

David said, "Blessed is the man against whom the LORD counts no iniquity" (Ps. 32:2). Now we have no more consciousness of sins unpaid (see Heb. 10:2), nor "a fearful expectation of judgment, and a fury of fire that will consume the adversaries" (Heb. 10:27). If anything remains with us, it is a contrite awareness of where we were, and a new, passionate appreciation for "the Lamb [of God] who was slain" (Rev. 5:12).

In my teens, I had a favorite pair of khaki trousers that were strictly for church. "I want to wear those to school today," I told my mother. She wasn't keen on the idea, but I assured her that I was practically grown up at age sixteen, and could manage my own clothing, thank you. But at sixth hour art class, the girl sitting next to me accidentally knocked a bottle of India ink into my lap. I had to go home that day with a stain the size of Texas on my pants, and tell my mother about how her "big boy" wasn't able to manage his clothing after all. "Maybe it'll come out in the wash," I timidly suggested. She gave me an annoyed smirk. No detergent in the world was going to undo that stain. The trousers were demoted from church wear to lawn-mowing clothes.

Nothing was ever going to launder the sin off your conscience, either. But now the cross has expunged your sin record, and you have been notified of it through the preaching of the gospel. Having believed, you can be counted among those who "have washed their robes and made them white in the blood of the Lamb" (7:14).

Massive Upgrade

Now, the previously bullied, neglected, anemic, stained, conscience that was forced to do its job from the back of the bus, has become the very bow of the ship of the Christian walk. Something has clearly happened. In Acts 2:38, Peter commanded his listeners to "Repent and be baptized every one of you in the name of Jesus Christ for the forgiveness of your sins," but he added a promise: "and you will receive the gift of the Holy Spirit."

Receiving the Spirit, as we have already seen, triggers the second birth. This is nothing less than the resurrection of the deadened human spirit, and the bringing to life of one of its chief functions, the conscience. The Spirit not only convicted the conscience unto repentance, but enlivened it by His gracious presence. In this "repentance that leads to life" (Acts 11:18), the conscience then rose above its former station. All our lives it had only acted as a witness to the limited righteousness of the human world, but now, as Paul wrote, "my conscience bears me witness in the Holy Spirit" (Rom. 9:1).

This is something new, and signifies a massive upgrade not only unto new standards, but aligned upon new tastes. Heard says, "When a man's spirit . . . is really regenerated of the Holy Ghost, the sure and certain mark that a work of grace has begun is a certain sensitiveness to sin and a certain fear of offending God, arising not so much from fear of the consequences as because we hate sin even as God hates it."[22]

Paul highly valued this inner dynamic. He summarized his own experience, saying, "I have lived my life before God in all good conscience up to this day" (Acts 23:1), and, "Our boast is this, the testimony of our conscience, that we behaved in the world with simplicity and godly sincerity, not by earthly wisdom but by the grace of God, and supremely so toward you" (2 Cor. 1:12).

The apostolic desire to live every day with a newly cleansed and enlivened conscience provides an example for us all. But, as we will see, it is an aspiration with a certain amount of vigilance attached to it.

6

Conscience—A Guide to Care and Maintenance

Oh, for a heart to praise my God,
A heart from sin set free,
A heart that always feels thy blood,
So freely shed for me.

—Charles Wesley

IN THE SUMMER OF 2014, I went on a camping trip with friends to the Boundary Waters area of Minnesota. I had been warned ahead of time about mosquitoes and leeches, and I'd heard a little something about bears. Nobody had said a word about mice. It wasn't a problem for a few days, until some of the guys started noticing holes in food sacks.

When we ignored it, the situation got worse. Small shapes scurried around the campsite. And then we started seeing them in our tents. Apparently a mouse will risk life and limb for dinner, so it was officially "on" when the little varmints discovered trail mix in our supplies. They began running across our chests while we were sleeping, looking for snacks. They even gnawed a hole through one guy's shirt pocket! (He'd stowed a pack of peanuts there, thinking it would be safe.)

By the time we got serious about the mice, they had virtually lost their fear of man. You could approach your tent with a flashlight and see them sitting outside the tent door, like people waiting in line for free concert tickets. Finally we put all the food products in a bag and hoisted it by rope over a high tree branch. The problem subsided. Thinking back on it, if we hadn't done anything about the situation, we'd have ended up in sleeping bags full of mice—and a ruined trip as well.

This is what I see happening when a Christian decides to "take a break" from Jesus. The lapse always involves the conscience. We start letting little things go, making excuses, ignoring problems. And then there's a mounting outbreak of sin.

In the meantime, it's hard to enjoy anything related to church or the Bible. You feel yourself losing boldness when people ask you about your Christian life. Your position on certain moral issues grows soft. Everything and everyone seems bent on judging you. It makes you angry. You start to think about those hypocrites at church and it makes you rage. Your favorite verse stops being John 3:16 and starts being Matthew 7:1—"Judge not, that you be not judged"—a sentiment that suits you just fine, but for all the wrong reasons. You used to seek truth. Now you only hunt for affirmation.

Once this habit of life begins, it might be months or years before something happens that shakes you back to your senses. And by that time, so many "mice" will have accumulated, you won't know where to start dealing with the infestation.

While our eternal salvation was a mighty one-time event that needs no help to remain potent, our spiritual condition must be cultivated and maintained. If we want to fully enjoy salvation in the vector of day-to-day life, and bring glory to God, we must be done with passivity. We should develop a holy vigilance for what is happening within, beginning with the registration of conscience. This is critical, because it is the first and most simple exercise related to inner life.

A Gauge of Quality Fellowship

In Christians, the conscience is a psychological *and* spiritual part meant to optimize our fellowship with God. It not only witnesses to general standards of right and wrong, but also works under the influence of God's truth and the indwelling Holy Spirit to keep us walking according to Christ. "The conscience in man may be likened to a balance," Baird says. "In unregenerate natures it can make, successfully, the larger discriminations, but, when quickened and made spiritually sensitive, it is capable of much greater refinement and deals with the more delicate matters of motive and principle."[1]

Beginning with this newly calibrated conscience, we can start to realize the potential of the Christian experience. John wrote, "These things we write to you that your joy may be made full" (1 John 1:4, NKJV). And the very first means of making our joy full involves learning that "God is light" (1:5). This is good news to us, the same way light is good news to a field of crops, or to a city after a long nighttime crime spree, or to a person suffering from a vitamin D deficiency. God is bright, refreshing, energizing. "In Him is no darkness at all" (1:5). There is nothing about Him that withers or depresses, nothing that contains the gloom of evil.

Furthermore, "If we say we have fellowship with him while we walk in darkness, we lie and do not practice the truth" (1 John 1:6). This is logical. Since God is light, we can't claim to have a robust relationship with Him while living in sin. No one draped in darkness can claim they're standing under the strength of a noonday sun. If they do, they're either willfully lying, self-deceived, or just don't know what light is.

"But if we walk in the light, as he is in the light, we have fellowship with one another, and the blood of Jesus his Son cleanses us from all sin" (1:7).

> **THE LIGHT OF GOD MANIFESTS OUR DEEDS, OUR ATTITUDES, OUR MOTIVES. THERE ARE NO FIG LEAVES TO HIDE BEHIND.**

Notice the "if" in verse 7, because it means the apostle is about to address something conditional. "If" we walk in the light of God, then fellowship—that is, true interactions—will take place between us and Him. "If" we walk in the light.

This may sound unsettling, because light exposes things (see Eph. 5:13). The light of God manifests our deeds, our attitudes, our motives. There are no fig leaves to hide behind. Therefore, with neither pretense, nor excuse, we willingly stand before him "naked and exposed" (Heb. 4:13). Such vulnerability sounds terribly awkward, yet His light—the brilliance of His presence—spares us from fruitless introspection, second-guessing, and self-condemnation. No human search or checklist can substitute for the light of God. Nor does God need our help to uncover our transgressions, as though we must root through daily track records—*Did I use profanity today? Have I fallen into hating that person at work again?* Or a million other permutations. Introspection of this sort only generates anxiety—a mock sense of conviction. No, our part is to walk in the light. He does the rest. Come to God and let the radiance of His Person do the work. Proceed as though everything is fine. Don't pick at yourself. His personal shining will illuminate anything that needs to be addressed.

Yes, Paul did say, "Let a person examine himself" (1 Cor. 11:28), but it was an instruction to those in Corinth who had established a habit of not walking in the light. They had experienced a wonderful beginning, and been enriched in all knowledge (1:5), but their attention had shifted away from their inner life. The Corinthians had become mindful of dramatic spiritual gifts, yet blind to the obvious fact that they were visiting prostitutes, and suing one another in court! Paul hoped to shake them awake. It reminds me of the days back when I helped my little daughter find something in her room—her shoes, or a toy, that was right in front of her, but somehow escaping her sight. "Look hard," I told her, knowing that with a minimum of effort she would finally see it. I've also done the same thing a time or two, when, distracted, I searched the entire house looking for car keys—*that were in my hand*. Paul hoped that with a minimum of self-examination, these Christians would see the obvious sins they were committing.

Sometimes we simply don't want exposure of this kind. The prospect of light is intimidating to a sinner, as John's gospel says, "everyone who does wicked things hates the light and does not come to the light, lest his works should be exposed" (John 3:20). But what horrible thing will occur when light does its exposing work? What can we, as Christians, expect to happen? The answer is, "We have fellowship with one another, and the blood of Jesus his Son cleanses us from all sin" (1 John 1:7). God's emphasis is on fellowship—fellowship restored and strengthened, not alienation. He therefore illuminates our conscience for the sake of maintaining a powerful inner life. Do we really want to avoid that?

Although verse 7 doesn't use the word "conscience," we know from earlier study that whenever sin appears, conscience is always involved. We might at this point think of it like a plate of glass, through which God's light shines and bathes us in glory. But as with an actual window, the brighter the light, the more spots appear on the glass. Light doesn't create the spots; it exposes them. If we ignore the stains, smears, and blemishes for too long, then like a window assaulted by weather and dust particles, your ability to see through it will become impaired over time. Your view of God's glory will dim.[2] Given enough negligence, that dim glow will fade to a barely discernible glimmer. Most believers who have experienced backsliding (myself included) agree that at this point, the Christian life will seem to have lost its luster. Little will remain that we find compelling anymore, because a mud-stained, opaque plate exists between us and God.

But as sin is manifested in the conscience, the blood of Jesus cleanses. This is the gospel realized in our daily inward experience. A sinful person can fellowship with God in the brilliance of His glory because of the blood of Jesus. None of us should ever be paralyzed by fear of God's light, because the blood of His Son is there, and it washes us relentlessly.

When the light of God shines through a clear conscience, it facilitates fellowship with God, and with others who fellowship with Him. The positivity and joyfulness that breaks out can actually be a spiritual defense against some forms of depression.[3] When we walk in the light, we see God for who He is. Consider the creatures in Revelation who are "full of eyes all around and within"; they see the glory of God, "and day and night they never cease to say, 'Holy, holy, holy, is the Lord God Almighty, who was and is and is to come!'" (Rev. 4:8). They can't help it—the sight of peerless worth and majesty stirs them to praise. The more the light of the glorious God floods your inner being, shining through a spotless conscience, the more you will find yourself walking above things that formerly weighed you down.

Light brings everything into the open where nothing is hidden. However, this does not mean everything that might be wrong with you is made manifest. Such an avalanche of conviction would be disastrous for you. Watchman Nee says, "Conscience is a God-given *current* standard of holiness."[4] Even if it is crystal clear, we cannot assume we have arrived at absolute perfection. A good conscience merely assures us that so far as our knowledge goes, we are perfect, that is, we have arrived at the immediate goal, but not the ultimate one.[5] God has much more to say to us, but He must deal with us as believers who are in varying conditions and places of understanding. He therefore allows imperfections in us that have not been brought under His light, and for the time being remain unknown to us.

The condition of your conscience, therefore, becomes incredibly important. When troubled, it delivers warning of a decline in the quality of your fellowship. When peaceful, it shows that as far as you know, you are living faithfully before God.

Reactions to the Light

For all the blessings that conscience can offer, we still find ourselves arguing with it. This is dangerous. John warned, "If we say we have no sin, we deceive ourselves" (1 John 1:8). When light shines deeply enough to illuminate a private, cherished sin, we often dispute the protestations of conscience, and sometimes violently. For example, King Herod had enjoyed hearing the sermons of John the Baptist until the day John dared preach about sexual ethics. The message offended the king, because he had been living with a woman in adultery. Rather than repenting, and facing the complications of dealing with his sin, he threw John into prison.[6] Contemporary analogies of this account are not hard to find. One need only think of preachers being fired for landing on the wrong side of political correctness, church members moving from congregation to congregation to escape Scriptural accountability, and experts who invent hermeneutical schemes for redefining Bible verses they find backward or embarrassing. There are also the age-old responses of bribing one's conscience, self-justification, blame-shifting, and using religious attainments in other areas to silence conviction.

Paul taught that believers should be people "holding faith and a good conscience. By rejecting this, some have made shipwreck of their faith" (1 Tim. 1:19). He also wrote that when we refuse the protests of conscience, it can lead to an inward condition he called "seared," or cauterized with a hot iron (4:2). "Human skin frequently cauterized becomes thick, tough and leathery, and is rendered insensible to pain."[7] Such regular neglect of the conscience desensitizes us toward God and leads into progressively deeper bondage to sin.

Ultimately, all our resistance occurs because of our mistaken assumption that the grieved conscience could only lead us to one place—loss and misery. But Paul wrote that "godly grief produces a repentance that leads to salvation *without regret*" (2 Cor. 7:10). Pangs of conscience come with the intention of enriching, not impoverishing the wayward saint. Grief, however momentary, is the gateway into horizons far beyond what we currently know, like Josiah's repentance that led to a national revival, or David's repentance that set the stage for bringing Solomon to the throne, leading to the building of the temple.

> **THE HEART-LEVEL OPERATIONS OF CONSCIENCE ARE NOT THE PRODUCT OF AN OVERACTIVE IMAGINATION.**

A great truth lies right on the other side of what we dismiss as trifling concerns of conscience. The apostle John wrote of it, saying, "whenever our heart condemns us, God is greater than our heart, and he knows everything" (1 John 3:20). This reminds us that the heart-level operations of conscience are not the product of an overactive imagination. Behind them, the eternal God may be furnishing the very sense of conviction you are trying to write off. And He knows *everything*.

Consider the night light in your home that gives off a small, gentle glow. Its diminutive illumination comes from an electrical current traveling through wires from a gigantic power plant many miles away. The power behind your little bathroom bulb is great enough to run your entire city. Similarly, your small disquiet over something you've done, or are planning to do, may have a truthfulness behind it larger than the universe.

When we heed a bothered conscience, or repent because of an aggrieved one, we can experience the immediate effect of strengthening fellowship with God. Any inward rebuke, therefore, must be settled. This is why John went on to write, "Beloved, if our heart does not condemn us, we have confidence before God" (1 John 3:21), that is, bold, fearless faith.

Understandably, the light of God will make us aware of things within that we'd rather not see. Years back I lived in a house that had a bug problem. I'm not crazy about spiders, centipedes, and all their kinfolk, and thankfully, I seldom saw any during the day. But one time I was doing some late work and went down to my basement office at two in the morning. Big mistake. When the light came on, I saw an enormous brown spider perched on a box next to my desk. After shaking off the chills, I took a swipe at it with a rolled up magazine, missed, and knocked it inside the box. The thing was large enough to make an audible thud when it landed in the bottom. After dousing it with half a can of bug spray, I tucked the box flaps together, and then threw the whole package into the trash, making sure the garbage truck carried it off the next day. (Did I mention I don't like spiders?)

Most of us don't know about the "wildlife" that lives in our basements, and may not want to know. Likewise, we may not want to see what is in ourselves, either. When the light comes on, we have a habit of looking the other way. Yet, in fighting or dismissing our consciences, we show our ignorance of the ongoing power of the blood of Christ to cleanse us. We also forget that cleansing restores us to fellowship, and elevates us to still greater vistas. God's call to repentance is not a curse; it is His kindness (see Rom. 2:4).

Light Through the Word

Light is not so mystical an experience that it shines without rhyme or reason. John describes it as traveling a descending order, becoming available in increasingly practical ways. Thus light (see 1 John 1:7), comes through truth (see 1:8), which is packaged in the Word (see 1:10). If you are truth deficient, having little of His Word deposited in your heart, then at best, your inner life will be swamped in twilight.

It is not uncommon to hear people speak of "their truth," meaning whatever feels right to them. The most common characteristic of "their truth," though, is that it avoids any actual dealing with sin, even to the complete denial of it.

"If we say we have no sin, we deceive ourselves and the truth is not in us. . . . If we say we have not sinned, we make him [God] a liar, and his word is not in us" (1:8, 10). The link between God's Word of Truth and our attitudes toward sin is unmistakable in these verses.

And the Word of Truth for us begins in the pages of the Bible. It enters us through prayer, meditation, reading, hearing, and study, then becoming the language by which the Holy Spirit speaks to us. It illuminates our inward parts. This is why Psalm 119:130 says, "The entrance of your words gives light" (NKJV). Our light source originates *outside* of us—outside our subjective ideas, our cultures, our political biases, and the popular opinions to which we subscribe. And it is just as well. Truth becomes suspect when it is radically individualized. Strom says, "Any process of ethical choice which occurs entirely within the mind of the agent remains vulnerable to circularity and possible fallacy."[8] Mortal concepts are full of internal contradictions, and *un*reality, which is why God said to us, "My thoughts are not your thoughts, neither are your ways my ways. . . . For as the heavens are higher than the earth, so are my ways higher than your ways and my thoughts than your thoughts" (Isa. 55:8–9). Our brains are not the point of truth's origin, neither could they ever be.

When exposed to the Word of God, Baird compares the conscience to a glow-in-the-dark toy which, when held under bright light, glows furiously in the dark.[9] A conscience thus enlightened protects us from being shaped by unbalanced religious thoughts. Many of us spent formative years in churches that emphasized beliefs having little or no scriptural support—legal requirements like diet, dress, observance of days, hair styles, ownership of televisions, beards, and hundreds more. These so-called convictions can burden an entire community of believers, driving some of the members to despair. But nothing brings clarity like the plain sense of Scripture. It calibrates our conscience, keeping us from unnecessary additional burdens.[10]

But the same Word of Truth that sets us free also makes us "slaves to righteousness" (Rom. 6:19). God never intended for us to drift into liberal indifference to His holiness. This has often been our answer to legalism—to claim unfettered freedom, even to the extent of antinomianism (meaning "against law"). Today's society, including many Christians, have fallen into a near idolatry of love divorced from the Person of God, and grace as disconnected from truth. Such extremes also became evident during the Protestant Reformation, when Luther, himself a champion of personal conscience, made a surly observation of his Protestant brethren:

"They live like dumb brutes and irrational hogs; and yet, now that the Gospel has come, they have nicely learned to abuse all liberty like experts."[11] We should not answer one extreme with another, nor do we look for a compromise in the middle. Instead, we stand upon the Word of God.

Paul Strohm, author of *Conscience: A Very Short Introduction*, presents the saga of King Henry VIII, as he attempted to get out of the marriage to his longtime queen, Catherine, and marry his romantic interest, Anne Boleyn. Henry wished to justify his decision based upon personal conscience, and private communion with the Holy Spirit. Sir Thomas More, councillor to the king, at first wavered in favor of Henry, but eventually saw through the king's dilemma for what it was— the development of an evil conscience, which More called "damnable" and "an errant individual . . . against common faith."[12] On the heels of this statement, Henry ordered More executed. Too bad the king never grasped the spirit of Luther's famous sentiment—"I am bound by the Scriptures I have quoted, and my conscience is captive to the Word of God." Perhaps he would be famous today for something more than his eight marriages. And for executing Sir Thomas.

In order to properly school our conscience, we should use all means at our disposal to understand the clear sense of Scripture. We absorb the Word through prayer and reflection; through the enrichment, checks, and balances of godly companions; by reading healthy literature; by listening to the Word preached; and through study according to the rules of good interpretation. We wish, in other words, to say together with the Psalmist, "Your word is a lamp to my feet and a light to my path" (Ps. 119:105).

Agreeing with Our Conscience

The biblical alternative to concealing or denying our sins is to confess them to God: "If we confess our sins, he is faithful and just to forgive us our sins and to cleanse us from all unrighteousness" (1 John 1:9). Confession is the moment of truth and turning point for a believer. It's like a reality television program such as *Restaurant Rescue*, when the owner, who has mismanaged his establishment to the point of collapse, finally listens to the expert and admits where the problem lies. Only when he acknowledges the truth, and his complicity in the mess he has made, can the real magic of turnaround begin.

However, confession hardly seems the best thing to do with God. Why would drawing His attention to our sin solve anything? Wouldn't it make things worse? But that concern is actually laughable, because it assumes God is ignorant of our transgressions until we bring them up. In reality, we do not draw God's attention to them, *God* draws *our* attention to them. Jesus is "he who searches mind and heart" (Rev. 2:23). Before we are willing to label anything as sin, He already knows there is something wrong. In His light, we should confess it.

The Greek word for "confess" is *homolegeo*. *Homo* means "same," and *legeo* means "to speak." When we confess, we should speak the same thing our conscience speaks—no more and no less. Look at David's confession and repentance in Psalm 51. We don't find excuses, or tiptoeing around the issue, but a full-out admission of guilt. He had tried to bury his sin of adultery and murder for nine months, and when confession finally emerged, it had neither the ring of trite apology, nor liturgical wording, nor political spin. Nothing but brutal self-honesty marked his words.

Our English word "confess" implies a previous reluctance to come clean. Fear and tentativeness often causes us to blunt the force of a confession even when it is privately to God. The desire for saving face can become so strong a force that what begins as a confession turns into an excuse, complete with tears of pity for ourselves. We long to be a victim, rather than a perpetrator, believing that confession of wrongdoing on our part must be avoided at all costs.

Much to our surprise, the confession of dark secrets illuminated by God's Word, leads not to increased guilt, but to His forgiveness and cleansing. John cites the unexpected reason for this outcome: God is "faithful and just to forgive us our sins and to cleanse us from all unrighteousness." Faithfulness and justice would hardly seem to be characteristics that motivate forgiveness. They appear much better suited for judgment. God is faithful to do what is right, and it is right for Him to find sinners guilty. However, the blood of Jesus has been shed for our sins. As a believer, you are now on the other side of that cross, and it is right for God *not* to make us pay for sins that Christ has already paid for. If He did, it would suggest that the cross of Calvary was insufficient, and insult the payment His Son had made for us. Thank God that He can be counted on (He is faithful) to do what is right (He is just).

The forgiveness and cleansing that comes after confession is not some new work of God, but an application of what He has already done through Jesus. It is a memo to the stricken conscience, a fresh, inward awareness of the cancellation of our sin debt on Calvary. *What about this sin?* the troubled conscience asks, and then recites a litany of failures.

> *I lied about how much I make a year because I wanted everybody to admire me.*
>
> *I hate the woman who works at the front desk.*
>
> *I would do anything to have his/her spouse.*
>
> *I've been too lazy to pray.*

To each, God says, "Yes, I forgive it. I forgive because I am faithful to the blood covenant of My Son. I forgive because it is the right thing to do. Now, resume walking in the light."

Confession applies redemption in real time and makes us conscious of it. It appropriates the *objective* truth of redemption and applies it to our *subjective* experience.[13] And the conscience, having received a fresh application of the gospel, finds satisfaction. It has not been bribed or twisted, numbed, or seared. It has been *answered.* The promise that God will forgive and cleanse us translates into two results. Forgiveness means a weight has been lifted off our conscience, a burden of guilt discarded, so that we can "mount up with wings like eagles" (Isa. 40:31). Cleansing, on the other hand, refers to the removal of stains from the window of our conscience, resulting in the fresh sight and celebration of God's glory.

The Christian who maintains conscience in such a way will make astounding progress in spiritual growth and conformation to Christ.[14] Typically in the aftermath of forgiveness and cleansing, small personal revivals break out. Some are truly life-changing. The first time I met my wife-to-be, I was a new Christian—happy and bright. A few months after marriage, though, I let myself go to the extent that I was dark and angry most of the time. Although I didn't direct any animosity toward her, I did a lot of yelling at our dog, who liked to tear things up and wet the carpet. My cursing and temper tantrums went on just long enough for my wife to wonder if I was the same man she had married. I had also begun to behave at work like I had prior to salvation, although my coworkers didn't mind, since they loved my R-rated comedic wit. Looking back on my few brief months as a Christian, I thought, *Well, that didn't last long.*

But when I finally answered the corrective protest of my conscience, and had a thorough, verbal admission of guilt, I was revived to the extent that everyone noticed. I went back to my normal self, bright, upbeat, and walking in the light of God. My wife was relieved. My coworkers were puzzled, but welcomed my fresh kindness and work ethic, and a few of them became interested in the gospel.

Even more, I had learned an incredible new lesson. In my earlier life, I had had a couple of false starts with religious living—proto-Christian experiences I call them—and had fallen off the righteousness wagon every time. Without being born again, there was no way I could pretend to be a Christian for long. I would always reach a place where I would abandon my attempt to be a better man, like the guy who just can't stop cheating on his kale diet. With each of those defeats came a crushing sense of failure. I would always get a few days out, a week, maybe, before coming to the end of my self-improvement program.

Eventually, though, I met Jesus, and was born again. Equipped with an enlivened spirit, I told myself, "This time I'm going to do it right." Yet, as if on an egg-timer, some of my old failures began to reemerge. So did my impulse to give up. I figured if I couldn't have a perfect, self-manicured

Christian life, I would forget the whole thing. That was the debacle I mentioned earlier, right after I had gotten married.

But my humiliation, repentance, and return from that tar pit taught me my approach had been all wrong. The secret to following Christ wasn't about my ability to control my way to glory, to succeed in being a Jesus cadet, or in keeping a squeaky clean record. I needed the regular application of the gospel found in the simple dynamic of light-blood-confession-fellowship. Due to the grace of the gospel, there was no reason for me *not* to have a quality relationship with God.

That was thirty-five years ago, and I am still here following Him, precisely because the gospel has been effective. For the rest of your life as well, great care notwithstanding, you will at times commit sin. That means the blood of Christ applied through confession will need to be a regular feature[15] of your inner life.

When Paul said he had lived in all good conscience before God, he didn't mean he never sinned, but he paid attention to his inward state, and dealt with his conscience according to the blood of Christ. The normal Christian life is one of repentance, ongoing realignment, and fresh beginnings that lead to higher places. This is why Revelation chapters 2 and 3 recycle a drumbeat of "Repent" to the churches. At any given moment, it seems either Christians need a thorough housecleaning, or they're close to needing one. This is similar to people who have a hoarding disorder. As they stockpile trinkets and amass mountains of dirty clothes and assorted trash, weirdness begins to settle into the fabric of their world. And once the conscience falls into such neglect, collecting offenses and sins of various sorts, so the Christian's inner life degrades.

However, our bodies are temples of the Holy Spirit (see 1 Cor. 6:19), vessels of glory. From the moment our eyes open in the morning, we hope to be strengthened with power through his Spirit in our inner being, so Christ can dwell in our hearts through faith, we come to know the love of Christ, and we are filled with the fullness of God (see Eph. 3:16–19). Our conscience aids greatly toward this end, disagreeing with the things that don't correspond to His magnificence, and peacefully allowing all that does.

With this internal gatekeeper satisfied, the way will be open for further spiritual experiences to take place. However, in order to navigate the inevitable misunderstandings that arise from conscience issues, we need one final round of adjustment.

7

The Conscience
Gone Haywire

No weapon that is fashioned against you shall succeed,
and you shall refute every tongue that rises against you
in judgment.
This is the heritage of the servants of the LORD
and their vindication from me, declares the LORD.

— Isaiah 54:17

EVERY YEAR, THOUSANDS of people go missing in the woods of North America. Apparently, they wander off a trail to explore, or to take a bathroom break. Most of these return, though an alarming number are never seen again—alive, anyway.

Maybe upon becoming lost, they try to do the things they saw on survival programs, like thatching a hut, getting naked, spearing fish. These aren't things to do when you're lost.

Wildlife safety experts strongly suggest that when venturing into the forest, we should carry everything with us that we need in case of getting lost. Rather than try to construct a villa made of fir limbs to keep the elements off you, wear a raincoat. Don't try to start a fire in the wild by using a prehistoric bow; bring matches or a lighter. Rather than trying to hunt down and kill an elk with a homemade stone dagger, pack some energy bars.

And this last one is extremely important: bring a compass. It can mean the difference between heading in a straight line, or discovering you've walked in a grueling six-hour circle. At any rate, no matter how scared or lost you are, that needle keeps floating northward, always telling you in what direction you're headed.

Still, the compass, the ultimate simple directional tool, can run into challenges of its own. The little needle can be thrown off magnetic north by exposure to metal objects like wristwatches and car keys, or by an electrical source such as your cellphone, and thus give false readings.

Like the compass, our conscience was meant to be something simple and sincere. But just like the compass, it can encounter interference from various objects and situations, and bring confusion. Suddenly, what ought to be simple becomes downright mystifying.

For instance, the conscience that was at peace after a thorough repentance is full of misgivings twenty minutes later. Or there can be a collision of conflicting consciences among those in the church. Who is right? And finally, unexplained dark moods can plague a believer over sins that may never have even happened. These all come from competing "fields" that can adversely affect our conscience.

Thankfully, we can sort through these potentially confusing issues with God's truth, bringing recalibration and understanding to our inner life.

The Enigma of False Readings

During one colorful Old Testament incident, the Philistines encountered the punishment of God. Chafing under His displeasure, they invented laughable, ineffective solutions meant to calm His anger. "Who can stand before this holy God?" they had asked in futility, so some suggested a "guilt offering" (see 1 Sam. 6:3). And then the solemn recommendations of the pagan priests had begun—offer the God of Israel a new cart. Golden mice. Tumors cast in gold. (Some old-school commentators have suggested those "tumors" were actually hemorrhoids. Yes, golden hemorrhoids, offered to God.)

My friends and I had a good laugh over this bizarre Philistine guessing game one morning during a men's Bible study, but I wonder how many Christians endure similar torments. What happens when confession of sin fails to "work," and afterward a certain dread continues—an unsettled fear of not having done enough? For many of us, strange days begin right here.

This, therefore, is a problem worth exploring, for at some time in the future, a repetitive or deeply troubling sin may emerge in our lives that creates special pain and shame. Registrations of guilt can become so severe it could lead to a downturn in our spiritual health, and challenge our trust in the blood of Jesus. Believers who have experienced this situation know the second-guessing that takes place. They have confessed their sin and experienced the peace of the Lord's blood in their conscience, but condemnation returns, causing them to wonder if that sin must be confessed afresh, this time with tears. Having obeyed that impulse, self-reproach creeps in once more, suggesting that we might have still gotten off the hook too easily and should penalize ourselves more severely.

Those of us who enter this vicious cycle, especially those more emotionally fragile, may feel they're struggling against quicksand. Guilt seems to resurrect as surely as Jesus from the tomb, and though we banish it ten times a day, it keeps coming back. Even while you attempt to bring these things to the Lord, the blood of Christ seems laughable in the face of your wrongdoing. The power of guilt and condemnation have come calling, and we begin to frantically search for another answer. "How can I stand before this holy God?" we catch ourselves wondering, just like the Philistines of old.

> **THE GOOD JESUS HAS DONE ON THE CROSS COUNTS FOR MORE THAN THE EVIL WE HAVE DONE. THE CROSS IS OUR MAGNETIC NORTH.**

There are no special tricks to solve this problem other than our insistence upon the truth of the gospel: the good Jesus has done on the cross counts for more than the evil we have done in our flesh. The cross is always our magnetic north. Without it, just as with an actual compass, our needle will swivel around wildly. The worst thing we can do is entertain these false readings, feeding them and obeying them. Learn to say no to them instead, while standing on the truth of Calvary.

This, or course, doesn't mean we should minimize sin. Your sin is so serious Jesus had to die for it. Don't carelessly walk back into its embrace, telling yourself, "No problem; I'll just repent later." There are plenty of consequences you can incur that can't be undone, like an unwanted pregnancy or an abortion. Maybe in a moment of weakness, you said or did something that seriously damaged another person's life. Perhaps something you did caused another person to lose their life. Maybe you betrayed your spouse, assaulted someone, unrighteously caused someone to lose their job. Or, perhaps you revisited a sinful pattern you had fought for a long time, like pornography, drugs, alchohol, or gambling. None of these matters are inconsequential. Having fallen into them, there is no guarantee you will emerge without significant scarring, or at the very least, a radically altered life.

The last thing you want to do is rationalize your sin as "no big deal." Don't lie to yourself. Cleansing never comes from dishonesty. Learn to tell yourself the largest truth possible. That is, from the beginning of the world, God instituted the thought of blood sacrifice, rejecting anything else as unworthy (see Gen. 3:2, 4:3–5). As His redemptive plan unfolded, He saved His entire people from condemnation with the blood of a lamb (see Exod. 12), maintaining His fellowship with them through the blood sacrifices of Leviticus. When at last He Himself showed up, He did so as "the Lamb of God, who takes away the sin of the world" (John 1:29). Today, the power of His cross is the centerpiece of the Christian life (see 1 Cor. 1:18), and will forever be exalted by God (see Phil. 2:5–11; Rev. 22:1).

You must preach this sermon to yourself, because your conscience will only witness to the truth it has been shown. It is not simply the forgiveness of Jesus or the love of Jesus. It is the *blood* of Jesus. Blood demonstrates the severity of the situation. His payment was not for mere "slips" or, much less, accidents. Had the sins He intended to pay for only included occasional profanity or peevishness before morning coffee, He might have been able to avoid the bloody nightmare of the cross and find an easier way to deal with such "tame" offenses. But He knew the enormous darkness of the human heart—a heart that produced the Holocaust, every form of sexual deviance, hate for one's fellow man, the utter inability to love, and refusal to forgive. He knew of our idolatry of self, the wicked glee we feel when we exact revenge, and our submerged, evil motives that are present even while doing allegedly good things. If we were in any sense hopeful, His blood would have been a gross overpayment. The truth of these words must overwhelm your conscience.

After Peter's denial of Jesus, the Lord not only forgave the hapless disciple, but went after him and restored him. We never hear of Jesus showing up after his repentance, taunting the man, challenging him to repent again for his infamous lapse. Instead, we find inside the future ministry of the apostle, the death of Christ looming large to the point that his entire first letter was dominated, chapter by chapter with the thought of Calvary: "The precious blood of Christ" (1 Pet. 1:19); "He himself bore our sins in his body on the tree" (2:24); "Christ also suffered once for sins, the righteous for the unrighteous" (3:18); "Christ suffered in the flesh" (4:1); "the sufferings of Christ" (5:1). Peter apparently learned that what Christ has done must always speak louder to our consciences than our failures.

Some sins we commit will result in painful consequences that we must live with for the rest of our lives. However, even in those situations, the blood of Jesus removes the restriction upon our inward flow of fellowship with Him. It frees us from a state of perpetual condemnation. This is the message a malfunctioning conscience needs to hear.

Satanic Interference

In a number of places the Bible describes a real and continuing war waged on the saints that at times becomes palpable.

Since it is beyond physical sight, most of the world, including careless Christians, walk around oblivious to its existence. In saying this, I don't wish to feed religious paranoia. Some believers have become hypersensitive to satanic forces and look for supernatural reasons behind every case of stomach flu or car trouble. Some are even quick to cite satanic attack as the reason they lost a job, when the blame might lie with chronic lateness or workplace incompetence. As Christians, we should avoid becoming superstitious or developing a morbid fascination with the powers of darkness. Though we shouldn't be ignorant of Satan's tactics, we do not need to be distracted by them, either.

Concerning his battle plan, the devil's weapon of choice is linked to his very identity. "Devil" literally means accuser or slanderer. The Christian conscience, therefore, makes an appealing target for him. We are people who value righteousness, love Jesus, and wish to please Him. New life has sensitized our consciences, but we are still imperfect—constantly prone to gaffes, seasons of backsliding, and deliberate sins. A sensitized conscience within an erring body seems to be a bad combination. It becomes child's play for satanic accusations to slip by undetected—impressions of doom and failure that we mistakenly assume to be the conviction of the Holy Spirit.

Were it not for Scripture, we would have no idea what this hidden drama looks like as it plays out, concealed as it is from the naked eye. Zechariah chapter 3 brings to light one graphic example of satanic attack, and the complications the people of God often endure.

> Then he showed me Joshua the high priest standing before the angel of the LORD, and Satan standing at his right hand to accuse him. (Zech. 3:1)

The devil's accusation here seems to simultaneously go in multiple directions—both to Joshua as well as to the angel of Jehovah, who represents God. Thankfully, as shown in this confrontation, God does not agree with it.

> And the LORD said to Satan, "The LORD rebuke you, O Satan! The LORD who has chosen Jerusalem rebuke you! Is not this a brand plucked from the fire?" Now Joshua was standing before the angel, clothed with filthy garments. (3:2–3)

Clearly, in verse 3, Joshua's "filthy garments" signified some sort of corruption. But notice that the LORD responds to Satan neither with a sentimental defense of Joshua ("I love this man"), nor a lame acquittal ("Well, no one's perfect"). He does not appeal to optimism ("There's a lot of good in Joshua"), nor does He deny the fact that Joshua's garments are dirty ("Satan, you are a liar!"). Instead, the LORD's defense of the man revolves around His own work of salvation.

In this case, Joshua represented the people of Israel after they had come out of captivity in Babylon. Those who had returned were not perfect, a fact which the devil was eager to point out in front of God. The LORD, however, dismissed the satanic denunciation out of hand, based on the fact that he had chosen his people and plucked them out of the fire of Babylonian judgment. His discipline had been flawless, and the trajectory of His work would yet be even more glorious. Rebuked and shamed, Satan falls silent. But God's further message to Joshua tells him that he has been purged of sins and dressed with purity.

> And the angel said to those who were standing before him, "Remove the filthy garments from him." And to him he said, "Behold, I have taken your iniquity away from you, and I will clothe you with pure vestments. (Zech. 3:4)

As the facts of the verses show, the grace of God not only restores us to fresh fellowship with God, but unto service. Joshua was refitted with priestly garments.

This exchange sets the tone and template for our defense against the devil's accusations. In the same fashion as the high priest Joshua, but on an infinitely higher level, if anyone today sins, "we have an advocate with the Father, Jesus Christ the righteous. He is the propitiation for our sins" (1 John 2:1–2)—that is, the blood covering that answers all claims of justice upon us.

> JESUS' CROSS ALLOWS OUR ONGOING BOLDNESS AND FELLOWSHIP WITH GOD, REPELLING THE ATTACKS OF THE DEVIL.

Knowing this, the apostle Paul instructed the Ephesians in the art of spiritual warfare, telling them to put on the breastplate of righteousness (see Eph. 6:14). The breast represents the broadest, easiest target for an adversary. Even a clumsy attack can manage a hit on the torso, and be instantly fatal if it strikes the heart. Paul advises a metaphorical plate of iron, the impenetrable righteousness of Christ, for our protection. It is the righteousness that was secured for us through the blood of Jesus. His cross alone allows our ongoing boldness and fellowship with God, repelling the attacks of the devil. It is so final in its effect that in Romans 8, Paul asks the famous rhetorical question, "Who shall bring a charge against God's elect? It is God who justifies" (8:33). When the supreme authority in this universe has declared you righteous in Christ, there is no further ground for argument, evidence, or even speculation. He has spoken and that is all.

Therefore, you need not reason with Satan, nor attempt to sort through his case against you. The debate would turn into a tar baby anyway, as he countered your every defense with fresh indictments. In fact, Zechariah 3:1 does not even allow him to lay out the sordid details of his accusation. Neither should you.

The devil wishes to overwhelm us with excessive sorrow (see 2 Cor. 2:7), miring us in emotions of guilt, regret, and remorse, but never true repentance. In addition to a repetitive, reinforced sense of guilt over an issue, he can also kindle a crippling sense of condemnation over nothing at all. Under those circumstances, believers are left wondering why a dark mood has settled on them, and whether they have offended the Lord in some particular way. This leads to fruitless introspection and ultimately fear. Paul warned the believers in Corinth not to be outwitted by Satan, for "we are not ignorant of his designs" (1 Cor. 2:11). Over-sensitized consciences can often fall into such traps, especially those who already have a tendency toward anxiety. I will have more to say about these abnormalities of feeling in Chapter 10.

Satan's long-term purpose is to switch our focus from Christ to ourselves. In response to our sins, we will try harder to find resources within our own flawed personalities, and fail ever harder, until we give up in complete despair. However, once we look away by faith to Christ, we will see nothing *but* hope, and, Wiersbe says, "thus repent, confess our sins, and find cleansing and restoration of fellowship."[1]

Indeed, according to Revelation chapter 12, this is the way victorious Christians overcome the devil: "The accuser of our brothers has been thrown down, who accuses them day and night before our God. And they have conquered him by the blood of the lamb and by the word of their testimony, for they loved not their lives even unto death" (12:10–11).

When we oppose Satan, we are not attempting to win a victory as though one did not already exist. We conquer through the blood of Christ, a triumph gained at the cross. We claim his victory for ourselves and use it against our enemy. Only then will our consciences calibrate properly.

A Record of Wrong Toward Others

Satan can cause a supernatural wrinkle in the operations of our conscience, but so can unresolved transgressions toward other people. Paul sought to have a conscience void of offense toward God *and* man. In the Bible, we find examples of people making public confessions of sins, as well as restitution of materials they have obtained through unrighteous means. These include Zaccheus, who confessed his sin of illegal gain, saying, "if I have defrauded anyone of anything, I restore it fourfold" (Luke 19:8). In principle, we should seek to reconcile with or reimburse those whom we've wronged. However, for those situations that involve extenuating circumstances, where an innocent person is exposed to open shame or danger, we may want to fall back on Paul's injunction to "Work out your own salvation with fear and trembling, for it is God who works in you" (Phil. 2:12–13).

In order to make room for your involvement with the Holy Spirit, the Bible does not always give detailed instructions on how to rectify past wrongs, what to do, how, and when. Some sins hidden in the heart, like hate and lust, are simply not appropriate to disclose. Confessing them to the people toward whom we feel these things can lead to great stumbling, and give rise to possible further sins. In principle, when and if public confession of fault occurs, it should always proceed under the Spirit's leading, and according to His wise discretion.

Still, in cases where we are choosing not to disclose our sins against others, we must always challenge our true motives. Are we only acting in order to spare ourselves shame, and possible repercussions? When criminal acts are in question, this becomes a great test. Murder, manslaughter, rape, theft, or sexual abuse can carry jail time. Still other sins could at least affect public reputation, and loss of titles, and some, like infidelity, can affect marriages. Confession can be costly, but concealing the sin can be as potentially disruptive to your inner state as keeping a dead cow in your basement.

All these situations require us to look to the Lord for wisdom. We must know He has forgiven us, but we can never assume we are entitled to forgiveness from the people we wronged, especially if the deed was grievous. Justice may choose a route less painful for us, and for this we thank God. But if it wields the sword, we can only trust God's hand of discipline in the matter.

During the early part of my Christian life, I entered a season of backsliding, and did some shoplifting. When I turned back to the Lord later, I was deeply troubled over the event, and knew I couldn't keep the merchandise. I brought it all back, and risked having charges pressed against me (though the retailers chose not to do so). Even as the entire process freed me, it deeply humiliated me. The shame alone was enough to break me from ever doing it again.

However, not every situation plays out so graciously. A man in our church who had been in the grip of pornography for a long time, finally came to a point of release from the sin. He confessed it to the Lord, but his conscience still felt unsettled. He eventually determined that the Lord was requiring a third person to be part of that confession—his wife. When he finally confessed to her, it was a "discussion" that went ballistic. "I'm sorry" and "It will never happen again" wasn't doing the trick. The marriage took a while to heal.

Sometimes a person you have hurt badly will reject your apology, and want nothing to do with you, ever again. In this world of sinners, such things happen. Do not offer Band-Aid apologies, and never give lectures to the person you've hurt about the virtues of forgiveness. You played fast and loose with someone, and they don't owe you anything. Do your best not only to apologize, but reconcile with them in a meaningful way.

Laura is a believer who has a problem with gossip. At work she made some "observations" about Sally to some of her coworkers in the office. The talk spread, and now Sally is in danger of losing her job. Laura confesses her sin to God, but is still troubled. She approaches Sally with an apology, but Sally tells her what she can do with that apology.

Well, there is something else Laura can do. She can tell her coworkers—and the boss—that she grossly exaggerated what she said about Sally. When she does, the whole office loses respect for her. The boss decides that Laura should not be promoted. But, thankfully, Sally will no longer be fired. In fact, Sally gets the promotion, and Laura must now report to *her*. Maybe with time, Laura's contrition for what she did will convince Sally of her sincerity. Maybe not. But one thing is for sure, Laura made her repentance in the matter as complete as she could. Her fellowship with God continues.

Paul says, "If possible, so far as it depends on you, live peaceably with all" (Rom. 12:18). There are times, though, when it may no longer depend on you. Remember that not all people we sin against will understand the concept of grace, and therefore no matter what, they will not forgive. Sadly, our sin against them created damage, but their lack of grace guarantees that the damage done to them will be permanent. That being said, loving your neighbor as yourself will minimize how much we sin against others, and will therefore largely avoid the tangled web of complications that follow. The best advice is to "'love your neighbor as yourself.' Love does no wrong to a neighbor; therefore love is the fulfilling of the law" (Rom. 13:9–10).

Even so, none of us will leave this earth without having offended someone else, and sad to say, deeply hurt them. Jesus commanded, "If you are offering your gift at the altar, and there remember that your brother has something against you, leave your gift there before the altar and go. First be reconciled to your brother" (Matt. 5:23–24). The "remembering" mentioned here is the conscience, interrupting your worship, because you have somehow violated the relational triangle of God, you, and "your brother." This cannot be put right until the offense is settled. That is why Jesus says, following reconciliation, "*then* come and offer your gift [at the altar]," because only then will the fellowship of inner life continue. Our compass needle will be free of interference.

A Log Jam of Unforgiveness

Undealt-with wrongs toward others can cause us noticeable conscience problems, but even more so when we, as the offended parties, fail to forgive. The Savior warned in the strongest possible terms about disruptions of our inner life arising from an attitude of unforgiveness. When one makes a life of holding grudges, of nursing grievances, of recounting past wrongs, he or she will not find much grace when seeking forgiveness for their own sins. As Jesus said, "If you forgive others their trespasses, your heavenly Father will also forgive you, but if you do not forgive others their trespasses, neither will your Father forgive your trespasses" (Matt. 6:14–15). This graphically describes a conscience seeking to be right with God, but failing to find peace, because it refuses to know peace with another person. Although the grace of Christ assures us of eternal salvation, only the extension of that grace to others assures us of an unhindered, ongoing fellowship with God.

> **PEOPLE WHO DO NOT FORGIVE NEVER HAVE A CLOSE WALK WITH GOD.**

The blood of Jesus will not seem effective in the experience of those who insist on abiding in anger. This is why people who do not forgive never have a close walk with God. As the saying goes, "Withholding forgiveness is like drinking poison and hoping the other person dies." In this case, the offended party in the fellowship triangle refuses to be brought back into fellowship. Perhaps they require further demands, and worse, revel in the pity and special attention that comes from victimhood. They may become addicted to this dark elixir, but will never fully know the grace that says, "as far as the east is from the west, so far does he remove our transgressions from us" (Ps. 103:12).

My brother and I used to enjoy damming up the creek behind our house. We would throw tree limbs, sand, and rocks into the water, then pack it tight. A reservoir would develop on the high side of the dam, but the current down-stream would slow to a trickle, where small fish wiggled desperately for relief. Yes, we were mean kids, but when the situation reached crisis level, we would kick the dam apart, restoring the flow of life-giving water. An attitude of unfor-giveness in a Christian can create just such a blockade in his or her inner flow, and choke off their spiritual joy. However, forgiveness of others releases a torrent of grace that funnels through our conscience, and invigorates the dried-up areas of our being. The reviving effects of it might lead you to ask why you waited so long to remove the barrier. When we channel grace to those who wrong us, our conscience will have no problem registering grace and forgiveness for us from God.

Consciences in Collision

Though the idea of individual conscience is critical, none of us exists in a vacuum. Wherever Christians have failed to learn this, and think of themselves as island nations, trouble is sure to be present in the church. You can't have a "Christ and me" attitude, in an exclusive, solitary relationship where your personal convictions trump all others.

Our unity is found in the great essentials of the Christian faith—"one body and one Spirit . . . one Lord, one faith, one baptism, one God and Father of all, who is over all and through all and in all" (Eph. 4:4–6)—but in the church we still often find ourselves sitting atop a powder keg of differ-ing opinions. Worse, many of these issues have ceased being mere point of view or personal conscience; we have elevated them in our minds into genuine articles of faith.

We're all aware of the worship wars that once shook the church—acoustic versus electric, strings versus percussion, acapella versus any instrument at all. We've also encountered struggles over which version of the Bible is approved by God, and which are watered-down pretenders. And don't forget arguments over whether Christmas is a pagan holiday, pork is dirty, or education should be public, private, or home-based. Some quarrels revolve around esoteric things like the banning of certain colors, facial hair, motorcycles, pets, or holdings in the stock market. Beyond our interpretational connect-the-dots, Scripture hardly remarks on any of these.

Sadly, it is unsurprising when division runs rampant among us. Paul, therefore, identifies the first step in keeping a cohesive community within the faith: "Let not the one who eats despise the one who abstains, and let not the one who abstains pass judgment on the one who eats, for God has welcomed him" (Rom. 14:3).

Handling his charge in order, we first address not despising the conscience of others. Paul himself, though utterly committed to the holiness, righteousness, and truth of the gospel, possessed a breadth of conscience that was startling to his contemporaries. He said, "I know and am persuaded in the Lord Jesus that nothing is unclean in itself" (14:14). For instance, he had no compunctions about the spirituality of food products. He looked at all such things through the grid of the cross, and saw no unclean meats, only a Savior who had inaugurated a new creation (see 2 Cor. 5:17). When the conscience of a believer is shaped this way, he or she can live in maximum freedom and flexibility. The gospel, deeply and powerfully understood, could enable a Jewish man like Paul, of the strictest sect of the Pharisees, to peacefully maneuver throughout the ancient world, in and out of churches located in any cultural context.

There were others, though, whose relationship with God dangled on the thread of religious convictions like the consumption of certain foods, wearing particular fabrics, and observing certain days as sacred. No gospel lens existed between these people and a host of religious concerns. In fact, many early Christians understood that Christ had died for their sins, but never saw the cross as radically altering amoral activities of life, or ceremonies related to them.

Paul's advanced apostolic understanding enabled him to say, "far be it from me to boast except in the cross of our Lord Jesus Christ, by which the world has been crucified to me, and I to the world. For neither circumcision counts for anything, nor uncircumcision, but a new creation" (Gal. 6:14–15). According to his view, the cross and the empty tomb had fulfilled the demands of ceremonial law, had terminated the entire old universe, and then germinated a new one. Religious minutiae was unlikely to ever hijack his conscience.

Conscience relies on education, and Paul's had been educated to a lofty extent, indeed. Without exposure to substantial Bible truth, we will come to think many things are unclean that are actually clean, and vice-versa. This, of course, does not mean that Scripture teaches moral relativity, only the relativity of conscience as dealing with items it does not spell out, or practices and prohibitions Christ has fulfilled.

The conscience is an individual, inner life matter that is self-contained, so dealing with it involves simple honesty with oneself, and obedience to what one knows is right. However, in a community of faith, where consciences between people can differ significantly, convictions must be tempered with love. For instance, suppose you encouraged someone to join you in doing something they thought was sinful. Maybe you playfully derided them, because they were reluctant to participate. Finally, they gave in, and although it was nothing to you, it was a sin to them. This happened in the first century, when one believer would lead another, weaker one to eat certain foods he believed were unclean. Paul wrote, "If your brother is grieved by what you eat, you are no longer walking in love. By what you eat do not destroy the one for whom Christ died. So do not let what you regard as good be spoken of as evil" (Rom. 14:15–16). The grievance referred to came from the weaker "eater" experiencing an internal upset of fellowship with God.

In a contemporary example, there was a man who had a fierce addiction to sports television. Under the conviction of his conscience, he dealt with the problem by getting rid of all his cable sports channels. But later, he accepted weekend hospitality from an older Christian man, who kept his television on sports events the entire time. By the time the weekend was over, the younger man had become embroiled in his previous habits again. For him it was a return to sin. I could also mention the believer who does not want to touch playing cards due to an earlier gambling habit, but being jeered by Christian friends, he gives in. His conscience will now say he violated a vow he had made to Christ about never again playing games of chance.

To those of us who have never wrestled with these problems, they may seem juvenile. We are tempted to despise them. But in each case, where a person has grappled with God on some dilemma, and reached a conclusion, contradicting it becomes grievous. He or she may feel they have betrayed Jesus. We might respond that all a Christian needs to do is claim the blood of Christ, and be done with it. This is true, but falling into some sins for some people can become unusually damaging. It takes them months to shake the feeling of being a Judas Iscariot who has sold out their Lord. The apostle Paul used the word "destroyed," to describe it, because in some cases the erring believer may even feel they have committed the unpardonable sin. Good scriptural knowledge disallows such thinking, but, "Not all possess this knowledge" (1 Cor. 8:7).

> **I WILL NOT LEAD YOU INTO DOING
> SOMETHING YOU FEEL IS WRONG,
> EVEN THOUGH I KNOW IT'S FINE.**

Don't be the Christian who inadvertently influences another believer backward into sin. If you do so, Paul says, "You are no longer walking in love" (Rom. 14:15). You didn't care for the other person's relationship with Christ. Instead, you adopted the selfish attitude of personal freedom. Perhaps you have quite a bit of legitimate freedom within the Christian faith. That is good, but as Paul said, don't let your good "be spoken of as evil" (14:16). The bottom line of conscience in the faith community is not always, "*I'm* okay with it!" Rather, the standard is in Romans 14:19: "So then, let us pursue what makes for peace and for mutual upbuilding." In terms of conscience, we support one another's relationship with God, and try not to do anything to cause another to stumble. In other words, I will not lead you into doing something you *feel* is wrong, even though I *know* it's fine.

When today's typical Christian reads these sentiments of concern for one another, it sounds unreasonably binding. Few of us know enough about the faith journey of someone else, or their conscience issues, to know how to encourage them forward. Besides, in today's Western culture, it seems that nothing is more important than gratifying individual freedoms. Yet in order to avoid conscience running amuck and serving the forces of selfishness, we must know how to possess it in the body of Christ.

Remember that Paul spoke a balanced word to both strong and weak alike. Those seated on the other side of the aisle, then, must also consider their attitudes and conduct. Though discriminating consciences typically think of themselves as spiritually strong, the Bible actually labels them as "weak"—sensitive to a great many things Scripture neither condemns nor condones. Yet these same consciences are typically certain in their judgments. Their exacting standards easily brand others as irresponsible, worldly, frivolous, vain, uncommitted, and unspiritual. Small matters escalate quickly, and such believers find every hill to be one worth dying on.

Jesus warned about the over-scrupulous nature of some religious people, as they "tithe mint and dill and cummin, and have neglected the weightier matters of the law" (Matt. 23:23). Mint, dill, and cumin are spices. Even in a tiny pile of them used for cooking, stringent Pharisees would mark off one tenth for God. These people would fail, though, to observe "justice and mercy and faithfulness" (23:23)—"Penny-wise but pound foolish," we might say. "They should have done them," Jesus said of the weightier things, "but not neglected the others," that is, the minor ones. In this way He called us to acquaint our consciences with grander themes, so that they would control our hearts.

Given the amount of time Jesus spent dismantling or adjusting external legalisms of various kinds, and Paul's confrontation of pinched hearts and pettiness in the church, it appears weak consciences among the people of God are common. By settling into self-designed standards and poorly understood truths, some of them were even judging the apostles! Paul had to tell the Corinthian believers, "But what we are is known to God, and I hope it is known also to your conscience" (2 Cor. 5:11). Their smallness made them contentious, almost impossible to reason with. He told them, "you are restricted in your own affections . . . widen your hearts" (6:12–13).

If you find yourself passionately opinionated about certain things that do not directly touch the essentials of the faith, obey your conscience in them, but go sparingly on judgment toward others. As you grow in your knowledge and apprehension of the Word of God, you may learn later on that your obsessive passion about something was misplaced, if not wrong. Additionally, we should learn to tell the difference between conscience, and mere personal opinion. Narrow-hearted individuals have sometimes held entire congregations hostage over issues such as having a coffee station in the church lobby, or various other concerns of that nature. It has nothing to do with the violation of their conscience, only their desire to control other people and situations. Don't be the kind of person who cries, "Conscience!" whenever church decisions don't go your way.

Knowledge affects conscience. This is partly why those who are overly permissive and careless at the beginning of their faith become more discerning later, under the influence of the Word. Alternately, by that same Word, others who begin with rigid, unyielding standards learn breadth of heart. "Not all possess this knowledge" (1 Cor. 8:7), Paul warns, and so rather than blindly trusting we are correct in all things, especially the trifling matters that often damage church fellowship, we should seek to grow in the timeless truth of Scripture. As we interact, and sometimes even constructively debate one another, perhaps we could distill Paul's words in both Romans and First Corinthians down to the now famous saying, "In essentials unity, in non-essentials liberty, in all things love."

The conscience can become complicated. Being a human product on the one hand, it responds to psychological processes as simple as moral education. Being a spiritual product on the other, it is influenced by God Himself. And so the possibility of imperfection exists, and differing levels of awareness. Perhaps this should be so, for our inner life with God must flex and grow, both personally and interpersonally. We certainly should possess a good and clear conscience (see 1 Tim. 1:19; Heb. 13:18), without registration of offense toward God or man. However, even having this condition only means we are good and clear *as far as we know*. God is infinitely holy, beyond our capacity to comprehend all of His perfections.

Paul wrote,

> But with me it is a very small thing that I should be judged by you or by any human court. In fact, I do not even judge myself. For I am not aware of anything against myself, but I am not thereby acquitted. It is the Lord who judges me. Therefore do not pronounce judgment before the time, before the Lord comes, who will bring to light the things now hidden in darkness and will disclose the purposes of the heart. Then each one will receive his commendation from God. (1 Cor. 4:3–5)

When it came to moving around within the faith, and of decision-making in ministry, the final verdict was not with onlookers who judged Paul, nor even Paul himself. God would have the final say.

In the meantime, during these days of growth and no small amount of navigational challenges, conscience should still be heeded. And the possibility of our conscience being wrong, like the compasses we talked about earlier? It happens. One hiker reported that during a forest walk, the mountain that should have been in front of him was behind him. That's a fairly severe mistake in bearings. By comparing his compass to others in his group, he realized that his device had been compromised by the metal snaps on his backpack. Thus, an almost negligible magnetic field was enough to swing the compass needle off, and situate a mountain in the wrong place!

We don't want to end up aimed in false directions by the defective readings of our conscience. Surprisingly, though, you will learn as much by diagnosing and recalibrating it as by simply using it. That in itself is a great reason to continue learning and growing. Having navigated through confusing circumstances and the various fields of difficulty, we will be prepared to inwardly enjoy the blessings of heaven. Nothing will restrict our inner life and the unfettered glory it will now offer us, as we will see in the upcoming chapters.

8

Worship—
Enjoying God Forever

*How sweet all at once it was for me to be rid of those fruitless
joys which I had once feared to lose! You drove them from me
and took their place, you who are sweeter than pleasure.*

— Augustine of Hippo

THE PAST CAN BE humbling. While going through a
trunk of old photos I found a photographic reminder
that I hadn't been born loving God. The old Kodak picture
was a family shot taken on the front porch of my house
when I was fourteen, right before going to church.

My mother stood in the middle, pleasant, smiling, holding my baby sister. Posed next to her, my other sister beamed
with simple radiance, as did my younger brother. Then, there
I was, with a look that could have wrinkled paint. I was sul-
len that morning, mainly because I hated church. I wasn't
exactly gonzo for God, either. I believed He was out there
somewhere, and I should respect Him. But I couldn't help it.
I didn't like Him, at least not the way I liked horror comics
and pizza, guns and fishing, model airplanes and off-color

jokes. When I saw the photo of my angry, skinny, younger self, it jogged my memory of those days when there were cultural claims all around me saying, "Jesus is wonderful," but nothing within me that agreed.

Not knowing what else to do, I continued to swim in the southern religious world with great difficulty, dog paddling with a bowling ball tied to my ankle. Later I learned that the extra weight, the relentless downward pull, was coming from a deadened human spirit. Worship cannot rise without resurrection life.

This is most often why people have a hard time appreciating worship, or, as they say, "getting into it." Otherwise, why would there be so many jokes about falling asleep in church, or daydreaming during prayer? According to the Westminster Confession of Faith, "The chief end of man is to glorify God and enjoy Him forever," yet the enjoyment part seems to keep getting lost in the religious shuffle. We end up mistakenly learning that our chief end is "To glorify God and be *bored* with Him forever."

Even authentic Christians have difficulties with worship, finding it intangible, nebulous. That's why we have historically packed our meetings with extras, like physical objects, ambience, and stylistic concerns. We work overtime to make worship interesting for youth, assuming it won't be without laborious entertainment strategies. We also rig the deck for ourselves and newcomers to guarantee an outcome, what we call "pumped," or "jazzed," or "stoked." If we're honest, we have to admit we get people hooked on the things we use to prop up flagging worship, rather than the worshipful connection itself that they're supposed to have with God.

Suppose we stripped away the buildings, the equipment, the lights, the celebrity personas, the budgets, and everything else that has come to define "worship" in Christian settings. What would that leave us? The answer is simple. We would still have everything we needed for worship that would rock our world, beginning with, most importantly, a spirit enlivened by the new life in Christ. I am not advocating a return to primitive, zero-tech church life, as though we were living in the first century. I'm pointing out that before anything else, true worship comes from our second birth at the price of Jesus' blood, by the life-giving power of the Holy Spirit. Anything beyond this—audio-visual technologies, sacred

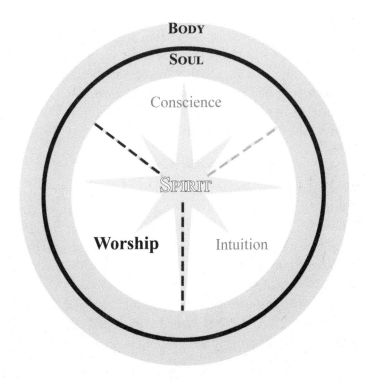

spaces, etc.— might be nice to have, but comparatively speaking, they could never be more than side dishes.

When I finally came to saving faith in Christ, it quickly proved to be more than a one-time event. New birth turned into a trickle of wonder, a continuum that kept flowing in the midst of my previously stale heart. I found it hard to describe the experience to others.

But when I had difficulties explaining it, they tried to explain it to me. "You got religious." "Sounds like you're a churchman now." Some remarks were less charitable: "You've been brainwashed." "Sounds like you joined a cult."

The real cause for confusion came from the fact that most of the folks around me had never witnessed worship come alive. I had never felt it before, either. No doubt my experience was immature, and often inaccurate, but it was *living*, nonetheless. All who have been born again (or, as we might also call it, saved or regenerated), experience a similar spring-like awakening of admiration, love, and zeal for the Person of Christ that keeps on going from that moment to the grave, and on into eternity.

The Miracle Continues

Worship that emanates from a life not of this world must, by definition, be incredible. No one spoke of it in a more compelling fashion than Jesus. In fact, it's no accident that John chapter 3, where Jesus discusses the miracle of the new birth, flows right into chapter 4, where He discusses the miraculous nature of worship.

On a trip through Samaria, Jesus met a woman at a well, and asked her for a drink of water. In turn, she'd registered surprise, since Jews normally had nothing to do with Samaritans.

Jesus answered her, "If you knew the gift of God, and who it is that is saying to you, 'Give me a drink,' you would have asked him, and he would have given you living water." The woman said to him, "Sir, you have nothing to draw water with, and the well is deep. Where do you get that living water? Are you greater than our father Jacob? He gave us the well and drank from it himself, as did his sons and his livestock." Jesus said to her, "Everyone who drinks of this water will be thirsty again, but whoever drinks of the water that I will give him will never be thirsty again. The water that I will give him will become in him a spring of water welling up to eternal life." (John 4:10–14)

Like a lot of people, the woman's entire prior experience with the things of God had been bound up with places and traditions, handed-down teachings, controversies, and personal failure. She had no idea that the man sitting in front of her was the giver of something far better than anything she'd ever encountered in religion. *If only you knew*, He said, *You wouldn't waste any time asking me for it.* His grace would have said yes, and given her the remarkable "living water," which, as it became evident later, was a fitting symbol of the Holy Spirit.

Having heard the word "water," though, she was still attached to the idea of literal liquid, and wondered how Jesus could draw it out of the well without a bucket. That was obviously something the patriarch Jacob had not been able to do. What manner of man was this, then, who was offering a drink of something far superior to what people had been drinking at that very spot for centuries. She had been taught to revere the ancients, but they too, including father Jacob and his sons, heads of the tribes of Israel, had also traveled to this well, like everyone else, and none of them had found *living* water.

Jesus clearly spoke of the Holy Spirit like no one else ever had. Even we who have had this Scripture for two thousand years still primarily conceive of the Spirit as a force who provides powers and interesting gifts and peculiar experiences.

> I'VE KNOWN CHRISTIANS WHO CLAIMED
> TO BE SPIRIT-FILLED, YET WERE DRIVEN
> BY THIRST FOR THINGS OF THE WORLD.

But Jesus here emphasizes the Spirit's baseline ability to *quench thirst*. I've known Christians who claim to be Spirit-filled because of the gifts they manifest, and yet these same souls were driven by thirst for things of the world—everything from romance (like this woman), to materialism, to entertainment. Their thirst dominates them, although during the church hour they try to exhibit the opposite.

Not only was the water promised here peculiar in meeting the needs of the soul, but was to be an ongoing experience. Jesus said that an initial drink of it would lead to its installation within the person who drank of it—a spring of water, available continuously and welling up, becoming deeper and fuller over time.

And so being intrigued by this description, she made the only sensible request:

> The woman said to him, "Sir, give me this water, so that I will not be thirsty or have to come here to draw water."
>
> Jesus said to her, "Go, call your husband, and come here" The woman answered him, "I have no husband." Jesus said to her, "You are right in saying, 'I have no husband'; for you have had five husbands, and the one you now have is not your husband. What you have said is true." (John 4:15–18)

Though Jesus had promised to give her living water, He hadn't instantly complied when she asked for it. Instead, He made an apparently random request to see her husband. The Lord, who searches every human being, knew the complex corridors of the woman's heart. He was aware of iniquity in her that would have blocked her very first gulp of living water.

This probably became a crisis moment for her, however brief. She thought her sexual sin had been safely concealed from this man. And with any of a thousand other strangers, the opaque truth she told about being unmarried would, indeed, have hidden her real situation. But this was not some stranger who could be fooled with a fig leaf. Regardless of how she had reasoned in the past, justifying her multiple divorces, and the illegitimacy of a live-in lover, the eyes of Christ saw through the facade. It was a detriment He could not ignore.

And now she stood in the blistering, awkward exposure of the light of truth. She knew better than to defend her sin. Nor did He launch into a scolding lecture. It was a perfect moment of heart-level transaction, where sinner stood convicted, but Savior stood forgiving.

This moment should remind us how often we have allowed unconfessed sediment to accumulate and clog the flow of our spiritual supply. Under those circumstances, nothing much seems alive within, certainly nothing approximating a "spring of water welling up."

But as we saw in the previous two chapters concerning conscience, what a difference honest repentance makes before Jesus! If He forgave the woman here based upon the power of His death that had not yet come, how much more for us, based on His redemptive death already now accomplished.

She said, "Sir, I perceive that you are a prophet" (John 4:19).Weak as it was, this was her confession of sin. She acknowledged His true assessment of her past as divine discernment, not a mere guess or deduction. Under this sudden light of God, it would have been useless for her to protest that she had been misunderstood or unfairly judged. The omniscient gaze of God makes no such mistakes. Real repentance means we submit to His judgment, own our sin, stop feeling sorry for ourselves, and move on to the greater issue of worship (which she does): "Our fathers worshiped on this mountain, but you say that in Jerusalem is the place where people ought to worship" (4:20).

If she had introduced this theological controversy to deflect his attention away from her sin, the Lord graciously went along with it. Worship had been His original concern in the dialogue, anyway. Still, the Light of the World would not be manipulated. On His way to leading a humbled sinner to greater heights of blessing and revelation, He exposes sins; He also exposes ignorance. Jesus said to her, "Woman, believe me, the hour is coming when neither on this mountain nor in Jerusalem will you worship the Father" (4:21). Because of God's new work in Christ, arguments about shrines and pilgrimages were about to be rendered moot.

Worship was about to transcend everyone's limited understanding. And yet He did not allow the Jerusalem-versus-Mount Gerizim debate[1] to pass in silence. God *had* chosen Jerusalem for worship. The Samaritan scriptures were truncated, presenting a corrupted version of the Old Testament which severely limited what Samaritans knew of God. He told her, "You worship what you do not know; we worship what we know, for salvation is from the Jews" (4:22).

Jesus had no intention of presenting the new worship in a heretical framework. Though the Jews were far from perfect, God had granted them His divine revelation. His nature, His work, and His ways had been committed to writing and placed in their hands. The other nations of the world might worship various gods and monsters with utmost sincerity, but apart from God's self-revelation, their worship was blind.

And so Jesus recalibrated the woman's respect for the corpus of truth in the Jewish Scriptures, informing her that the salvation of the world would proceed from the Jews.

These words should be a serious warning to anyone who hopes to experience a robust inner life. We are not being called into a mystical swamp where we are free to ignore the books of the Bible we don't like. Nor have we the license to canonize the writings of Buddha, Gandhi, Confucious, or any extra-biblical voice that might allegedly have something to teach the people of God. Living water does not emerge from those sources; therefore, whoever tries to drink from them will "thirst again"—continue to have a dead spirit and dead worship.

Jesus added, "The hour is coming, and is now here, when the true worshipers will worship the Father in spirit and truth, for the Father is seeking such people to worship him" (John 4:23). Jesus' mention of "true worshipers" speaks of those who have experienced the new birth, an internal resurrection that enables worship in spirit. The formerly withered function of worship so characteristic of a deadened spirit is now alive, for living water brings living worship. Worship becomes true, and no longer a slavish copy of patterns and styles.

"True worshipers" also presuppose the existence of false ones. And sometimes this characterizes even the people of God as they sink into swamps of tiresome, empty religion.

Whenever this has happened in history, God found it terribly offensive and called out the people, saying, "You did not serve the LORD your God joyfully and gladly" (Deut. 28:47–48, NIV). He doesn't take responsibility for this problem; he doesn't say, "Well, I admit worship is not the liveliest pursuit—not like motocross." When the people of God begin going through the motions, no one is more disgusted than God Himself.

> "The multitude of your sacrifices—
>   what are they to me?" says the LORD.
> "I have more than enough of burnt offerings,
>   of rams and the fat of fattened animals;
> I have no pleasure
>   in the blood of bulls and lambs and goats.
> When you come to appear before me,
>   who has asked this of you,
>   this trampling of my courts?
> Stop bringing meaningless offerings!
>   Your incense is detestable to me.
> New Moons, Sabbaths and convocations—
>   I cannot bear your worthless assemblies.
> Your New Moon feasts and your appointed festivals
>   I hate with all my being.
> They have become a burden to me;
>   I am weary of bearing them.
>
>   (Isa. 1:11–14, NIV)

The last verse sums it up, where God basically says, "I'm done with this." False worship can come from sincere people—not just deliberate deceivers—who frequently find themselves grinding out religious tedium, bored with a distant God, driven by duty and fear. Nor is this a problem confined to the Old Covenant. Jesus warned that at His judgment seat He would not affirm the "Lord, Lord" mantra that false worshippers use (see Matt. 7:22), or tolerate alleged branches that bore no fruit (see John 15:5–6).

When Christ anticipates with enthusiasm the arrival of true worship and true worshippers as he does in the John 4 passage, He is essentially saying the wooden situation of Isaiah 1 does not need to be repeated anymore.

And as if to demonstrate, He granted a foretaste of living worship to this Samaritan woman. As she realized the truth of her sin, and later the identity of Jesus as Messiah, with joy she went and told her friends, "Come, see a man who told me all that I ever did. Can this be the Christ?" (4:29). It was such an apparently illogical thing to celebrate One who had exposed her shameful deeds, yet her first draught of living water had overcome any sense of personal embarrassment, and replaced it with wonder.

Truly she was experiencing worship without a mountain in Samaria, the temple in Jerusalem, or the well of Jacob— indeed, with nothing more than Christ, His word, and the Spirit. A drink of living water had gotten into her, welled up, overflowed, and turned into a river (see 7:37).

> ## THE STORY OF THE WOMAN AT THE WELL DEMONSTRATES THE POTENCY OF AN ENLIVENED SPIRIT OF WORSHIP.

The current reached the rest of the townspeople, creating a proto-church gathering of fellow believers who came and confessed their own new faith. "They said to the woman, 'It is no longer because of what you said that we believe, for we have heard for ourselves, and we know that this is indeed the Savior of the world'" (4:42). This case, perhaps more than any other in Scripture, demonstrates the potency of an enlivened spirit of worship.

The Samaritan Woman Revisited

The apostle Peter included all true believers in the Samaritan woman's dynamic when he wrote, "though you have not seen him, you love him. Though you do not now see him, you believe in him and rejoice with joy that is inexpressible and filled with glory" (1 Pet. 1:8). And the apostle Paul added that living worship not only revives those matters traditionally considered religious, but invests *everything* with a certain joy—"For everything created by God is good, and nothing is to be rejected if it is received with thanksgiving, for it is made holy by the word of God and prayer" (1 Tim. 4:4–5).

When the river of the water of life reaches flood stage, it saturates all around it: a neighborhood sunset, a pick-up game of basketball, the caress of a breeze, a forest hike, a pile of hot tamales, a love song, a puppy—all take on richer, deeper hues. Inner life invigorates human existence and all the mundane matters connected to it. As the hymn writer said,

> Heaven above is softer blue,
> earth around is sweeter green;
> something lives in every hue
> Christless eyes have never seen.[2]

When I had been a sourpuss fourteen-year-old boy, I hadn't wanted any of this. That front porch photo said it all. Like the character in Dr. Seuss's book, *Green Eggs and Ham*, "I did not like it in a house, I did not like it with a mouse, or in a tree, please let me be." But a short seven years later, having met Jesus and been made alive, I moved into the ending of the *Green Eggs and Ham* story, a heartwarming phase where the main character finally tries the dish he vowed to hate. He finds he likes it, and then categorically reverses all his previous rejection—"Yes I like it! I would eat it in a box and I would eat it with a fox and I would eat it here or there, and I would eat it anywhere!" His was the joy of discovery, and it was happening to me, with Jesus. Worship was alive, humming along on a wavelength both gentle and real.

I started liking God, as I did chocolate cake, John Wayne westerns, and collecting arrowheads. It seemed that suddenly He ranked way up there with Ray Bradbury books, big-game rifles, and ultra-light fishing tackle. He was at the front of the pack with all the cool stuff, seriously competing and even pulling ahead of them. Without any encouragement from a church (since I hadn't yet become a member of one), I liked Him more than my *Field and Stream* magazines, electronic chess set, and Led Zeppelin albums. Though no one had coached me into this status, I was a bona fide "fanatic."

And I hoped others would become the same. Those rivers of living water hadn't found themselves trapped inside me, as though swirling around a cul-de-sac. I set about mailing letters to family and cornering coworkers with the gospel.

After four or five years, I became a college campus preacher (minus the insults and theatrics). My low-level approach called for filtering through crowds, looking for the lone student who might want to talk with me about Jesus.

One afternoon I found a young man as he was returning from class. When I asked if he had a few minutes for the Bible, he smirked, then proceeded to unload on me every protest he knew from the skeptic's arsenal. I fielded his objections as best I could, shared with him the gospel, and saw him believe in Jesus—a flicker of faith that he at first tried

to suppress. We met again a number of times, always reading and conversing, until a few weeks later, when he finally
agreed to visit our campus Bible study.

We happened to be in John chapter 4. For the first time,
he read about the Samaritan woman, saw the promises of
Jesus concerning living water welling up into eternal life, and
dumbfounded, he burst out in the middle of the study, "Hey,
that's me!" The effervescence of salvation had been bubbling
up in him since the day he'd believed. Not long after, it became a river flowing out of him to someone else, continuing
the entire dynamic.

And yet how reluctant we are to enter true worship. We
want to guard things, to protect them from Christ. *What
about this or that issue?* we ask. *If I become a true worshipper, can I still do what I like? Will I be allowed?* Typically this
boils down to concerns over whether we can continue in an
entrenched sin of some sort. *Can I bring my baggage into this
new life?*

The Samaritan woman certainly had her baggage—five
previous husbands and a live-in boyfriend! Men were her
drug of choice. We've all heard that troll-like voice tell us
God is only interested in prying our cold, dead fingers from
around things we love and can't live without.

But you know those beloved hobbies that occupy the
number-one spot in your heart—where God ought to be?
The comic collection that generates so much excitement in
your life, or those new-release movies, or the mountain bik-
ing, or computer games, or photography, or fishing trips?
You may think you're in danger of God snatching them away
and throwing them under a bus. No, your real danger is in
losing your enjoyment of them.

The simple fact is, you can't expect model railroading or scuba diving to do what only God can do. Eventually hobbies prove they're exactly that—hobbies, and nothing more. They're a lot of fun, but they can't deliver life purpose, and they always become empty when they're elevated to the number-one spot. It's a hard reality: sweet peas taste better when they're sitting next to a thick, juicy steak, not when they're offered as the main course. In the same way, smaller things of life actually take on a more intense level of enjoyment when they're ranked where they belong.

With the Giver of life at the top, above all, He's perfectly positioned to pour living water downward. Everything underneath that cascading flow enjoys blessing. When the worship of God becomes our chief enjoyment, it has a transformative effect upon everything it touches beneath it.

More than Mere Experience

To further clarify, worship is the cultivation of a relationship, not just an experience. Unless this is made clear, you run the risk of dethroning Christ, and making your feelings the ruling authority in your Christian life. On being born again, we entered a *fellowship*, a live, dynamic participation between two people. We are told, "You were called into the *fellowship* of his Son, Jesus Christ our Lord" (1 Cor. 1:9); "Our *fellowship* is with the Father and his Son Jesus Christ" (1 John 1:3); we are now in "the *fellowship* of the Holy Spirit" (2 Cor. 13:14).

As believers, we have entered a relationship with the entire Holy Trinity. It is more than disembodied sensory experiences. That is why Jesus never said, "I will send you grace and mercy," or any other experiences, as though they were separate from Him. Instead, He told us, "*I* will come to you" (John 14:18).

The dyslexic approach of putting "feel-goods" first has led many a Christian into "worship shopping" from one church to another. But real worship revolves around its object, not its feeling.

God said, "You shall have no other gods before me" (Exod. 20:3), regardless of how they might get you into a partying mood. "You shall not make for yourself a carved image, or any likeness of anything that is in heaven above, or that is in the earth beneath, or that is in the water under the earth. You shall not bow down to them or serve them, for I the LORD your God am a jealous God" (20:4–5). Jealousy only occurs in the matrix of a relationship.

And if there was ever any doubt about God's desire for a relational bond between Himself and His people, nothing clears it up like the greatest commandment of all: "You shall love the LORD your God with all your heart and with all your soul and with all your might" (Deut. 6:5). You don't see the word worship here, nor do you need to, because this kind of devotion couldn't be anything other than worship.

The theme continues later in the New Testament, when Paul told those who had believed in Jesus that "I betrothed you to one husband, to present you as a pure virgin to Christ" (2 Cor. 11:2). His preaching the gospel to them had been like introducing them to a prospective husband, and when they said yes, they had in effect slipped on the engagement ring. This freshly initiated relationship was a marriage of glorious dimension, standing for all time as an example for earthly marriages to emulate (see Eph. 5:22). The marital love between a man and woman, therefore, is a shadowy expression of something superior. As Paul wrote, "This mystery is great; but I am speaking with reference to Christ and the church" (5:32, NASB).

The Song of Songs provides a window into the relational richness between us and Christ. Though many readers see the book as human romance, it is that—and infinitely more. In its pages, the Shulamite woman, an aggregate of believers, finds her beloved, Christ, "distinguished among ten thousand. / His head is the finest gold; / his locks are wavy . . . his cheeks are like beds of spices . . . his arms are rods of gold" (5:10–11, 13–14)—all descriptions rich with spiritual metaphor.

This is the Person with whom we have entered a relationship, and as the metaphors multiply, the Song of Solomon increasingly sounds like human beings who have been smitten with the beauty of their Lord. John Owen writes,

> To the soul, Christ is altogether lovely (Song 5:16). He is infinitely more preferable than the highest, greatest good. The soul sees all that is of the world, "the lust of the flesh, the lust of the eyes, and the pride of life," and sees it all to be but vanity, for "the world is passing away, and the lust of it" (1 John 2:16–17). These beloveds are in no way to be compared to Christ.[3]

THE SPIRIT'S MINISTRY SHOULD LEAVE US IN AWE OF CHRIST, AND NOT OF OURSELVES. HE IS OUR FOCUS, NOT OUR EXPERIENCES.

During my high school years, I occasionally overheard religious kids talking with each other about what went on at church over the weekend. I recall one conversation that began as a discussion about the Holy Spirit. A girl matter-of-factly told her friend, "You can't remember what you do when you're in the Holy Spirit, so I guess I don't know what I did on Sunday morning." It was as though to her, amnesia authenticated spiritual experiences. Her friend seemed intent on encouraging her, though. "You jumped this high off the ground," he told her, and held his hand at waist level. She seemed comforted by that news, even giddy over it, but I was utterly mystified. Granted, as an unsaved person, I had been ignorant as to any work of the Spirit, whether it involved jumping, yodeling, or walking on the moon. Sometimes you can't understand something if you don't have it.

Then again, it's possible not to understand something even when you do have it. Jesus said concerning the Holy Spirit, "He will glorify me, for he will take what is mine and declare it to you" (John 16:14). The Spirit's ministry should leave us in awe of Christ, the Son of God, and not of ourselves doing peculiar things. Whether we shout, or jump, dance, or sing, or fall on our knees, it ought to be a worshipful response to the perfections of God. Long after the event is over, what remains impressed upon our hearts are the glorious things we have beheld in Him. He is our focus, not our experiences. Jonathan Edwards championed this thought, saying, "spiritual emotions arise out of the loveliness of spiritual things."[4]

Justin Buzzard reminds us that, in a world of wonders great and small, "the Creator gave us eyeballs, fingertips, nostrils, holes in our ears, bumps on our tongues, synapses in our brain, and curiosity in our hearts as tools to explore with."[5] It makes sense that this same God who obviously encourages exploration, would reserve Himself as the most supreme object of all to search out. Truly, "The hour . . . is now *here*" to discover and celebrate Him.

Equipped with a living spirit of worship, and particular avenues He has provided, we will do this.

9

Worship—
Cultivating Enjoyment

I passed by the field of a sluggard,
by the vineyard of a man lacking sense,

and behold, it was all overgrown with thorns;
the ground was covered with nettles,
and its stone wall was broken down.

Then I saw and considered it;
I looked and received instruction.

A little sleep, a little slumber,
a little folding of the hands to rest,

and poverty will come upon you like a robber,
and want like an armed man.

— Proverbs 24:30–34

WHOEVER THOUGHT of packaging garden seeds in those little paper envelopes was a marketing genius. Could there be a better deal? Simply push the seeds into the soil with your finger, and in a few months you'll have beans, tomatoes, and carrots, just like the color photo on the front of the pack. Huge numbers of us have probably made the purchase at least once in life, and then engaged in a plant-and-forget endeavor, where we figure rainfall would do most of the work. If we add anything to the effort, it will amount to making sure no one drives the riding mower over the new plants. However, the rest of us, comprising a smaller category, take the time to do weeding, watering, and fertilizing.

At the end of the growing season, the person who did nothing will find his unstaked tomatoes lying around on the ground, spoiling. The bean vines have piled up in wads, and the carrots have been partially consumed by rabbits. He tells himself that he suspected all along that garden produce was overrated. Meanwhile, the other guy, the conscientious gardener, has reaped a small harvest of tasty vegetables, and his garden will continue to produce them for some time.

Both groups of people planted the same vegetables, but had opposite outcomes. Cultivation made all the difference.

Christians today have developed a bad habit of criticizing spiritual disciplines as being, oddly enough, unspiritual. The word *discipline* sounds suspiciously legal to a generation of believers whose Christian lives, like the neglected garden, have largely been a plant-and-forget proposition.

As a result, it has become vogue to brand regular Bible reading and prayer as antithetical to a relationship with Christ. We've learned to label anything habitual as programmed, robotic, or heartless. If one must make oneself read the Scriptures, it is said, that is a violation of authentic worship, and a mere religious work of law. The given alternative tells us to "just let it happen," or, "follow the Spirit's lead," and service will take place. Church attendance will occur. The Scriptures will somehow be read. Prayer will happen. This approach has become popular among us because, well, it's easy.

But Francis Schaeffer writes, "We do not come to true spirituality or the true Christian life merely by keeping a list, but neither do we come to it merely by rejecting the list and shrugging our shoulders and living a looser life."[1] Ryrie adds, "There is a kind of quietism abroad which rules out any activity on man's part as being 'of the flesh.' The slogan of this kind of teaching is 'Let go and let God.'"[2]

> ## WE RECEIVED THE NEW LIFE IN CHRIST FREE OF CHARGE, BUT WE ENJOY IT BY PAYING ATTENTION TO IT.

It sounds spiritual and sincere, but such a lop-sided emphasis creates passivity and finally, spiritual poverty. The Bible is full of directives designed to guide believers into spiritual formation and greater depths of experience. These could hardly be considered optional, nor can linguistic or spiritualistic wrangling undo the tone of command surrounding them. In a field of crops, "God gives the growth," although human agents must still plant and water (see 1 Cor. 3:6). Spiritual life does not work independently of the people who receive it.

We received the new life in Christ free of charge, but we enjoy it by paying attention to it. This calls for disciplined practice, and none more vital than that which is related to the Word of God and prayer. I don't choose these two arbitrarily, as if other biblical practices are unimportant. We have already touched upon confession, and upcoming chapters in this book will deal with Christian community and good works. Word and prayer are primary here, because in the Word, God speaks to us; in prayer we speak to God.[3] Every other practice proceeds from within the context of this fellowship, this two-way communication.

Encountering God in the Scriptures

Healthy worship thrives when we pick up the Bible in a regular way. It is like fertilizer to our inner life, because when we encounter the Word, we encounter God.

> In the beginning was the Word, and the Word was with God and the Word was God. . . . And the Word became flesh and dwelt among us, and we have seen his glory, glory as of the only Son from the Father, full of grace and truth. (John 1:1, 14)

The experience of the Word firstly involves encountering an expression of who God is ("and the Word was God"). This is chiefly what a word does—it communicates what is within the speaker. Without God's Word, we would be utterly lost as to His nature, work, plan, and character. Sustained proximity to it, though, makes us aware of His glory ("and we have seen his glory")—the summation of His splendid attributes—and provokes within us, even rewards us, with godly awe.

Furthermore, in the Word we find *grace* (see 1:14), an assurance of God's powerful love and generosity, His willingness and ability to do for us and be for us what we cannot do and be. We also meet with *truth* in the Word (see 1:14)—reality about past, present, future, the actual state of mankind, and of God Himself. The experience overall sanctifies us (see 17:17).

And of course, our coming to the Word places us squarely in the path of God's *eternal life*. Jesus said, "It is the Spirit who gives life; the flesh is no help at all. The words that I have spoken to you are spirit and life" (6:63). Of course, anything alive has a particular operation, even if only at the microscopic level. The living Word of God is no exception. It works. It performs. It accomplishes. "For the word of God is living *and* active, sharper than any two-edged sword, piercing to the division of soul and of spirit, of joints and of marrow, and discerning the thoughts and intentions of the heart" (Heb. 4:12).

This is inner life in high gear, as the Word operates to pierce, discern, and divide your inward situation. It sets aside your truth, which is often a confused mass of relativistic preferences, from His truth, which is the reality of all things moral, ethical, and spiritual.

The Word is a universal constant that becomes deeply personal to you, without becoming confused with you or by you. It can be so effective to all people, in all situations, because the gracious Person of Christ wields it as a sword, performing internal surgery, just as the high priest of the Old Testament prepared sacrifices for God.

Maybe you're not so excited at the prospect of your soul being operated on, much less having things cut out of your life. But if it's spiritual cancer, that is, idolatrous attachments threatening your faith, you might change your mind. Or, if you've struggled for clarity in some area for years, you'll probably welcome that sword to separate in you what is spiritual from what is not.

I recall facing an old temptation that had on many occasions defeated me. I often wondered why. For some time I had stood on the truth of Jesus' death for my sins. But that day, the living word came to me from First Corinthians 10:13: "He will also provide the way of escape." *This is it, John. Follow the exit sign I've given you and you'll be out.* I did just that, and for the first time in a while, felt I was standing under a clear sky.

I had been right to confess my failures, trust in redemption, and lean on the Lord's love, but I had slipped into an unconscious habit of making a home in defeat. The sword of the Word exposed this mindset as being a rut I had fallen into. It reminded me that when it comes to sin, I am to think of escape and freedom, not resignation and imprisonment. Worshipful praise rose from my heart that day like incense.

And all of this commences with an opened Bible. The Word we find within it is effective toward our inward condition precisely because it embodies the glorious, gracious, truthful, personal vitality of God Himself. Neglecting it, therefore, is out of the question.

Certain brands of neo-orthodox Christianity try to portray a vast distance between spiritual Word and written Scripture. This is an extreme misunderstanding of Second Corinthians 3:6, where Paul apparently juxtaposes Spirit and letter. The apostle certainly did not wish to lower the Christian appraisal of Scripture, much less invalidate it. He was correcting the Corinthians, who had fallen into a lifeless, Pharisaical understanding of the Bible. When they opened the Scriptures, they saw it as opening a ceremonial handbook, or a manual of behavior. The apostle hoped to return them to the life-giving power of the Spirit when they handled those same Scriptures.

However, people often have other reasons for differentiating the Word of God from Scripture. Kevin DeYoung observes, "Some people don't like written texts and propositions because they imply a stable, fixed meaning, and some people don't want truth to be fixed. They would rather have inspiration be more subjective, more internal, more experiential."[4]

Some of these same people have also implied that parts of the Bible are merely the products of human ideas, and are thus less the word of God than other parts. It is hard to imagine this attitude leading anywhere but what DeYoung calls a "compromised Christianity."[5]

No doubt, there are nuances between the Word as the Person of Christ, and that same Word captured in human language and written down in Scripture. None, however, validate the idea that Word and Scripture are completely separate. Jesus Himself treated the Word of God and the written Scriptures as synonymous. When He schooled the devil in the wilderness, He said, "Man shall not live by bread alone, but by every word that proceeds out of the mouth of God" (Matt. 4:4). Yet the words he quoted were Scriptures from the book of Deuteronomy. Not once does Jesus downgrade the written Word. Notice that even the devil does not challenge Him on this point, with arguments like, "Men wrote it." Satan may pretend to question the Bible in front of us, yet in front of Christ he didn't bother with such games. The whole universe knows that Scripture is the Word of God. Only confused human beings waffle on the subject.

Jesus furthermore paired Scripture with the eternal power of the Word. He told the Saducees, who did not believe in resurrection, "You are wrong, because you know neither the Scriptures nor the power of God" (Matt. 22:29). He often rebuked stubborn listeners by asking, "Have you never read . . . ?" (12:3, 5; 19:4; 21:16, 42; 22:31).

He even chided His own disciples as they dallied with doubt.

> And he said to them, "O foolish ones, and slow of heart to believe all that the prophets have spoken! Was it not necessary that the Christ should suffer these things and enter into his glory?" And beginning with Moses and all the Prophets,

he interpreted to them in all the Scriptures the things concerning himself. (Luke 24:25–27)

Finally, in John 10:35, He revealed His unqualified trust in the inerrancy of the written Word when He said, "the Scripture cannot be broken."

Like Jesus, we also should hold a high view of Scripture: It is the actual word of God through human writers, who were prepared by the Holy Spirit through a rigorous work of discipline, transformation, and revelatory knowledge. When they wrote, God considered it His own word, preserving it from embedded mistakes, ignorance, myths, or falsehoods. He did all of this without dissolving the personalities and life experiences of the human authors. Scripture is the self-revelation of God, given to us in written human language.

> ## THE BIBLE SPEAKS TO US IN THE CONTEXT OF THE HUMAN EXPERIENCE, YET OFFERS A PORTAL INTO THINGS UNSEEN.

Imagine what would happen if a probe landed on Mars, craned its camera around, and saw a book lying on the ground. The excitement back here on Earth would reach a fever pitch. Governments would spare no expense retrieving that book, and thus acquiring extraterrestrial intelligence.

And yet we have here on Earth a document containing wisdom from beyond this world. It is written in human language; we do not need a sophisticated cipher to understand it. It speaks to us in the recognizable context of the human experience, yet offers a portal into things unseen. Most exciting, though, is the fact that, as Timothy Ward says, "God has invested Himself in His words, or you could say that God has so identified Himself with His words that whatever someone does with God's words . . . they do directly to God himself."[6]

All of this should remind us what a tremendous resource we have in the Bible, where Scriptures lie packed with the power of the Word. Our habitual involvement with it enriches worship from skim milk to fine cream.

Balanced Worship—Intellectual and Spiritual

"Be transformed," Paul said, "by the renewal of your mind" (Rom. 12:2). That is exactly what happens as we interact with the written Word. Our intellect is incredibly important to the quality of our worship. Tim Keller notes, "The mystic wants to attend only and directly to God, not to words and ideas about God,"[7] but God told us to love Him with all of our minds, meaning He is not interested in blind, ignorant worship.

Clueless devotion brings no glory to God. John Piper has compared this to a young man who chooses a woman to love, yet with no depth of insight about her. His "heat" is impressive, but he does not know who she is, nor what she has done, her character, her dreams, or her attitudes.

We typically call such a thing infatuation, and no mature adult holds out any hope of such a relationship lasting. Nor, in this case, is it a glory to the woman. She has become the object of someone's fixation, not due to anything attractive in her or about her, but due to an admirer's vapid obsession.

God wants to be loved for reasons related to His glory, for facts illuminated by the Holy Spirit and savored by the gaze of both faith and intellect. The believers in Corinth missed this point and got the wrong idea about worship. Their devotion became utterly self-serving, ecstatic, and ultimately clueless. They descended into an exercise of tongues-speaking, void of an understanding of what they were worshiping.

Paul tried to help them by using himself as an example: "For if I pray in a tongue, my spirit prays but my mind is unfruitful" (1 Cor. 14:14). An unfruitful mind is a mind without understanding. Paul added, "I will pray with my spirit, but I will pray with my mind also; I will sing praise with my spirit, but I will sing with my mind also" (14:15). And so he revealed his own worship as being a unified exercise of his mind, the place of renewed understanding (see Luke 24:45), and his spirit, the place of deep revelatory fellowship with God (see Eph. 1:17).

When we encounter Scripture, its words, information, ideas, and concepts enter our minds. This is part of the reason why we encourage everyone to read and study well. Though poorly educated people can certainly be born again and worship the Lord, our Creator has supplied us with a mind, a powerful instrument capable of reflecting, imagining, reasoning. We thus benefit from developing memorization and listening skills, as well as reading comprehension. None of this, however, requires us to be born academics. A simple passion for God and even rudimentary Bible study can help us enlist our minds for the experience of worship.

I remember the first time I attended a church meeting after having been born again. My sedate, liturgical background could not have prepared me for the sheer experience of . . . *volume*. Although the gathering that night was not in the strict definition "charismatic," people were hollering. The idea was to shout praises and such until you felt something.

I participated, but at the end of the session, it seemed as if I had forced an emotional state upon myself. I was tired

and hoarse without knowing why. And therein was the problem. As a group, we had neglected to furnish one another
a reason for such exuberance. There had been no appeal to
the mind with the truth of God. It was a classic case of "cart
before the horse," and, in fact, a cart *without* the horse.

Whether you worship corporately at a church meeting or
privately in your basement at six in the morning, Scripture reli-
ably maps and marks a route to God-shaped worship. "I'm not
a reader," many of us defensively say, as though being a book-
worm was a prerequisite to opening the Bible. But think of a
non-nonsense blue collar worker, a confirmed non-academic,
who has received a love letter from his girlfriend. His reading
list over the last year has been little more than Pizza Hut menus
and X-Men comics. Yet he pours over this ten-page letter word
by word, sentence by sentence, and reads it multiple times.

Twice she used words he didn't understand, so he
promptly looked them up in the dictionary. He wonders
why his sweetheart has chosen this word, and not another.
He hunts for meanings, hints, promises, declarations, and
revelations of her heart. Yet after all this, he would still not
call himself a "reader." That is because this document is different. It is written to *him*. It is not recreational reading. It is
relational reading.

When we open the Bible, it's not the same way someone
might burrow into a clunky, thousand-page novel for sheer
love of books. We read, knowing the Scriptures are written
to *us*. It is the correspondence of Christ to His believers. All
other volumes are written to those who find pleasure in liter-
ary pursuits. You gain access to them because of your library
card. You gain access to the Bible because of your faith. God
is not seeking "readers." He is seeking worshipers.

Learn to Savor the Glory

The Bible calls for a certain willingness to linger in its pages
and immerse oneself in its content. Although a number of
ways may achieve that end, simple meditation is probably
among the best of all practices. Meditation is biblical, being
mentioned some fifteen times in Scripture. This may come
as a surprise to those of us who automatically associate the
practice with gurus, shaved heads, candles, robes, chanting,
and yoga. Biblical meditation is the polar opposite of the
pagan eastern variety. While those other approaches seek to
empty the mind, biblical meditation seeks to fill it with the
Word of God. After having read a passage, we utilize our
mind (and later, our mouth) to actively "chew" on the words
we've read. S.D. Gordon says,

> Meditate means to mutter, as though a man were repeating
> something over and over again, as he turned it over in his
> mind. We have another word, with the same meaning, not
> much used now—ruminate. We call the cow a ruminant
> because she chews the cud. She will spend hours chewing
> the cud, and then give us the rich milk and cream and but-
> ter which she has extracted from her food. That is the word
> here—ruminate. Chew the cud, if you would get the richest
> cream and butter here.[8]

Furthermore, the Hebrew word for meditate, *hagah*, can
also be translated "growl" or "chew." Consider the way the
prophet Isaiah used *hagah*: "As a lion or a young lion growls
[*hagah*] over his prey" (Isa. 31:4). There is nothing relaxed in
this picture, only a hungry beast trying to get every shred of
nutrition it can, even to the breaking of bones to access the
rich marrow within. This is far more active than the passivity
we usually associate with meditation. Likewise, our handling

of the Word is no casual, calm endeavor. We turn it over and over in our mouths, re-speaking, and tasting its truth.

This exercise brings it bundled with the power of the Holy Spirit into our inner life, where it has provocative effects: "This Book of the Law shall not depart from your mouth, but you shall meditate on it day and night, so that you may be careful to do according to all that is written in it. For then you will make your way prosperous, and then you will have good success" (Josh. 1:8).

Meditation on "the book" brings prosperity and success in doing "all that is written in it." Andrew Murray, author of *The Inner Chamber and the Inner Life*, writes,

> It is in meditation that the heart holds and appropriates the word . . . so in meditation the heart assimilates it and makes it a part of its own life. The meditation of the heart implies desire, acceptance, surrender, love. Out of the heart are the issues of life; what the heart truly believes, it receives with love and joy, and allows to master and rule the life. The intellect gathers and prepares the food on which we are to feed. In meditation the heart takes it in and feeds on it.[9]

The garden of our inner life and worship requires this kind of tending.

Handling with Care

Spiritual disciplines can only develop through practice. We must proceed, therefore, into more pragmatic considerations. How do we handle the Word in order to arrive at the depths of experience we have already spoken about?

First, slow down in your reading. Our typical speed is almost certainly too fast to "taste" anything in the Word. This exercise is not about the quantity of factoids we can load into our brains, nor are we trying to satisfy a reading plan. Our goal must be quality, and you will begin hitting that goal when you reduce your reading speed by half. Save your "read through the Bible in a year" plan for another time. The blessed person of Psalm 1, who "meditates day and night" in the Word of God, "is like a tree planted by streams of water that yields its fruit in season, and its leaf does not wither" (1:2–3). It prospers seasonally, by slow absorption of nutrients through its roots, rather than a rushed, artificial process.

> **MEDITATE ON THE WORD. SLOW DOWN. LINGER THERE. CHEW ON THE WORDS.**

During this slow reading, you will find it easier to notice some things in the text standing out more than others. This may be the Holy Spirit drawing your attention to a thought or theme. Linger there. Chew the words by speaking them out. While doing this, you are preparing for powerful, effective prayer (more about this in a few moments).

Aside from simply reading through a passage, there are other meditative ways we can chew on the Word. One of them has to do with going through a verse multiple times, while emphasizing a different word each time. This method yields a bushel of complementary thoughts that highlight even further the overall meaning of the verse.

"**In** Him was life, and the life was the light of men"
(Within Christ, not outside of Him).

"In **Him** was life, and the life was the light of men"
(Him Personally, not religious systems).

"In Him **was life**, and the life was the light of men"
(energy, vitality).

"In Him was life, **and** the life was the light of men" (additionally, consequently).

"In Him was life, and **the life** was the light of men" (unique, unparalleled).

"In Him was life, and the life **was** the light of men" (truly, effectively).

"In Him was life, and the life was **the light** of men" (unique illumination).

"In Him was life, and the life was the light **of men**" (the entire human race).[10]

Donald Whitney, author of *Spiritual Disciplines for the Christian Life*, adds, "Of course, the point is not simply to repeat vainly each word of the verse until they've all been emphasized. The purpose is to think deeply upon the light (truth) that flashes into your mind each time the diamond of Scripture is turned. It's simple, but effective."[11] When we handle the Word this way, it is like turning a precious stone over and over, to admire its many facets. While we're doing this, our souls simultaneously see and taste the glory of God, similar to the way we would savor a delicious meal.

However, we must remember that the message appearing to us will not be one that creates a personalized meaning foreign to the text. The Spirit will speak and apply the passage to you, but only according to the intended truth of it. All too often, "new teachings" turn out to be old heresies. We protect ourselves from this danger by paying attention to the overall understanding of the verse, and its immediate context. There is enough rapturous joy available in truth properly understood to keep us busy for eternity.

Jonathan Edwards described his own experience:

> The first instance that I remember of that sort of inward, sweet delight in God and divine things that I have lived much in since, was on reading those words, 1 Timothy 1:17, "Now unto the king, eternal, immortal, invisible, the only wise God, be honor and glory forever and ever, Amen." As I read the words, there came into my soul, and was, as it were, diffused through it, a sense of the glory of the Divine Being; a new sense, quite different from anything I had ever experienced before. Never any words of Scripture seemed to me as these words did. I thought within myself, how excellent a Being that was, and how happy I should be, if I might enjoy that God, and be rapt up to him in heaven, and be as it were swallowed up in him forever![12]

Embrace God's sixty-six books, and savor His glory. Through His Word, His holiness inspires, His love warms, His righteousness instructs, His faithfulness secures, His goodness satisfies, His wisdom humbles, His power emboldens, His mercy relieves, His grace gladdens, and His wrath terrifies. The sum of His glory makes a human being worship.

And that is when we start talking back.

Prayer—Responding to the Glory

It is impossible to overstate the importance of prayer in cultivating the inner life and worship of a believer. We sometimes try to help people learn this discipline by telling them to simply start talking to God. "Speak from the heart," we say; "Be honest." And so they do, extemporaneously, in halting words, as though they were trying to recite a French vocabulary list. Prayer is an awkward, foreign language to them, because their hearts are still full of childish ignorance, lusts, and self-centeredness. Sometimes even folks who aren't Christians participate as well, giving little speeches heavenward, telling

God what to do and how to bless. Occasionally they use a ton of words, writing them out ahead of time and then reading them, so as not to sound foolish if they must say a word of "prayer" at public events.

Jesus talked about this when he said to the disciples, "And when you pray, do not heap up empty phrases as the Gentiles do, for they think that they will be heard for their many words" (Matt. 6:7). Prayer becomes an exercise in straining out phrases, inventing sentiments, filling time, and trying to impress God (or others) with religious sincerity. That's hard— so hard that God would be cruel if He actually required it.

Remember that He Himself took the first step in the prayer conversation: "Long ago, at many times and in many ways, God spoke to our fathers by the prophets, but in these last days he has spoken to us by his Son, whom he appointed the heir of all things, through whom also he created the world" (Heb. 1:1–2). Anytime you open the Scriptures, God basically invites you into a conversation He already began long ago.

The deeper you enter the text, the more you sense the joy of divine accomplishments, the outrage of sin, a hope invulnerable to disappointments, confidence in the face of doubt, self-sacrificial love, and divine sovereignty. Within His words to us are the very words and concepts we use to talk back to Him. God gave us the Bible so we would enter the conversation, and know how to pray. That is why we spent so much time on meditation in the last section. Once the Word and prayer combine within us, a new relational dynamic forms in our lives. Andrew Murray says,

> Prayer and the word are inseparably linked together: power in the use of either depends upon the presence of the other. The word gives me matter for prayer, telling me what God

will do for me. It shows me the path of prayer, telling me
how God would have me come. It gives me the power for
prayer, the courage of the assurance I will be heard. And
it brings me the answer to prayer, as it teaches what God
will do for me. And so, on the other hand, prayer prepares
the heart for receiving the word from God himself, for the
teaching of the spirit to give the spiritual understanding of
it, for the faith that is made partaker of its mighty working.[13]

Once you have carefully received and understood the
Bible's communication, it becomes a powerful way of interacting with God. The prayers that emerge out of it are not a
slavish rehash of what you've read. They are formed in you,
like a loaf in an oven, and offered back to God in the shape
of worshipful confession, praise, thanks, or petitions. When
we practice prayer this way, biblical inner life begins to hum.

"But I Want God to Give Me Something"

The average person sees prayer and petition as virtually synonymous. Why pray unless there is something to ask for?
Prayer simply to enjoy the presence of God seems to border
on aimless subjectivity. After all, even Jesus told us to "Ask,
and it will be given to you" (Matt. 7:7).

Requests of many kinds often flow out of the word-prayer
dynamic described in the last section. Genesis 18, for instance,
shows God visiting Abraham, and sitting with him over a
meal. He speaks a word to the man concerning two upcoming
things, the birth of Isaac, and the destruction of Sodom.

Abraham finds the promised blessing of a son befuddling,
and seems not to know what to say about it. But God's dis-
closure about the dramatic overthrow of the evil city seizes his
immediate attention, because his nephew, Lot, is living there.

This begins a ping-pong dialogue between Abraham and God, as Abraham pleads for the salvation of the righteous in that doomed place (see Gen. 18:23–32). God had made known His word, and Abraham, struck by part of it, responds with prayer. The prayer, though, has left off of mere savoring, and become a desperate request, an intercession for Lot's life, although Abraham never mentions Lot's name. God, who does not need that missing information, later delivers Lot from the city moments before it is destroyed in a fiery apocalypse.

But how about the times when we don't obtain what we asked for, when God seems tightfisted, or silent? The Christian who is obsessed with a particular desired outcome, may have fallen into a form of idolatry, a hunger for something that has become even more important than God himself. And if God doesn't come through to provide it, he or she can fall into severe disillusionment, depression, even a faith crisis—further proving that some form of idolatry was connected with the thing they were asking for.

Yet insisting on our perceived needs can actually short-circuit what God wants to do in our lives. Much of what I honestly think I need is the tip of an iceberg. I am hardly conscious of the more profound areas that lie beneath—the places God pays all His attention to day and night. When I pour copious amounts of prayer energy into my concerns, I often find that God is not as concerned about them. He is far more interested in root issues.

It may come as a surprise to many of us that there is no such thing as unanswered prayer, only prayers answered in ways different than we expected. On one occasion, Jesus said, "If you then, who are evil, know how to give good gifts to your children, how much more will your Father who is in heaven give good things to those who ask him!" (Matt. 7:11). The obvious point is that God knows better than we how to give good things. If He withholds something we think would have been good, then that means either it would not have been good for us at all, or it would not have been good at the particular time or in the particular way we requested it.

But for the purpose of our study, we need to ask what God gives, if He doesn't give what we specifically asked. Luke mirrors Matthew's account, but adds one small detail: "how much more will the heavenly Father *give the Holy Spirit to those who ask him!*" (Luke 11:13). God views the Holy Spirit as the most desirable grant we could ever receive, and therefore a more than acceptable swap for anything we asked for in particular, but didn't get.

In 2009, I entered the world of church planting. Anyone in this ministry soon becomes familiar with the anxious feeling that you're never doing enough, and it can descend into workaholism. Around every corner lurks the tantalizing promise of success—a large, thriving church—if you are willing to put in more hours than a married man ought, and if you're amenable to skimping on "extras" like personal spirituality. I pored over church-planting literature, hoping to capture the same "miracle grow" experience they all described.

Though I was careful to follow their paint-by-numbers approach, God steadfastly refused to ante up with the hundreds of new folks necessary for a big success. The harder I tried, the more He dug in with a resolute "No." Frustration developed in my heart. The more I drilled down in prayer about it, the more things on the surface remained the same. In fact, each time I drifted toward these topics during my daily devotions, my joy would dry up.

An oil gusher came later that year. And no, I don't mean that my church plant suddenly hit the big time. For many years I had understood and labored into spiritual disciplines, trusting that simple repetition of techniques would be good enough. But the filling of the Spirit is a progressive matter, with life lessons attached to it. God was apparently wishing to demonstrate His superiority over anything on my want list. And so He laid aside my original petition for numerical success something not good—at least not for the time being.

> ## GOD IS CONCERNED WITH OUR INWARD STATE MORE THAN ANYTHING ELSE.

And what did God give that was better? The Holy Spirit. He brought an enhanced sharpness to my interior life, and an ability to praise and pray for kingdom concerns. Divine glory eclipsed human success. While my interest in growing our church has certainly not disappeared, it has been adjusted. These days I have higher aspirations in my heart than headcount.

Many of our prayer disappointments would be alleviated if we remembered that God is concerned with our inward state more than anything else. Author Philip Yancey writes,

> Like Peter, we may pray for food and get a lesson in racism; like Paul we may pray for healing and get humility. We may ask for relief from trials and instead get patience to bear them. We may pray for release from prison and instead get strength to redeem the time while there. Asking, seeking, and knocking does have an effect on God, as Jesus insists, but it also has a lasting effect on the asker-seeker-knocker.[14]

And so, even the simple process of petitioning God, of learning to receive, and receive *better* than what we asked, cultivates our inner life in profound ways.

Enjoyment in the Practical Lane

As we pray and thus cultivate worship, we'll need to pay attention to some associated best practices. One of them has to do with being honest. Practice authenticity when you pray. Jesus spoke of those "who devour widows' houses and for a pretense make long prayers. They will receive the greater condemnation" (Luke 20:47). He also said, "When you pray, you must not be like the hypocrites. For they love to stand and pray in the synagogues and at the street corners, that they may be seen by others. Truly, I say to you, they have received their reward" (Matt. 6:5). Some people can put on quite a show in public when they pray, but when alone with God, minus a human audience, their long, loud prayers lapse into silence. Relationships thrive on honesty, especially when it comes to us and God. He is the truest true, and so prayer and gamesmanship cannot coexist.

Since authenticity is so desirable, you'll also want to avoid stilted, mechanical prayers. When Jesus taught the disciples to pray the Lord's Prayer, He said, "Pray this way," not "Recite these words." That means He presented a scaffold for them, a framework that neophytes could use to develop their prayer life. We find in this model structure concerns for the Father's name, His will, His kingdom, our needs, forgiveness, forgiveness of others, and deliverance from evil. All of these represent springboards into possible areas of prayer. But neither the exact wording of the Lord's Prayer, nor any other recorded prayer, was meant to be a straitjacket for us.

Prayer is a flexible, elastic exercise. You will find God ready any time of the day or night to hear it. Jesus prayed during the events of the day (see Matt. 11:25); He also prayed the whole night (see Luke 6:12). Paul charged us to "Pray without ceasing" (1 Thess. 5:17), but the apostles also apparently prayed at fixed times (see Acts 3:1).

If you're just beginning the habit of disciplined prayer, some sort of measurable objective is appropriate. Set a goal you can grow into, but not one so challenging it won't be sustainable—five or ten minutes, perhaps. Obviously, as you practice, your ability to pray will grow. You will begin to chafe against your previous five-minute limit, as though you were outgrowing an exoskeleton. That's when you'll probably need to get creative. Finding an extra ten, fifteen, or twenty minutes might require adjustments to your schedule—like getting up a little earlier in the morning.

Guard your focus during that time. Minimize distractions like cell phones and other electronic devices. And people, as well. There is definitely a time for public prayer, during which we hope to encourage and build up one another (see 1 Cor. 14:), but devotional prayer needs a private dimension, one that allows a direct, person-to-person bond to form between God and the believer.

All true relationships of depth have boundaries of privacy. Not everything within it should be on display. Jesus modeled this Himself: "And after he had dismissed the crowds, he went up on the mountain by himself to pray. When evening came, he was there alone" (Matt. 14:23); "And after he had taken leave of them, he went up on the mountain to pray" (Mark 6:46); "But he would withdraw to desolate places and pray" (Luke 5:16).

Praying in the presence of other people tends to generate self-consciousness. If it doesn't lead us into showing off, it can go in the other direction, inhibiting us to the point that it strangles real prayer. Knowing our propensities for these weaknesses, Jesus said, "But when you pray, go into your room and shut the door and pray to your Father who is in secret. And your Father who sees in secret will reward you" (Matt. 6:6). For us, "in secret" means finding a quiet place—a laundry room, a basement, or a bathroom. A parked car might work as well, or taking a walk in a secluded area.

These points about prayer have traveled far from telling someone, "Just start talking to God." Though that admonition might be fine for a brand-new Christian, as growing believers we need a further commitment if we want to milk all the potential out of communing with the Lord.

Indeed, at first the word "disciplines" seems better fitted to the military than to Christian spirituality. The idea of grace as a formless liberty sounds more appealing and poetic, in a bohemian sort of way. But consider Paul's charge to the elders of the church to be "hospitable, a lover of good, self-controlled, upright, holy, and *disciplined*" (Titus 1:8). He also said of himself, "I *discipline* my body and keep it under control, lest after preaching to others I myself should be disqualified" (1 Cor. 9:27). These verses indicate that a relaxed, plant-and-forget version of the Christian life is not apostolic.

Powerful worship requires intentional practice. Our inner life may be a garden full of organic reality; however, it still needs intentional gardening. And that means it needs the attention of a conscientious gardener.

10

Worship Falling Flat

I'm alone Lord
alone
a thousand miles from home.
There's no one here who knows my name
except the clerk
and he spelled it wrong
no one to eat dinner with
laugh at my jokes
listen to my gripes
be happy with me about what happened today
and say that's great.
No one cares.
There's just this lousy bed
and slush in the street outside
between the buildings.
I feel sorry for myself
and I've plenty of reason
to. Maybe I ought to say

I'm on top of it
praise the Lord
things are great
but they're not.
Tonight
it's all
gray slush.

— Joseph Bayly, *Psalms of My Life*

IF YOU REMEMBER Fruit Stripe gum, you probably recall how at first it would deliver an intense burst of flavor. Thirty seconds later, though, every bit of that flavor would disappear, and you'd be left chewing something that tasted like hard putty. The only way to get the taste back was to try another stick, and so on, until you had powered your way through the whole pack. By then, the gum was gone, and your jaw was sore. That's probably when you started to give up on Fruit Stripe.

The Christian life often seems to lose its amazing flavor as well. The initial glow of salvation subsides, and we—unconsciously, at least—begin to hunt for some alternate high. We all know how damaging this attitude can be in high-stakes situations like marriage, when your spouse doesn't seem so magical anymore. Or employment, when the alarm clock goes off and you decide you're not "feeling" that job like you did before.

However, skipping church services or choosing Netflix over Scripture doesn't deliver instant life collapse like those other things. We might even feel justified in taking a break. For many of us, when we answered the call to faith in Christ, at the back of our minds we were signing up for thrills, chills, romance, comfort, and inspiration. And if that ceases, isn't a hiatus called for? When the vending machine stops paying off, only a fool keeps putting coins in it, right?

Watchman Nee frames the problem of a disappointed believer when faith stops delivering emotional goods:

> His most beloved joy suddenly vanishes. He rises as usual in the morning to read his Bible yet where is the former sweetness? He prays as before but finds himself exhausted after a few words. He feels as if he has lost something. Not long ago he was judging others for being far behind him in the spiritual race, but now he considers himself to be one of *them*. His heart has turned cold; the earlier sense of a fire burning within has been smothered. No longer is he conscious of the presence and proximity of the Lord; instead the Lord appears to be quite remote from him. He now begins to wonder where the Lord has gone. To suffer becomes a real suffering now because he cannot sense any more of the former joy he had in suffering. Moreover, he has lost interest in preaching; he no longer feels like continuing on after saying but a few words. In sum, during such an episode everything seems to be dark, dry, cold and dead. It appears to the believer that he has been abandoned by the Lord in a tomb; nothing can comfort his heart.[1]

In addition to this bleak picture, external stresses may suddenly come along and compound the problem—a family member falls into an unexplained illness, a much-needed job is in jeopardy, grave marital difficulties arise. You can count on the devil to take advantage of moments like these, whispering in our ears with his own dark opinions, questioning the validity of our salvation, or hurling accusations in hopes of burdening us even further.

However, loss of spiritual feelings does not automatically mean anything is wrong. It may even signal God's intention to develop our inner life and growth in new and previously unexplored ways.

To establish this claim, we first need to say that emotions, in and of themselves, are not a problem. Well-meaning books and teachers have often counseled Christians to ignore, even discard emotion as fraudulent spirituality. Such a wholesale dismissal of a valid part of our being runs counter to common sense, not to mention what the Bible actually says. Jesus promised that "my *joy* may be in you, and that your *joy* may be full" (John 15:11). Paul wrote that "we have peace with God through our Lord Jesus Christ" (Rom. 5:1). Other verses refer to boldness and confidence, hope, love, and grief over sin (see Eph. 3:12; Col. 1:27; Rom. 5:5; 2 Cor. 7:10)—all of which would be meaningless if feelings were not somehow involved.

Yet it's common to find Christians growing nervous over words like "experience" and "feelings." Some of this concern is justified; believers can often develop peculiar religious mindsets, mostly derived from their particular church culture. Experiences—miracles and amazing coincidences which they cannot wait to tell others about—are the focus of their lives. They would do well to heed the old saying, "a tree overfull of leaves will not have much fruit."

> **EMOTIONALISM IS NOT THE PRESENCE OF STRONG EMOTION. IT IS THE ABUSE OF IT.**

Our misgivings, though, should be more about *emotionalism* than emotion. Emotionalism is an approach to life and worship where feelings predominate over our mind and will, eclipsing the intellect and short-circuiting responsible decision-making. Ruled by passion, our worship runs off the rails into idolatry, strays into strange teachings, and produces disorder in Christian meetings. Emotionalism, then, is not the presence of strong emotion. It is the abuse of it.

Remember the case of Nadab and Abihu in Leviticus 10? These two sons of Aaron, in rash excitement, ran into the Holy Place of the tabernacle and offered "strange fire" (10:1, KJV)— incense not authorized by God. Their uncontrolled zeal got in the way of their fear of God, their respect for His holiness, and the position the Law of Moses had assigned to them. That day, God answered with judgment upon these two.

The cure for emotionalism is not the removal of emotion, but the proper placement of it. Sensations, feelings, passions *follow* God and His truth. They don't come first, as if they were the engine pulling worship along. We actually need our God-created capacity of emotions in tow, following behind Him, so they can praise His perfections, mourn our sinfulness, and celebrate His cause. Only with a rich emotional dimension can we love or rejoice, dance before His glory, or sing of His victory. Rognlien writes,

> Whatever our predisposition toward emotion, it is impossible to deny that feelings comprise a major aspect of who we are as human beings and play a significant role in our faith. The Bible is not simply a dispassionate account of historical facts and theological ideas; it's also a passionate love story, filled with every kind of human experience and emotion.[2]

The new life we have received enriches and repositions emotion, but does not annihilate it.

Furthermore, our emotional palette is full of diverse possibilities. Jesus rejoiced (see Matt. 11:25), promised blessings related to happiness (see 5:2–11), had conversations with the Father that were punctuated with thanks (see John 11:41–42), and spoke of His own joy as unique and immovable (see 16:22); and yet the Scriptures call Him "a man of sorrows and acquainted with grief" (Isa. 53:3). He was not superhuman, but acutely felt the pain of this world.

Jesus wept when Lazarus died (see John 11:35). He experienced great distress in the garden prior to his crucifixion (see Mark 14:33), and petitioned the Father with tears (see Heb. 5:7). He experienced humiliation on the cross that could only be captured in the psalmist's words, "I am a worm, and not a man" (Ps. 22:6). He expressed profound pain in the cry, "my God, my God, why have you forsaken me?" (Mark 15:34), signaling the most profound sense of loss, as He was made sin for us, and the Father turned His face away from Him. Our Leader, our Captain, the Lover of our souls, has experienced both the heights of joy and the depths of emotional despair during His life, as well as at His death.

Much of Scripture seems calculated to provoke feelings in us of various kinds, and never of only one kind. Brian Steven Borgman says the Bible uses "vivid, descriptive, emotional language, not simply designed to inform, but to move. God wants us to feel the truth."[3]

True worship involves a spectrum of emotion, such as in the book of Psalms, where we find everything from joy to thanksgiving, to hope, to lament, to resentment, to frustration, to anger, and to despair.

The functions of the human soul related to worship—mind, emotion, and will—work like a three-legged stool. They depend on one another, and in harmony with our regenerated human spirit, become a holistic inner life. You cannot remove one leg and have a stable platform. If we attack or even diminish emotion, it will certainly lead to extremes of the mind (intellectualism), or the will (legalism).

One of the central characters of the old TV series *Star Trek* was an alien named Spock. His main personality trait was a denial of emotion, operating on the level of pure logic. Spock was always lauding the virtues of highest reason, while avoiding the shame of emotion. In order to make the character work, however, the show's creators concluded they had to make Spock half-human. A fully logical being would come off as wooden—like a mannequin reciting lines. Besides, it would look problematic, even contradictory, to portray high intellect operating in an emotionless vacuum.

And yet some people aspire to that standard, even considering it spiritual. Faith, to them, means an unchanging calm, cool, detached demeanor. To them, tears are evidence of a breach of trust. Joy is a sign of shallowness.

That works for a computer. Or for those with misguided religious attitudes. But not for normal human beings who desire a rich worship of God. Our hues and mixtures of emotion are not a problem, because God meets us in all of them. "He who descended is also the one who ascended far above all the heavens, that he might fill all things" (Eph. 4:10). Christ has filled both depths and heights, and is accessible at either extreme and every place in between.

This runs contrary to the saccharine, upbeat caricature we sometimes promote in Christian circles—the kind that leaves no room for hurt, or loss, or the blahs. As it stands, there is no need for us to pretend we never struggle. Life-changing experiences often occur in places of great honesty.

Emotion is one of humanity's most enduring features, and once aligned with our enlivened spirit of worship, extremely valuable. Until that time, though, our feelings will seem transient and troublesome. We hope for rainy days to be few, blizzards still fewer. Droughts, never. We dislike these erratic moods, yet they are the very way through which God furthers His work in us.

Encouraging the Newly Born

The immediate joy of a new believer is the first hug, the first kiss, God delivers to his new child. Although the intensity of the encounter differs according to the circumstances and personality of the believer, God often grants these felt encouragements parallel to faith in order to make His invisible presence known. This may go on for an indeterminate period of time, during which the young Christian obeys the Lord, prays, reads the Bible, and goes to church because it feels good. His or her proximity to God is palpable. Faith indeed feels as though it is riding a wave, with little or no effort involved.

More seasoned believers might refer to this stage as "the honeymoon with Jesus" (and unfortunately, sometimes they do so with a sour spirit). It is as though they hope to settle down the brash upstart whose zeal for Christ stands out everywhere he goes. But this is God's work, His glory.

It is not uncommon for new life to move a person to sell all, to make radical changes, and to begin laying a foundation that will last through the ages. "Jesus only, Jesus ever" is the banner cry. God is well pleased, and He lets the believer know it—through feelings, of course. At this point, to the believer, there is no difference between a happy mood, and the eternal, indestructible joy of the Savior. It's all the same.

And so, it seems the lovely tulips on the stems are there to stay, indefinitely.

Establishing A Deeper Life

But then, shockingly, the flowers fall off. At the beginning of faith, joy gushed effortlessly. It alerted the new believer that eternal life had come. As Jesus promised, it welled up, and flowed like a river. Yet one day, that steady torrent dwindles.

Just days after I was born again, that very thing happened to me. I woke up expecting my regular dose of happiness, and found nothing. The New Jerusalem seemed a ghost town, complete with an empty throne and a dried-up river.

Actually, the joy of Christ was still there in me, unmoved as Jesus promised, but I was more attuned to my own mood. I assumed that whatever I felt must naturally be the same as what God felt, that the normal state of things was for heaven itself to be aligned upon me. But when my undisciplined emotions moved, affected as they were by early-morning blahs, I followed them, and believed in them, not God.

One of my earliest lessons thus became clear: that my emotional state and God could be two different things. For me, it was the beginning of a new learning experience. Author J.I. Packer wrote,

> God . . . is very gentle with very young Christians, just as mothers are with very young babies. Often the start of their Christian career is marked by great emotional joy, striking providences, remarkable answers to prayer, and immediate fruitfulness in their first acts of witness; thus God encourages them, and establishes them in "the life," but as they grow stronger, and are able to bear more, he exercises them in a tougher school.[4]

Since emotion was as yet my only barometer of spiritual health, I attempted to resuscitate the golden feelings of the past few days. They returned, but sporadically, appearing and disappearing over a year or so, until I finally paid them no more attention.

During that time, my focus gradually shifted. Rather than trying to use the Bible to rescue my lost euphoria, I began to drill down into Bible verses, learning about the character, the work, and the will of God. My prayer, that had once kept an obsessive eye on my feelings, now grew into a fuller praise.

SPIRITUAL DRY TIMES OFTEN FORCE THE ROOTS OF NEW FAITH TO GO DEEPER.

I also paid more attention to what I was bringing to Christian meetings than what I got out of them. This yielded another kind of joy, but not the type I had to chase around, corral, and coddle.

Spiritual dry times often have the effect of forcing the roots of new faith to go deeper, and provoke searches that are more profound. This won't happen if a believer remains in a "Candyland" of sorts, where surface emotions are abundant. Jesus spoke of this danger in Matthew 13:20–21, saying, "this is the one who hears the word and immediately receives it with joy, yet he has no root in himself, but endures for a while, and when tribulation or persecution arises on account of of the word, immediately he falls away."

God allows and even creates tougher learning environments to wean us from surface faith, and encourage us to be "rooted and built up in him and established in the faith" (Col. 2:7). This means being drawn away from surface life, down into the depths of inner life. In Archibald Alexander's words, "The flowers may have disappeared from the plant of grace, and even the leaves may have fallen off, and wintry blasts may have shaken it, but now it is striking its roots deeper, and becoming every day stronger to endure the rugged storm."[5]

Exposing the Need for Grace

Strip the leaves off a tree, and it will immediately become apparent how much fruit is actually on the branches. Similarly, when feelings fall away, we are left face-to-face with our true spiritual condition. In our search to know God, we often discount the importance of realizing who we are, including our unflattering aspects. Other people may have long noticed, or sensed at some level, our shortcomings. Perhaps a few of them tried to tell you, but you responded with anger, claiming they unfairly judged you, like Job's three friends. You begin wondering what is wrong with everyone else.

Yet you notice the same situations recurring in your life, sometimes differing only in the details. They keep lining up on the same theme, the one you refuse to face, or have been oblivious toward. Your frustration abounds. Resentment builds. No one understands. For some reason unknown to you at the moment, God refuses to remove the hardship.

The apostle Paul alluded to this kind of experience, when a long-term suffering struck his life. Although he didn't disclose the exact nature of it—whether spiritual, psychological, or physical—he did say, "Three times I pleaded with the Lord about this, that it should leave me. But he said to me, 'My grace is sufficient for you, for my power is made perfect in weakness'" (2 Cor. 12:8–9).

Eventually, Paul was also made aware of the purpose behind the affliction: "to keep me from becoming conceited because of the surpassing greatness of the revelations, a thorn was given me in the flesh, a messenger of Satan to harass me, to keep me from becoming conceited" (2 Cor. 12:7). While Paul's apprehension of deeper, mysterious things of the spiritual realm were good for the church and its edification, these very things tended to inflate his self-appraisal. The Lord grounded his apostle, reminding him that he was at the mercy of God's grace just as much as anyone else.

As we encounter our own personal limitations, it often brings us feelings of deep disappointment, dissatisfaction, and occasionally, humiliation. We wish for a complete range of spiritual gifts, only to find that we have few, perhaps only one. Even those with many gifts find that the success they achieved for the Lord often evaporates, leaving disillusionment in its place. We face the harsh realities of physical weakness—illnesses, or the reduction of our natural powers through aging.

We also feel the limitations inherited from our family of origin—places, backgrounds, and family drama that have significantly shaped us, sometimes in ways we don't desire. We wish to be free of time constraints, and long for the freedom to do things we want, but are constantly squeezed by the tyranny of a twenty-four-hour day. We all know financial limitations, regardless of how wealthy we may be, because there is only so much money available.

Your natural personality has boundaries related to introversion and extroversion, and possibly a range of problems inbred or acquired that create difficulties in moving forward, or even feeling stable. Our marital status or family situation limits us, for better or worse. And your job will at times seem to shackle you, forbidding the sweet, fulfilling freedom your soul desires.

These circumstances annoy us at first, then infuriate us, then drive us to cynicism. But at last they humble us. In fact, this kind of suffering closes off our escape routes and options. With all bridges out and alternative roadways blocked, we grieve, then dejectedly choose grace, because it is the only way left open. Unbeknownst to us, we are choosing the pathway to the depths of inner life and indomitable joy.

Overcoming the Environment

When happy feelings disappear, God is at work as much as He was when the believer was flush with sensations. For a long time a Christian can become accustomed to taking his cues and deriving his joy from things going his way—an idyllic job, a devoted spouse, perfect health, accomplished children, a thriving ministry. Under these circumstances, praises flow easily, but, as the devil said to God about Job, "Does Job fear God for no reason? Have you not put a hedge around him and his house and all that he has, on every side? You have blessed the work of his hands, and his possessions have increased in the land" (Job 1:9–10). That allegation both maligned Job's motives, and devalued God. But—dare we say it?—there might have been a kernel of truth in the matter.

Secure circumstances can become an unconscious crutch for the child of God. He or she is never so aware of that fact than when the environment unexpectedly shifts and God seems to disappear. The traditional five stages of grief set in (denial, anger, bargaining, depression, and acceptance), but with Chistians, hopefully a final one as well—learning.

Paul alluded to particular lessons related to finance when he wrote, "I have learned in whatever situation I am to be content. I know how to be brought low, and I know how to abound. In any and every circumstance, I have learned the secret of facing plenty and hunger, abundance and need. I can do all things through him who strengthens me" (Phil. 4:11–13).

He had to learn such things, because without them, his Christian life might have been indistinguishable from his circumstances. When things were running even keel, Christ would have been on the throne. But when the money ran out before the end of the month, when stomach flu struck, when problems in the church surfaced, the Savior would have appeared a ninety-eight pound weakling, incapable of meeting the challenges.

When Paul spoke of learning to be content in whatever situation he found himself, he did not mean to recommend passive indifference. Instead, he meant a state in which a person learns not to be mastered by his or her environment. Certainly, if Paul could have improved his situation, he probably would have done so. And so should we. But often we find circumstances forbidding any change.

This is where our problems usually emerge. In our helplessness, we find ourselves mad at God, resentful of others, stymied, miserable, sleepless, swarming with schemes, and developing an ever-growing willingness to compromise. Yet learning, not escape, is needed here.

Paul also wrote of his life or death struggle in Ephesus.

> We do not want you to be unaware, brothers, of the affliction we experienced in Asia. For we were so utterly burdened beyond our strength that we despaired of life itself. Indeed,

we felt that we had received the sentence of death. But that was to make us rely not on ourselves but on God who raises the dead (2 Cor. 1:8–9)

The apostle expressed here that at some deep, unconscious level, we all rely upon ourselves. We trust our emotional resources to weather the storm and manipulate the outcome. If we can't, we languish in sorrow. God must therefore train us in a new reliance, with eyes fixed upon His Son, who is the Master of all sufferings, and Lord over all trouble.

> **STABILITY ONLY COMES WHEN WE ARE ANCHORED IN THE UNCHANGING ONE.**

The blessed result of our discipline will be that "We walk by faith, not by sight" (2 Cor. 5:7). Then we will find the joy unique to the Person of Christ without elaborate outward scaffolding. This was how Paul could sing hymns of praise while in dungeon stocks—"sorrowful, yet always rejoicing" (6:10), he called it—and how the early church could continue those first three hundred years while falsely accused, attacked, and martyred. When our feelings are shackled to the erratic situations of life, what could we expect but mercurial highs and lows? Stability only comes when we are anchored in the unchanging One.

Training the Will

Though we might have experienced a significant number of emotions related to our new life, only our ability to follow through, to endure, truly counts as powerful in God's eyes. He endeavors therefore to train our will by withholding the emotions we have come to depend upon.

God's intended goal is for us to respond by doing things according to faithfulness, without needing inspirational feelings to return and sweep us off our feet. "I remind you to fan into flame the gift of God, which is in you" (2 Tim. 1:6), Paul instructed Timothy. The younger minister had apparently been overcome with melancholy, and like many of us, was waiting for the cloud to lift on its own.

More than a few churches have discovered in their ranks a majority that have not learned the skill of self-feeding. They still lean on church bands to stir them and sermons to nourish them. It is like the description of the lazy man in Proverbs 26:15 (NIV)—"A sluggard buries his hand in the dish; / he is too lazy to bring it back to his mouth." And this is precisely what happens when the will of a Christian goes untrained. Such believers have no energy to perform even the most basic self-feeding disciplines, because they don't "feel" motivated. Critical things like Bible reading and church attendance are allowed to fall by the wayside, simply because they have not been flooded with the feelings they think necessary to do any of it. It is all over until, inexplicably, they experience another jolt of encouragement.

Little wonder then, that God starts rationing emotional snacks, because beyond a certain point, they hardly contribute to our maturity. At this point, joy will sink to more sublime levels at our core, where it syncs with the One "who for the joy that was set before him endured the cross, despising the shame, and is seated at the right hand of the throne of God" (Heb. 12:2). God's grace in us begins to stimulate endurance rather than enthusiasm.

This reflects a monumental turning point in a believer's life, for we must "run with endurance the race that is set before us" (Heb. 12:1). God knows our faith journey is not a sprint that can be accomplished on sugar highs. It continues every day, seven days a week, at home and at work, while sick or healthy, wealthy or poor, young or old. Only a steady, habitual approach to it will yield the fruit of spiritual formation.

> Therefore, since we have been justified by faith, we have peace with God through our Lord Jesus Christ. Through him we have also obtained access by faith into this grace in which we stand, and we rejoice in hope of the glory of God. Not only that, but we rejoice in our sufferings, knowing that suffering produces endurance, and endurance produces character, and character produces hope, and hope does not put us to shame, because God's love has been poured into our hearts through the Holy Spirit who has been given to us. (Rom. 5:1-5)

In His wisdom and understanding of the human condition, God has called us into sanctified diligence undergirded with deep joy, rather than sustained moods of inspiration that sweep our surface. Eugene Peterson refers to this concept as "a long obedience in the same direction."

Jesus paid the price for us to enter His abiding joy. When our awareness of His presence wanes, we should never call it abandonment. Such a thing has never happened to any child of God, save the unique, firstborn Son of God Himself. Only He has truly experienced being forsaken by God, as He underwent the sufferings of the cross. Our feelings of abandonment, then, are false.

These seasons of sorrow are calculated to bless us, to usher us into a greater fellowship of life with God. Is there anything worthwhile in the valley, where purple shadows lie? Where waters run deep? Where the air is cooler, and thicker, and the shepherd promises to be closer?

We think not, but we are wrong.

What to Do While We Wait

Difficult spiritual seasons cannot be rushed, and during those times, positive feelings prove elusive. What we do during the wait can make all the difference.

1. Deal with Obvious Things

From the outset we would do well to consider how much of our situation lies in our own hands. Before we assume God is moving us into more demanding areas of worship, we ought to ask whether we have neglected dealing with a known sin or with our own feeding on the bread of life. This we have already covered in earlier chapters, and will not repeat here. Quite often with the resumption of these basics, disturbances to our inner life smooth out, and we continue on our way.

But a dry emotional state might also occur due to psychological or even physiological causes. Clinically diagnosed depression and other associated conditions like anxiety and bipolar disorders can require regular medication to control. I realize Christians are all over the opinion board on this issue. There is no doubt that our society has become over-diagnosed and over-prescribed, but even legitimate cases receive censure in some Christian groups. Their dogma states it is wrong to seek pharmaceutical aids, even if one has suicidal thoughts or becomes delusional or violent.

One man told me his adult daughter was on such treatments, but when she heard from her pastor that she should depend instead on the healing of the Holy Spirit, she stopped taking her medication. Within several days the girl was saying and doing things that damaged her marriage and all the rest of her familial relations. She began claiming odd religious experiences, and everything normal vanished from her life.

Church leaders who dispense blanket advice to cease medications are often nowhere to be found when those lives collapse, leaving hapless friends and family to pick up the pieces. They are good at making pronouncements, but poor at helping shoulder the burden of the outcomes they create.

When we are saved, we do not instantly lose all infirmities. Instead, we believe First Peter 2:24, that promises, "By his wounds you have been healed," and we look forward to any remaining or ingrained illnesses not currently healed to disappear when the Lord returns to glorify our bodies (see Phil. 3:20–21). In the meantime, after having been properly diagnosed and while under professional care, continue to take all necessary medications.

Apart from officially diagnosed conditions, many of us still deal with challenges. Even emotional conditions problematic to us before we met Christ, often must be wrestled with afterwards, like depression, anxiety, and melancholy. Being born again does not banish these or even suddenly re-order them. This process takes time and may even persist throughout one's life. Martyn Lloyd-Jones wrote, "I suppose that one of the greatest problems of our life in this world, not only for Christians, but for all people, is the right handling of feelings and emotions."[6]

I include myself in this category. I've always been a bit high-strung, but in 2008, I began to experience panic attacks. Because these involved crushing chest pressure, and oxygen starvation, I feared they were signs of a developing heart condition. After several rounds of tests at the hospital though, my doctor determined they were not.

Looking back on it, I realize I had internalized pressures around me related to a church split, unwanted changes in ministry, and even positive experiences. Since that time, I have had numerous relapses, but I've also found that a combined care for mind, body, and spirit is an absolute must. I practice techniques when my mind begins going to dark places (some of these based on Scripture, others on secular advice). I also avoid too much caffeine and sugar, get exercise and light, and make sure I continue walking closely with the Lord.

Some of our emotional challenges appear because they are directly linked to our daily habits, such as our diet. For instance, Robert was often moody, even hostile toward members of his small group. The believers around him thought it a mystery, until they discovered he habitually consumed huge amounts of caffeinated tea (he had earlier revealed he had a severe sensitivity to caffeine). His moods were no attack of Satan, nor even special work of God. A simple alteration of diet would have caused Robert to balance out.

In times of emotional crisis, we might want to ask ourselves the simple question of what we've been consuming.

> **OVER-TIRED PEOPLE RARELY FEEL SPIRITUAL. SCHEDULE BREAKS AND PERIODS OF REST FOR YOURSELF.**

Fatigue can also easily destabilize us. Many a productive man or woman who cannot tolerate the thought of "wasted time," ignores the principle of sabbath-keeping. But without rest, tempers shorten, focus blurs, and inspiration becomes lean. Regardless of talent, no one can continually operate while constantly drained of energy.

We typically refer to this condition as *burnout*. Its victims include even those upbeat souls who seem never to run low of vigor—people involved in full-time vocational ministry, highly leveraged moms, super-CEOs, and can-do activists. We don't function well as machines. Over-tired people rarely feel spiritual. Schedule breaks and periods of rest for yourself.

In principle, don't be quick to spiritualize every low tide moment. The situation may only amount to psychological and physical limitations that need attention.

2. Avoid Spiritual Junk Food; Feed on Truth

Times of spiritual apathy are famous for generating fog and a dullness of discernment. As a result, we might hunt for something new and exciting to break us out of our malaise, exposing ourselves to all sorts of quesitonable content. Many books, for instance, that sell like toilet paper in a pandemic, seem to offer fascinating new takes on Christianity. Actually, they only advocate a return to previous errors in church history, a fact most twenty-first-century readers wouldn't know (and perhaps the writer of the book didn't know, either).

Nor would they be aware of the fact that the engaging, witty author has allowed an erosion of biblical authority in his or her own life. Later, when their landslide finally comes, it does so in a deconversion story. That is when the author comes clean with their fan base, declaring they are now officially a pseudo-Christian, if not an atheist, demote the scriptures to the level of inspirational writing, banish hell as barbaric, apologize for their past endorsement of the Bible's sexual standards, and hope now to lead you down the primrose path to "greater enlightenment."

Paul wrote of this problem when he said, "But avoid irreverent babble, for it will lead people into more and more ungodliness, and their talk will spread like gangrene. Among them are Hymenaeus and Philetus, who have swerved from the truth, saying that the resurrection has already happened. They are upsetting the faith of some" (2 Tim. 2:16–18). Key thoughts from this warning: Some alleged ministries amount to mere religious *babble*. They characteristically lead people away from biblical morality—*ungodliness*. They enjoy rampant popularity—*spreading*—and are like an infection—*gangrene*. These teachers aren't afraid to take swipes at even major truths like *resurrection*, and the result is a *faith upset*, or overthrown.

John, who also wrote at a time of truth turmoil, advised, "Let what you heard from the beginning abide in you. If what you heard from the beginning abides in you, then you too will abide in the Son and in the Father" (1 John 2:24). During the time your emotions seem perplexing, learn to align your mind on truth—the unalterable, fixed truth of Scripture. This beginning, and touchpoint of faith is linked to the Son and the Father.

Paul exemplified this attitude while imprisoned at the end of his life. He told Timothy, "When you come, bring the cloak that I left with Carpus at Troas, also the books, and above all the parchments" (2 Tim. 4:13). He may well have been calling for copies of the scriptures, demonstrating that even at the end of his life, and though swarming with emotional upsets, he still sought the stability of the sacred writings, and the immovable truth that lay within them. He wrote,

> For the weapons of our warfare are not of the flesh but have
> divine power to destroy strongholds. We destroy arguments

and every lofty opinion raised against the knowledge of God, and take every thought captive to obey Christ. (2 Cor. 10:4–5)

We do not fight renegade feelings with trumped-up, manufactured ones, but conquer them with divine truth. "We overpower wrong feelings with right thinking," Borgman tells us. "This is not some naive approach that assumes a verse or two will do the trick. But how can we underestimate the power of the word? It is the word that can revive and give hope."[7] We fully embrace and steep in the truth of God's word to arrive at what Borgman calls "spiritual and emotional equilibrium."[8] As he further points out, "The feeling, Sovereign God of the Bible has revealed his glory to us in his word so we would not simply know him and think his thoughts after him, but also feel his feelings after him."[9] Indeed, such feelings are liable only to arrive much later. In the meantime, and through various seasons, as we suffer the absence of any noticeable faith emotion, learn not to be victimized by phantoms of untruth.

During dark times, we must practice not only agreeing with the Holy Word, but speak it to ourselves. The psalmists engaged in healthy forms of self-talk, as we see in Psalm 42:5—"Why are you cast down, O my soul, and why are you in turmoil within me? Hope in God; for I shall again praise him, my salvation." At the same time, this means halting our rabbity, anxious thoughts, and telling ourselves, "The Lord is in charge here." "I am obsessing on something unreal," and finally, "Stop it!" We need to affirm, and even speak authoritative truth that outranks feelings.

If you think this is a bit contrived, if not silly, remember that you internally speak a great deal of things to yourself daily. Most of them are so effective they can alter your mood for hours. Why not let the content of your message be the truth? Some of the best gospel preaching you will ever do will be to yourself.

3. Do the Right Things

If right thinking is beneficial during spiritual dearth, right doing is a step beyond. When Cain fell into anger and jealousy, God counseled him in the midst of his displeasure: "If you do well, will you not be accepted? And if you do not do well, sin is crouching at the door. Its desire is contrary to you, but you must rule over it" (Gen. 4:7).

The worst thing we could possibly do while in a spiritual low point is to burden ourselves with pity parties, tantrums, or simply giving in to the urge to vent dark desires. Right action might not unleash any sudden burst of power, but it certainly undergirds a general sense of well-being. Do necessary chores. Continue daily devotions in some form, even if you don't feel like it. Carry out responsibilities. When we let bills go unpaid, or leave homework undone in favor of Netflix binging, it exerts a predictable downward drag upon our spirit. The opposite effect happens when we say no to idleness and procrastination.

Another well-supported approach to spiritual self-care involves forgetting about yourself, and instead serving someone else. Many saints who suffer a spiritual setback experience a release when they get outside of themselves and seek the welfare of others. Isaiah the prophet wrote,

> If you pour yourself out for the hungry and satisfy the desire of the afflicted, then shall your light rise in the darkness and your gloom be as the noonday. And the LORD will guide you continually and satisfy your desire in scorched

places and make your bones strong; and you shall be like a watered garden, like a spring of water, whose waters do not fail. (Isa. 58:10–11)

4. Dwell Upon Grace

During dry spiritual seasons, believers can become morbidly introspective. Mulling over themselves, they arrive at the inevitable place of self-condemnation. Their religious performance and personal merits occupy them. This is graceless territory. I've known Christians, for instance, who have fallen under such a dark dread of the judgment seat of Christ that they can no longer think of rewards, but only punishment. This comes close to approximating what Paul called a "spirit of slavery to fall back into fear" (Rom. 8:15). During the earlier days when their zeal outshined others, they felt bright and confident. Now these emotions fail to buoy them, as they spend a lot of time pondering their failures. Actually, they were no more spiritual back when they were proudly wearing the badge of overcomer. The Christian life is not a showcase for mortal talents and success in religious endeavors.

> **WE DRAW NEAR TO A GOD WHO KNOWS WE DON'T HAVE IT ALL TOGETHER.**

Peter said, "God opposes the proud but gives grace to the humble" (1 Pet. 5:5). He will never pump grace upward to the conceited. Grace, like water, only flows downward. We will never have our hands filled while they are full of our résumés.

The writer of Hebrews counsels, "Let us then with confidence draw near to the throne of grace, that we may receive mercy and find grace in time of need" (4:16). In doing so, we draw near to a God who knows we don't have it all together. Even the thought of proving to Him otherwise serves to exacerbate our condition. He *knows* we often do things we say we don't believe in, and refuse to do the things we know we should. We are saved sinners at His mercy. Dry seasons are excellent times to learn about interacting with God solely on the basis of His giving and your receiving.

In the final analysis, we weren't meant to live on non-stop extravagant surface feelings. The new life we've received is a good land of hills with breathtaking vistas—*and* valleys. If we want to experience that life now, we must learn to hold onto the content of our faith, Christ, and not the product of it, joy. All of us are impressed with lightning strikes, but the Christian life is mostly a cultivated, increasing reality. No sustained euphoria can replace that.

Neither can bland spiritual seasons be controlled. When the cause appears to be something beyond our jurisdiction, trust that God is working. He's establishing you in a deeper life, and as long as He calls us sons, He will always exercise that right.

11

Enlivened Intuition

Oh, sacred union with the Perfect Mind,
Transcendent bliss which Thou alone canst give;
How blest are they this Peerless One who find,
And, dead to earth, have learned in Thee to live.

—Thomas Cogswell Upham (1799-1872)

I TOOK MY DAUGHTER, Elizabeth, to a library when she was five years old. While she looked at books in the kids' area, I browsed at a distance, keeping an eye on her through the stacks. I could see her, but she couldn't see me. At some point, another little girl climbed onto the library tabletop and started dancing. "Come on," the girl coaxed my daughter, "Get up here."

From my hidden vantage point, I studied the whole scene as it played out, wondering what my daughter would do. After all, her new little friend was having such a good time, and dad didn't seem to be anywhere around. Without flinching, though, Elizabeth said matter-of-factly to the girl, "My daddy would never let me do that."

I don't mind saying I was proud of her at that moment. She knew what to do (or, in this case, what not to do) by knowing *me*.

What does it mean to really know someone? That can be a complex, multi-layered question. To know someone requires facts, but it also calls for interpersonal contact and experience. And, of course, it should go without saying that for the greatest depth of understanding, a certain likeness of life is necessary. Though we might understand a great deal about dogs, for instance, we could not comprehensively know their world without sharing in the canine life.

Because they are bereft of truth, life, and experience, some of the largest world religions maintain (correctly, from their point of view) that God is unknowable. Their heroes might be said to have received communications from heaven, or performed various exploits for the sake of their religious cause, but none appropriated divine life. That would be clearly impossible, and indeed, the very idea of it did not occur to them, being blasphemous in the extreme. And so, not only do their holy writings fail to convey truth about God's nature and work (fulfilling the necessity of facts), but their ceremonial systems offer none of His spiritual vitality (fulfilling the necessity of shared life). Within those limitations, therefore, knowing God is a hopelessly cosmic endeavor.

The starting place for all heart-level knowledge of God begins with receiving the life that comes through second birth.

With Life Comes Knowledge

According to Jesus, "This is eternal life, that they know you, the only true God, and Jesus Christ whom you have sent (John 17:3). Eternal life *is* the knowing of God. I've categorized this entire book into separate areas of inner life—conscience, worship, and intuition. Actually though, the *entire* experience of eternal life is intuitive. Life enables that knowledge, defines it, initiates it. Without it, even a hundred advanced seminary degrees wouldn't help, because life is not only cognitive, but instinctive. A cat doesn't utilize cognitive knowledge when it sharpens its claws. It doesn't know that by rubbing its paws against a surface, slivers of retractable keratin will be honed to capture prey. Where spiritual life is concerned, it includes how God feels about sin, holiness, goodness, kindness, love, and a great many other attributes belonging to His nature.

> ## THE INCARNATION DEMONSTRATES THAT GOD DOES NOT WISH TO BE AN UNKNOWN QUANTITY.

But these realizations are not disembodied. Unlike the animal that does things without knowing why, eternal life enables us to know a whole Person in the moments of life. It even goes beyond projected knowledge, like my daughter used that day in the library—*My daddy would never let me do that*—or, the old evangelical question, "What would Jesus do?" Our enlivened intuition of God has more than facts and projections, and assorted experiences.

God does not wish to be an unknown quantity, and has thoroughly demonstrated as much in His costly act of incarnation. For that is where divinity and humanity met—God with skin, the Word become flesh—to be knowable, apprehendable. John wrote of this: "That which was from the beginning, which we have heard, which we have seen with our eyes, which we looked upon and have touched with our hands" (1 John 1:1). The interpersonal contact here of ears, hands, and eyes cannot be missed. Then John reminds us in the final phrase of that verse, that it is all "concerning the word of *life*." The Lord's incarnational presence was meant not only to be a historical reality, but to continue on into another level of experience with us: "I have been crucified with Christ. It is no longer I who live, but Christ who lives in me. And the life I now live in the flesh I live by faith in the Son of God, who loved me and gave himself for me" (Gal. 2:20).

In light of this, knowing God on a personal level becomes not only possible, but unavoidable. It is knowledge first hand, direct, and immediate. "We have the mind of Christ" (1 Cor. 2:16), Paul said. Though you will benefit from the external discipleship and instruction of the faith community, ideally, all such teaching will promote this new, intuitive knowledge that has come straight to you through being born again.

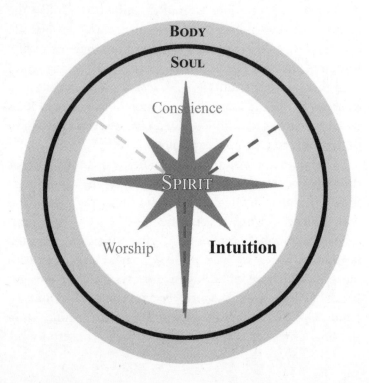

Knowing in a Remarkable Sense

This interior knowledge is a central promise to all who believe in Christ. The New Testament therefore repeats the promise God made through the prophet Jeremiah:

> For this is the covenant that I will make with the house of Israel after those days, declares the Lord: I will put my laws into their minds, and write them on their hearts, and I will be their God, and they shall be my people. And they shall not teach, each one his neighbor and each one his brother, saying, 'Know the Lord,' for they shall all know me, from the least of them to the greatest. For I will be merciful toward their iniquities, and I will remember their sins no more. (Heb. 8:10–12)

The "knowing" in this description is remarkable because it has been released from the barrier of corruption. Forgiveness of sins accomplished through the death of Christ not only guarantees escape from the lake of fire and the blessing of a cleansed conscience, but it clears the way for us to know God. As the verse says, "They shall all know me. . . . *For* I will be merciful toward their iniquities." Once the blockade of sins is removed, the knowledge of God floods forth.

Wherever sins have multiplied in a person's life, they generate a muddy, constant state of confusion. That is why a sinner, no matter how poetic, educated, eloquent, creative, pragmatic, and sensitive he or she may be, cannot know God while his or her sin remains unaddressed. These people remain in Adam, as if they were back in that awful moment of being closed off from the Tree of Life—when dark, sluggish stupidity encased their minds, estranging them from God. But let those sins come under the blood of Christ, and the knowing begins.

This is a knowledge not entirely the same as we gain through intellectual pursuit.[1] If it were, we wouldn't need the new covenant to know God, just an armload of study tools. The law written on human hearts as described here, is a divine work, outside the abilities of human effort. It is an internal work of grace—"the law of the Spirit of life" (Rom. 8:2). Paul refers to this in Second Cornthians, when he told the believers, "you are a letter from Christ delivered by us, written not with ink but with the Spirit of the living God, not on tablets of stone but on tablets of human hearts" (3:3). This is how we begin to know Him from the inside.

In saying these things, we do not mean to imply believers know everything there is to know about God. Even as Spirit-indwelt, redeemed beings, we are still finite, subject to imperfections and blind spots. It would be impossible, given our limited human capacity, to comprehend God's omniscience, nor could we override His kingly prerogative to conceal things He does not wish to disclose. Had the Corinthians known everything (and maybe the problem was they *thought* they did), Paul would not have had to chide them to repentance.

When the typical believer receives eternal life in Christ, the writing on their heart *begins*. It continues from that point onwards, through divine corrections, heady victories, and even seasons of confusion. Perhaps most of our lives are spent re-reading what He has already written on our hearts, applying it all afresh in the midst of new challenges.

After believing in Christ, I recall having a new sense of financial generosity toward strangers and friends. This was a fresh "oughtness" emanating from within. Even unsaved people participate in charitable activities, but I hadn't been one of them. That area of my life had been completely numb; the idea of giving anything to anyone never crossed my mind. Maybe in this new situation some deeply repressed memory of my Christian upbringing surfaced, something I heard or saw that came back to me.

At any rate, it was not clearly defined. I hadn't consciously remembered some preacher or saint who had modeled self-less giving. It seemed, rather, an inward encouragement to do something utterly unknown to me. My attempts were clumsy, completely unrefined by the truth of Scripture, yet I couldn't help but feel a joy aligning with this new orientation. A certain internal encouragement came with it. If I could have put it into words, it would have been God, saying, *This is how I am. This is how you will be.* The writing had begun.

And once something is written on your heart, it becomes exclusively yours. You can cover it up, and even try to deface it later. You can claim not to know it. But you still do, even if you're the smallest, newest, Christian on the planet. This dynamic has become yours. That's why God says it's unnecessary for anyone to tell you, "Know the Lord," because "they shall all know me, from the least of them to the greatest" (Heb. 8:11).

The Writing is a Voice

With this living law engraved upon our hearts, it becomes intensely personal to us—alive, spiritually communicative. Jesus said,

> He who enters by the door is the shepherd of the sheep. To him the gatekeeper opens. The sheep hear his voice, and he calls his own sheep by name and leads them out. When he has brought out all his own, he goes before them, and the sheep follow him, for they know his voice. A stranger they

will not follow, but they will flee from him, for they do not know the voice of strangers. (John 10:2–5)

What does this voice sound like? Does it literally occur in the brain of a believer, as if we were hearing music through headphones? Is it an audible voice coming out of thin air? Some believers give an enthusiastic "Yes!" I don't wish to invalidate anyone's personal experience, but when people hear the voice of God in the Bible, we are not told exactly how it occurs. Some deeply committed, spiritual, long-time believers have never received either audible voices, or articulated words within their minds. We want to be careful, therefore, to not make those experiences normal for everyone.

When it comes to what is typical for all of us, the voice of Jesus is *life-based*. It comes through our enlivened spirit, and makes His mind known to us. Jesus Himself describes it this way:

My sheep hear my voice, and I know them, and they follow me. I give them eternal life, and they will never perish, and no one will snatch them out of my hand. (10:27–28)

In these verses, we find the major items of His voice, the mutual knowledge of both sheep and shepherd, and eternal life all attached. Since eternal life is not an occasional presence, but a permanent, forever one, so is the knowledge of the shepherd and His voice.

The Voice is an Anointing

In John's later writings, he emphasizes not only the living voice of the Son, but the anointing of the Holy Spirit within us, conveying the mind of Christ. It is knowledge of a more intuitive variety, but does not mean we are granted the ability to know everything, nor possess God's every thought. Instead, this anointing assists us specifically in knowing how we ought to abide in Christ.

How do we, in the myriad complexities of existence, and often in the absence of detailed biblical instructions, know what attitudes to adopt, what courses to undertake, in order to walk in union with Him?

> But the anointing that you received from him abides in you, and you have no need that anyone should teach you. But as his anointing teaches you about everything, and is true, and is no lie—just as it has taught you, abide in him. (1 John 2:27)

The term "anointing" refers back to the oil of the Old Testament, which, when placed upon a king or priest, made them ceremonially holy. The apostle John borrowed this imagery to speak of the moving, sanctifying Spirit within us. The Spirit's operation causes us to inwardly know what is holy. He searches out the depths of God and reveals them to us. As used here, anointing specifically assists us to avoid being deceived by unholy teachings that threaten to pervert our understanding of Christ. It provides an attraction to holiness, and a repugnance to evil. If we are properly intuiting the mind of Christ through the anointing Spirit, we will inwardly recoil from corrupt versions of Christ, not embrace them.

It should go without saying that we also ought to have a sense of aggrievance within when we stray into various evil behaviors. This is why when John writes his first letter, highlighting love (2:8), righteousness (3:9), and God's presence (3:13), he speaks to us as though we already know what he means: "But you have been anointed by the Holy One, and you all have knowledge. I write to you, not because you do

not know the truth, but because you know it, and because
no lie is of the truth" (1 John 2:20–21).

> **WHEREAS THE BIBLE CAUSES US TO
> KNOW *ABOUT* GOD, THE ANOINTING
> CAUSES US TO ACTUALLY *KNOW* HIM.**

As the fixed, unchanging rule of our faith, the Bible ob-
jectively defines doctrinal and moral knowledge. However,
the anointing of the Spirit supplies the inward dimension of
that knowledge. Whereas the Bible causes us to know *about*
God, the anointing causes us to *know* Him. This intuitive
enablement is according to our differing levels of maturity—
"children," "young men," and "fathers" (2:12–14), but it fo-
cuses upon things such as holiness, righteousness, and truth,
which applies to all.

God's Will for Everyone is the Same

A great deal of confusion begins to occur when we assume
that God's will, referring to His eternal purpose, is the same
as His leading, which is personal and situational. The two,
though overlapping at key points, are distinct.

First, the Bible presents God's overarching will as applying to all His children. Take for instance, calls unto holiness
such as, "this is the will of God, your sanctification" (1 Thess.
4:3). He also calls everyone into the pursuit of spiritual practice and discipline—"Rejoice always, pray without ceasing,
give thanks in all circumstances; for this is the will of God
in Christ Jesus for you" (5:16–18). Other verses reflect His
grand desire for us to "be conformed to the image of His Son"
(Rom. 8:29), and "that through the church the manifold

wisdom of God might now be made known to the rulers and authorities in the heavenly places" (Eph. 3:10). These strategic revelations represent what God wants for all of us, at every time, in every place.

Yet we also find many instances of personal leading in the Bible. The Lord forbade Paul's entrance into Bythinia, but intervened through a dream to guide his apostle into Macedonia. He sent Philip to a desert road for an evangelistic encounter, sent Peter by a vision to the house of Cornelius. These and many other examples surround specific people, encompassing different places, and times. And, if we were to add all the less spectacular, life-based impressions of the Shepherd's regular guidance, we would quickly run out of room citing them in this book.

The point is, God's will and God's leading are not necessarily equal. One of them governs His will for us all. The other governs the situations of particular people. In the Lord's prayer, we find both aspects: "Your will be done" (Matt. 6:10), and "Lead us not into temptation" (6:13). Some Christians belabor the personal category, while having little or no interest in the category of God's comprehensive will. This has a crippling effect on them overall. Many a believer, while obsessing in prayer over which person to marry, or what school to attend, are in a hopeless fog. As far as they are concerned, God's eternal plan is to ensure their happiness. They are Christians, and love God, but lack an orientation upon any purpose larger than their own. Thus, the "leadings" they receive seem to emanate from nothing higher than their hopes, dreams, and appetites.

Dallas Willard writes, "My extreme preoccupation with knowing God's will for me may only indicate, contrary to what is often thought, that I am overconcerned with myself, not a Christ-like interest in the well-being of others or in the glory of God."[2]

It is difficult to change this self-orientation. Not only culture, but some pulpits today encourage people to follow their heart. It is as though no other will in the universe exists except theirs. Small wonder, then, when congregants casually announce they are "led" to move on to another church, or unmarried Christian couples are "led" to move in together. No struggle has gone on within them, no searching, or seeking. Indeed, why would there need to be any? If there had been any seeking on the subject, it was basically a religious formality. The deciding factor in the end was what they wanted from the beginning.

Besides, God-centered theology leaves some believers frankly underwhelmed. They cannot see the magnitude of blessing involved in it, nor the beauty. For instance, why does the church figure so prominently in the Scriptures, but not among so many inner-life-oriented individuals? Why does the Bible end with the arrival of a glorious city, and not with fulfilled individuals enjoying spiritualized hobbies?

The things that are larger than us tend to have the greater power. They bring structure and help our lives make sense— in ways that personal spontaneity cannot. If we want living, healthy, intuitive experiences, we must first value God's disclosed will as it occurs in the Word.

Jesus prayed to the Father in the garden of Gethsemane and said, "My Father, if it be possible, let this cup pass from me; nevertheless, not as I will, but as you will" (Matt. 26:39). In the first half of His prayer, He asked for a way out of His particular circumstances, revealing what He wanted. In the second half, He affirmed His loyalty to the will of God, its ascendancy over His life, and His submission to it. The Father's global redemptive purpose, His plan for all the ages, and His desire to elevate Jesus to His right hand, making Him Lord of all, had to eclipse everything else. It was a will that had been rooted in the Old Testament Scriptures, immovable as a mountain. No personal sense or feeling was ever going to set that aside. Even as Jesus prayed, He was clear. The Father had decreed the cross.

God's Leading is Personal and Individual

The will of God is like an ocean liner, moving irresistibly toward the distant port of fulfillment. Millions of lives are aboard it, with their various movements, directions, thoughts, plans. Not one of them assumes their onboard scheduled activities can invalidate the ship's direction. A decision to play shuffleboard on Deck A cannot change the cruise destination. Any hope to the contrary is delusional.

And yet, our God is personally interactive. He does not hit cruise control, and then leave us to our own devices. In fact, He often works out His overarching will through the myriad dealings He has with people—upon and around the general mass of humanity, and within the spirit of those of the second birth. You might say the captain not only sails the ship, but relates to all who are on board.

We are blessed when such interactions are recorded out loud for us in Scripture. One of Paul's first questions upon meeting Christ was "What shall I do, Lord?" The Lord's reply was not a detailed map of the future, but "Rise, and go into Damascus, and there you will be told all that is appointed for you to do" (Acts 22:10). His intention was to lay out the broad mission parameters that would define Paul's work, but parcel out the smaller specifics of the apostle's life and movement little by little, as needed.

Those details wouldn't become a template for everyone else, but only for Paul, the individual. The apostle himself later wrote that we all receive such customized attention: "For we are his workmanship, created in Christ Jesus for good works, which God prepared beforehand, that we should walk in them" (Eph. 2:10). Thus, we not only abide in broad, biblical principles, but expect personal leading.

Paul mentioned in another passage to the Corinthians, "Only let each person lead the life that the Lord has assigned to him, and to which God has called him. This is my rule in all the churches" (1 Cor. 7:17).

This dynamic brings color and vibrance to our daily Christian lives. "Some of the most meaningful times of adventure are the periods of working through major decisions," M. Blaine Smith reminds us. "Indeed, these are often the times when we feel most fully alive."[3]

In fact, God not only speaks uniquely to us as individuals, but in unique ways.

> Saul of Tarsus was a Pharisee—zealous, self-righteous, and proud. Are we surprised that he met Christ in a sensational and humbling fashion? God's first words to young Samuel, on the other hand, were spoken in a quiet, gentle voice in the stillness of the night. Encounters between God and individuals matched not only the person's character but also the circumstances. Saul's was a dramatic public experience. Samuel's was a gentle, private one. Still, each heard the Lord calling him by name.[4]

Leading in the Matrix of Relationship

It seems the way the book of Acts is set up, the apostles had a virtually unbroken experience of being led by God. But add real time back into it, and neither leading nor communication was constant with them as to what they should do in every small thing, and from moment to moment. Willard makes an excellent point that God's intent is "not to keep us constantly under his dictation. Too much intrusion on a seed . . . makes normal, healthy growth impossible."[5]

> DISCUSSIONS ABOUT GOD'S LEADING
> CAN CONTRIBUTE TO A NERVOUS
> SORT OF HYPER-SPIRITUALITY.

Although the voice of the shepherd is a constant with us all, it does not mean He seeks to micromanage in every affair. Such would quickly wear us out. Indeed, discussions about God's leading can contribute to a nervous sort of hyper-spirituality. Sincere souls who want to practice spiritual obedience are especially vulnerable to perfectionism, wanting to "get it right" in every small detail. I remember a friend in a restaurant who honestly tried to receive a word from the Lord about what to order. He eventually had to make up his own mind between chicken and ribs.

To many of us, God, it seems, is a God of scrupulous management details. It isn't difficult to imagine how this perception can oppress us with fears of making the wrong decision. Yet, God is not interested in puppets. While we find a number of guidance events granted during the movements of ministers in Acts, far more notable is the guidance we do *not* see—decisions governing the thousands of small, random movements otherwise involved. Paul tells us that "the spirits of prophets are subject to prophets" (1 Cor. 14:32), which means that God's method of doing things does not include forcibly overriding our will. Nor does He count every situation of life as a moral necessity.

Our enlivened intuition cannot operate in a healthy way if it is under a cloud of morbid terror, divine reprisals, or threat of catastrophe. Yet many believers expend considerable nervous energy trying to find God's guidance for their lives. Desperate, feverish prayers may indicate we have not cultivated a habit of walking in His presence, so we feel we must rush out and place a long-distance call.

This is not to say we shouldn't have occasional seasons of prayer for important crisis moments. But I have talked with many Christians who lose themselves in these prayers—that is, they lose all appetite for praise, thanks, or confession. With every day that passes without clarity coming to them, their mood sours a little more. God, they think, is toying with them. A sinful resentment builds within their heart. The Lord of glory now seems obtuse. They begin to pout, thinking, *Maybe I should drop out of church for a while. Let's see how He likes that.* Or, *I can't handle the Bible right now. Seems like all those promises are a bunch of baloney.* That is what happens when leading becomes bigger than God.

I can't number the times when leading came to me in the form of a winsome suggestion or a nuanced impression while I was occupied with otherwise normal interactions with the Lord. For instance, during a time of morning worship, I was in the book of Exodus, exploring God's care for the disadvantaged. I thought I would receive some inner clarity about what to do for those in my community. Instead, the

Lord gently rebuked me about my aggravation with some people I knew. *Your attitude is the problem here. Look how I am toward people.*

On another occasion, as I arrived at a park to do some sermon preparation, I saw a lady trying to change her tire. I have to admit, my first thought was to park farther away, so I wouldn't be drawn into helping. Just as quickly, though, the Lord seemed to say, *No! Here's your chance to show My love to someone.*

Another time, while I was in a church meeting, one of the attendants unknowingly said something that answered a question I had been waiting on from God. Instantly, came the deep, intuitive voice, *There. Were you paying attention?*

As a church leader during 2020, and the social paralysis of COVID, I felt pulled in many anxious directions. When I put the worries aside, and even the questions about what to do, an intuitive impression came as I was taking a trip through the book of Ephesians—*Pay attention to this.*

However, just as many times I have been mistaken. My sense of excitement was mostly mine, not the Lord's. And so, having gotten what I thought were marching orders, I left my devotional space thinking, *Wow, this is going to happen!* It either didn't, or it didn't happen the way I thought it would.

I recall the occasion when a church nearby needed a pastor. They had a lovely facility, and the congregation was just the right size, with extremely pleasant people. It was situated in the perfect location, and the outgoing pastoral couple encouraged us to follow up on the opportunity. My church was full of young families and open to a new adventure with that other, slightly older church, so I assumed we would be led into a church merger.

The Lord, in the meantime, never delivered any vetoes along the way. On the contrary, I felt emboldened and positively charged in His presence about the possibilities. After carefully studying church merger books, and talking privately with leaders of both congregations, My wife and I initiated a fellowship with the unified staff of the group we hoped to join. We drove away from the meeting that night aglow with how well it went.

In the days and weeks that followed, a few polite emails came, and then finally, *silence*. Months later, we got word that we had been one of many pastoral couples "eliminated" by their search committee. *What!?*

So much had seemed sovereignly arranged, including my own intuitive experience before the Lord, yet it did not total up to the result I had expected. In hindsight, I wonder if even in the midst of a close, ongoing relationship, we must learn a "yes" from a "Yes." One "Yes" might mean, "Yes, later," or, "Yes, in principle," or, "Yes to part of what you said."

My wife and I often discuss travel plans. We've been married for the better part of forty years, so we've both learned a yes from a Yes. Sometimes yes means, "Great idea for later." It might mean, "Yes, I like where this is going. Let's talk about this some more." But if I were to interpret her every yes as "Yes, get on the phone and book tickets," that could lead to a lot of turmoil.

All of this suggests we must come to learn the Lord's voice by experimentation, especially as the intuition of our enlivened spirit matures. The best field for this to occur is relational activity. God most readily steers those who are already in motion. Their momentum of worship, praise, love, and service makes it easy for course correction to take place.

Predictably, in many churches, the subject of spiritual gifting and ministries come up. Suddenly it seems everyone is galvanized by the thought of being led by the Lord into some area of service. Gift assessments have become popular tools, asking for a response to statements like, "On a scale of one to ten, when I have free time, I like to go visit someone." After twenty minutes of this, you can tally up the points, and decode what gift you have.

As a long-time church leader, I must admit I'm not crazy about these tests because, from what I've seen, few people benefit from them. Most of those who take tests like this are only doing so out of curiosity, with no intention of becoming more involved. It's as though they expect magic from the test result. But Paul told us it is *while* we present our bodies as a living sacrifice, and are transformed by the renewal of our minds, that we can test and know what is the will of God (see Rom. 12:1–2).

Typically, God does not have much to say to the idle and self-centered. They are waiting for something special to move them, something interesting or colorful. It must strike them as feasible, a thing within their ability to do. It must have a reasonable guarantee of success, with little or no sacrifice along the way. And so God remains quiet to most of them. Only in an active relationship with the Lord can we expect to discern, to intuit, His mind for us.

Failure to Follow

As we have seen, God's will for everyone has a powerful moral dimension to it. Failure to follow it is a rejection of His holiness, and is therefore sin. But failure to follow God's leading (except where it directly conflicts with His law), is largely a rejection of His wisdom, and while not technically sin, will create painful learning experiences.

I recall as a young Christian going to pick up my wife from work in downtown Cleveland. I was thirty minutes early, and decided to park on the street and wait for her. After sitting there for ten minutes, I noticed a bookstore a block or so up the street. I thought it might be nice to kill some time in there while I waited.

Instantly, I felt an odd, unexplainable *No* from within. It didn't make sense; the bookstore was not pornographic, so I would not be contradicting God's holiness or any of His eternal counsel by going inside.

After deliberating for long moments, I finally dismissed my intuition as a case of being overly sensitive. Besides, I really wanted to go to the bookstore. So I did. The *No* stayed with me. I ignored it some more.

Later, my browsing done, I went back out to the car— but it wasn't there! After walking around in a daze, I realized that from my exact position while seated in the vehicle earlier, I could not see a sign that said, "Tow Away Zone." The entire time I had been in the store ignoring the Lord, a hook and chain was being placed underneath my car bumper.

Was this a question of sin? No, not nearly as much as it was one of wisdom hard-earned—to the tune of sixty-five dollars (a small fortune in the late eighties for a family on a painfully tight budget).

No child of God should be spiritually careless. In sinful matters we grieve the Holy Spirit (see Eph. 4:30), but even if no sin is involved *per se*, our rejection of enlivened intuition is a rejection of wisdom, and will make life a lot harder than it ought to be.

The Bottom Line

If we want to strengthen our spiritual intuition, it largely depends on the other healthy functions of our spirit—that is, our conscience and our life of worship. Intuition is a cumulative product of spiritual health, rather than a crystal ball we consult. Since it is the sum total of all the other things that eternal life has put within us, and thus represents the mind of Christ, we must respond with an attitude of loving obedience. Christians who habitually disregard what they truly know within will discover that in moments of crisis, when they would benefit most from that inner assurance, they have almost nothing.

However, each time you heed the mind of Christ, it strengthens your inward processes. "For . . . if by the Spirit you put to death the deeds of the body, you will live. For all who are led by the Spirit of God are sons of God" (Rom. 8:13–14). According to this passage, the Spirit most often leads us to put to death the deeds of the body—not only evil, dirty things, but also foolish, ill-advised ones.

And if we obey, we live. Revivals of life will sweep our inner terrain. As the child of God grows more inwardly powerful, he or she begins to exemplify what it means to be called "sons of God."

We need reliable touchpoints, therefore, that promote inward spiritual knowledge.

This field of exercise is the place we will visit next.

12

Intuition Becomes Leading

The course of human history consists of a series of encounters between individual human beings and God in which each man and woman or child, in turn, is challenged by God to make his free choice between doing God's will and refusing to do it.
— Arnold J. Toynbee

It would be the greatest delight of the seraphs to pile up sand on the seashore or to pull weeds in a garden for all eternity, if they found out such was God's will.
— Alphonsus Liguori

ONCE UPON A TIME, before Amazon became a thing and the digital book took over, there was something called the Christian bookstore. You could walk up and down physical aisles and see rows of volumes categorized by theological subject. The best of these stores had a little coffee shop attached, inviting you to spend hours in caffeinated browsing. I did. As a result, I was introduced to all sorts of authors, subjects, and concerns I would otherwise have never discovered.

One popular topic that claimed a large amount of shelf space had to do with how to know the Lord's will for your life. The Christian press constantly seemed to pump out new titles on this subject, which meant the consumer appetite for it was consistently high. As soon as old titles disappeared, new ones would repopulate the gap they left. It seemed readers couldn't get enough of the subject, or, at least, weren't having their questions answered.

I bought a number of those books myself. I was often a bit confused by the concept of being led by the Lord, and, to be honest, at times I face similar quandaries today. The subject can be challenging, because in the Christian's experience, it is not merely a question of choosing between good and bad. Actually, those decisions are not hard to make. The difficulty comes in choosing between good and *better*. We can find ourselves lost in a thicket of information, confused about choices in education, career, or marriage, with options that all seem equally balanced.

Published advice ranges from the deeply mystical to pragmatically following "sanctified common sense." Which means, of course, that not all the advisers agree. One side dismisses the other's teaching as "mystical bunk, emotional subjectivity, and superstition," while the other counter-criticizes with charges of "bibliolatry, sub-spirituality, and dead legalism." On this kind of fragmented playing field of opinion, it's no wonder we are perennially unclear.

And some may wonder why we worry so much about it, as though it were some kind of needless preoccupation. Yet Paul tells us to test and discern what the will of God is (see Rom. 12:2). We have not been called into a passive fatalism, hoping that as we do nothing, everything will turn out.

Although there are seasons where we trust, where we "stand still and see the salvation of the Lord," we also understand that we have been called into *fellowship* with God, meaning a joint participation.

Besides, if God doesn't lead us in the affairs of life, something else will. This has been a problem since ancient times, when God asked the king of Samaria, "Is it because there is no God in Israel that you are going to inquire of Baal-zebub, the god of Ekron?" (2 Kings 1:3). Indeed, apart from God, there are plenty of alternate ways to navigate life. These include everything from witchcraft and the occult to human traditions, philosophies, angels, false apostles, false teachers, and false prophets.[1]

> ## THE MOST COMMON "LEADING" ARISES FROM THE DECEIT WITHIN OURSELVES.

Immaturity also leaves a believer ripe for erroneous directions; Paul warns us to "no longer be children, tossed to and fro and carried about with every wind of doctrine, by the trickery of men, in the cunning craftiness of deceitful plotting" (Eph. 4:14, NKJV). Peer pressure can mimic divine leading as well, catching Christians up in this or that religious momentum, similar to the way Barnabas was swept up in group hypocrisy (see Gal. 2:13).

But the most common "leading" arises from the deceit within our own selves, as we are "led away by various lusts" (2 Tim. 3:6). Paul reminded the Corinthians that prior to faith in Christ, they had been "carried away to . . . dumb idols, however you were led" (1 Cor. 12:2), and much like them, people today are carried away into politics, entertainment, work, and pleasure. Being led, then, is not some unnecessary fixation evangelicals have dreamed up.

We all follow something, even if it is only what we call our better judgment. At a low point in his life, David "thought to himself, '. . . The best thing I can do is to escape to the land of the Philistines'" (1 Sam. 27:1, NIV). "Thought to himself" means being virtually alone in one's considerations, forming a decision within the closeted personal space of me, myself, and I—without inquiring of God. Thus, David ended up in a compromised position, joining the enemies of God's people, being forced to degrade himself, and then losing all the bounty he had gained, together with that of his friends.

David learned the hard way that God's personal guidance preserves and protects, as he eventually wrote about in Psalm 23—"He leads me"—one of the greatest psalms of comfort.

Although there is some disagreement as to what method God considers most normal in leading us, Christian teachers have consistently distilled a few major themes:

1. Scripture

2. The indwelling Holy Spirit

3. Godly counsel from others

4. Circumstances and signs

5. Wisdom

Why are there so many venues through which the Lord might speak, and why must the experience be like assembling a jigsaw puzzle? The answer has nothing to do with His being complicated, and certainly nothing to do with a desire to tease us or play games.

God's composite manner of speaking has its advantages, because *we* are complicated—far beyond what we are aware of. Elihu said to Job, "God speaks in one way, and in two, though man does not perceive it" (Job 33:14). He loves to lead us, and to speak, but our blind spots, stubbornness, preferences, and personality quirks cause problems with our spiritual perception. Hence, He gives this assurance: "I will instruct you and teach you in the way you should go; I will counsel you with my eye upon you. Be not like a horse or a mule, without understanding, which must be curbed with bit and bridle, or it will not stay near you" (Ps. 32:8–9). God has therefore arranged a wealth of provisions to surround us, and assist in clarifying His living voice.

It Is Written

Our first resource lies outside of us, unchanging, free of vacillation, the shifting sands of culture, sin-tainted opinion, and political correctness—the Holy Scriptures. Jesus said, "Heaven and earth will pass away, but my words will not pass away" (Mark 13:31). God's sovereignty has overruled all corrupting influences, mistakes, and any alleged failure in transmission to give us a volume of sixty-six books that tell us exactly what we need to know about Him, His work, His nature, and His future. It shows us where we have fallen short of these glorious things, and how, through Christ, we enter them.

In settling a great many things, Jesus Himself said, "It is written." He answered the devil in the wilderness with just such a reply, and in so doing, placed the source of authority outside His own tired, hungry body. For those wanting an answer concerning the allowable grounds for divorce, He answered them with "What do the Scriptures say?" (see Matt. 19:3–6). This response drew their attention away from what the lusts of their flesh and the unfaithfulness of their souls was saying. No honest answer could come from within them, for their hearts were like a petri dish of marital infidelity.

Most controversies today among Christians could be settled the same way.

> From childhood you have been acquainted with the sacred writings, which are able to make you wise for salvation through faith in Christ Jesus. All Scripture is breathed out by God and profitable for teaching, for reproof, for correction, and for training in righteousness, that the man of God may be complete, equipped for every good work. (2 Tim. 3:15–17)

Guidance from the Bible on a given matter may not seem particularly exciting, especially if the seeker prefers more esoteric signs. Some singles who are considering marriage, for instance, are in such a stew of romantic sensations, it is doubtful they could gain any inward clarity from God. Sadly, some of them either neglect or reject the Scriptures as a reliable source of enlightenment. For instance, has the person they're considering believed in Jesus Christ and become regenerated? Are they divorced, but not on biblical grounds? God's leading can be obtained in this situation before a person even bends their knees to pray, because it is clearly spelled out in advance, in the Bible.

Obviously, considerations about marriage do not end with those few questions being answered. Nor does the Bible address every tertiary concern, like the budgeting style or child raising philosophy of a prospective spouse. The point is, big decisions require big authority, and no source has more than the Bible.

As we handle the Bible, we must still resist the temptation to read it according to our subjective bias. The forces of self-interest can lead us to shoehorn into Scripture whatever meanings we want, finding promises God has not given, and validation of things not permitted. We need to employ rules of good interpretation—but a graduate-level study of hermeneutics is not necessary. We just need to apply some basic, sound principles to govern our reading.

For one thing, context is key for good Bible reading. This rule applies to any work of literature or written correspondence—context determines ultimate meaning.

When it comes to the Bible, that means to first pay attention to what the verse says, not what it says to *you* (not yet, anyway). Having read it for meaning, we then read it sandwiched within the verses before and after. You may be surprised to find how much your understanding of the original verse changes by adding that little bit of surrounding context.

If you want even more perspective, draw back and read the larger unit of text (most Bibles have paragraphs and sections already built in; of course, the more strategic views occur at the chapter level). Finally, consider the covenant in which the verse is located (Old or New?). Study of this kind, along with good Bible study aids, will keep us from common interpretational mistakes, and making bad decisions based on them.

A serious Christian should have an appetite for understanding the Bible. For instance, you should know the things that continue between the Old and New Testaments, like the moral law and some parts of civil law. You must also be aware of the things fulfilled in Christ's crucifixion that are therefore

discontinued, like the ceremonial observances—diets, regu-
lations of fabric, animal sacrifices, and the like.

These are all questions of high-level context, and if we
don't know any of the answers, we will end up thinking God
is leading us into things His Son has freed us from. On the
other hand, we may conclude that God doesn't care about
some things He is definitely trying to lead us into. If you care
about the context of an office memo from the boss about this
year's bonus, you should care just as much for the context of
a Bible passage that could affect your entire life.

Another concern has to do with understanding the difference between Bible passages that are descriptive (narrating
events) and prescriptive (instructing us how to live). How are
we to understand and apply narrative details in Scripture?

STUDY A BIBLE PASSAGE TO RECOGNIZE THE CORE PRINCIPLE TO BE LEARNED.

For instance, Paul went into the Arabian desert after being saved. Are we to do the same? Must we try to walk on
water as Peter did in the Gospels? Simply adopting details
from the life of Moses in Exodus or the early church in Acts
can lead us down a path God never intended for us to travel.

Instead, study the passage to learn the underlying core
principle (faith, trust, righteousness, etc.). This is especially
important to note when descriptive passages intersect cultural
habits that no longer exist, such as head covering in First
Corinthians 11 and foot washing in John 13. We are left to
discern the core principle that gave rise to these prescribed
practices. The call to humble, self-sacrificial service underlaid
foot washing as a fitting example of the time. Head covering,

as espoused by Paul, was a practice related to the greater reality of authority, order, and sexual identity. We are to learn and practice these timeless principles, without necessarily copying the first-century cultural form of them.

Furthermore, don't claim biblical leading based on a single passage while ignoring other verses that balance and interpret it. The devil uses the Bible in such a way, finding one verse and quoting it in order to get what he wants (see Matt. 4:6). Jesus responded to that kind of "Bible study" by saying, "Again, it is written" (4:7), incorporating the fuller picture of God's mind. This means He saw the Bible as a whole, not atomized, unrelated pieces. Respect the wholeness of God's truth.

When we handle the Scriptures properly, they teach us about God's nature, and invite us to experience Him. However, we must not forget that they ultimately call us to obedience. We are to keep His Word. This is not to be confused with legalism; our living obedience to what is written demonstrates our oneness with Him: "Whoever keeps his commandments abides in God, and God in him. And by this we know that he abides in us, by the Spirit whom he has given us" (1 John 3:24).

Impressions of Life

Since this book is a survey of inner life, it would seem to make better sense to list the Spirit as our primary way of knowing the Lord's voice. Why, then, do we place the Bible first? Because it is the Lord's voice *outside* of you. The Bible is an external guide, although not a dead one. The same eternal life within us, written on our hearts, corresponds to the life we find captured within the written truth of the Bible. They should match. If I think the Spirit is leading me in a way that contradicts the written Word, I'm wrong. Religious people have been known to credit God for leading them into all kinds of violent, immoral behavior forbidden in the Bible, but the Holy Spirit will never lead us in contradiction to the Scriptures He has inspired.

On the contrary, according to Jesus, "the Holy Spirit, whom the Father will send in my name, he will teach you all things and bring to your remembrance all that I have said to you" (John 14:26). He reminded the apostles of what Jesus said, so they could write Scripture. He reminds us so that we can apply Scripture.

For example, a man who read Ephesians 6 last week remembers today the verse that says, "Honor your father and mother." A small, nuanced application comes to him from the Holy Spirit, shaped by the man's spiritual understanding. He interrupts his busy day, drives over to his parents' house, and mows the grass.

We can expect similar prompts of the Spirit, especially as He brings Scripture back to us. Obviously immersion in the Bible makes it easier for this to happen. When the voice of the Shepherd comes, it takes the shape of what He has already spoken.

These words are winsomely supplied. They rarely come to us like an annoying cell phone alarm. The internal reminding ministry of the Spirit has been called a "nudge" or a "hunch," but we prefer to describe it as an inward impression or life consciousness. Physical life, for instance, "speaks" to us when it is too cold, not with an intrusive weather report but with a simple shivering sensation. Our accompanying thoughts confirm it and make an application: we put on a coat.

Spiritual life also communicates through life conscious-ness—simple, Word-based impressions. Life and peace, as mentioned in Romans 8:6, exemplify such impressions. Life has to do with vitality, strength, and buoyancy. Peace is usually synonymous with calmness and satisfaction. Both come about because "to set the mind on the Spirit is life and peace"; conversely, death, an impression of heaviness, dark-ness, foreboding, and unrest, comes when we "set the mind on the flesh" (8:6). True to form, the more we contemplate sin, the more inwardly dead we feel.

Such internal phenomena often became significant fac-tors in Paul's apostolic movements. He writes concerning the news that Titus would bring him concerning the well-being of the Corinthian church:

> When I came to Troas to preach the gospel of Christ, even though a door was opened for me in the Lord, my spirit was not at rest because I did not find my brother Titus there. So I took leave of them and went on to Macedonia. But thanks be to God, who in Christ always leads us in triumphal proces-sion, and through us spreads the fragrance of the knowledge of him everywhere. (2 Cor. 2:12–14)

Paul's spiritual experience of unrest, and his response to it, became a glorious divine leading. In that case, his in-ner life prevented the good (evangelizing Asia Minor) from becoming an enemy of the better (protecting a church from being decimated).

The apostle was often richly conscious of inner life experi-ence, as when he wrote to the Philippians, "how I yearn for you all with the affection of Christ Jesus" (1:8). He was aware that his love for them emanated from a life union with the Savior. In a special moment he told his younger coworker,

Timothy, "I remember your tears," and "I am reminded of your sincere faith" (2 Tim. 1:4–5).

This remembrance was no doubt the result of the Lord's voice, similar to the way Jesus spoke of how the worshipper in Matthew 5 "remembers" an offended brother, and then goes to reconcile with him. Concerning such affections, Paul also confirmed to the Thessalonians that "you yourselves have been taught by God to love one another" (1 Thess. 4:9). In saying this, he did not consider himself a special class of believer, but one who shared an inner-life consciousness with all who possess the second birth.

Christians have made a lot of mistakes attempting to follow the "still small voice" (see 1 Kings 19:12–13, NKJV). This is something detractors, including a few well-respected Christian teachers, have been quick to point out. The cases that get cited usually involve Ouija-board-like experiences that portray inner-life leading in the most ridiculous—and dangerous—ways. It's not hard to see why so many negative opinions abound. But as J.D. Greear writes,

> These Christians might know who the Holy Spirit is and that He floats around in their hearts somewhere. They might even know He produces "spiritual fruit" in their lives, but they relate to Him in ways similar to how I relate to my pituitary gland; I know it's in there somewhere, and that it's necessary somehow for growth and life, but I have no real interaction with it. I've never spoken to or heard from my pituitary gland.[2]

And so, from an experiential standpoint, their plight ends up being similar to those disciples in Acts 19:2, who told Paul, "We have not even heard there is a Holy Spirit."

Some people shut themselves off to inner guidance because they are afraid of erroneous feelings. The solution to the problem of uncertain internal leadings, though, is not to fear or mock them, but as with prophecies, to evaluate and discern them: "Do not despise prophecies, but test everything; hold fast to what is good" (1 Thess. 5:20–21).

Feelings can come from diverse sources. Part of our spiritual maturity lies in understanding the difference between the ones that are soulish (emanating from purely mortal reasonings) and those that are spiritual. This comes about as we experience the inward work of the living, active Word— "For the word of God is living and active, sharper than any two-edged sword, piercing to the division of soul and of spirit, of joints and of marrow, and discerning the thoughts and intentions of the heart" (Heb. 4:12).

Thus, by constant practice, the power of our discernment is trained to distinguish good from evil (see 5:14). With the help of the Word, as well as that of the other healthy checks and balances to be covered next, we can begin to recognize life's inner leading. Learning curve and perceived risks notwithstanding, it is worthwhile to arrive at an understanding of the sense of life, for it brings registrations of immediacy, intimacy, and power.

What Others Say

Though it may sound counter-intuitive at first, we come to know the leading of our inner life better with help from the *outside*. We've seen how the Bible offers guidance and adjustment from a fixed objective standard. Now we'll take a look at how other believers can offer us objective points of view. This is especially beneficial in that they not only share the same eternal life in Christ as we do, but they know firsthand the challenges, excuses, victories, and failures that we experience in the currents of human circumstance and culture. In other words, they understand life in the trenches.

The Bible anticipates that many of us will have a hard time listening to others. That is probably why so much of the book of Proverbs makes such a case for it.

> The way of a fool is right in his own eyes, but a wise man listens to advice. (12:15)

> Where there is no guidance, a people falls, but in an abundance of counselors there is safety. (11:14)

> By insolence comes nothing but strife, but with those who take advice is wisdom. (13:10)

> Without counsel plans fail, but with many advisers they succeed. (15:22)

> Listen to advice and accept instruction, that you may gain wisdom in the future. (19:20)

The response from many Christians, especially the younger and self-confident, is all too often, "*God* told me," or, "*God* teaches me." These claims are true enough when spoken in context of the New Covenant, but when seasoned with individualistic pride, they sound more like "Talk to the hand," or, "Thanks, but I already know stuff." J.I. Packer described the attitude as,

> Isolated, defiant, and seeking in the name of spirituality to explore and express the depths of one's own being all the while refusing in the name of integrity to dance to any tune save one's own. It is a familiar mental mood into which our contemporaries are massaged by the lyrics of pop singers, debunking of the past by school and university teachers, self-help gurus and their programs on the media, loose talk about freedom, and much else along the same lines. Conditioned

by such a culture as ours, it is hard for Christians to learn the humility that should lead them to suspect themselves of insufficiency and therefore to seek advice when they should and value it properly when it has been given. This is our problem.[3]

For some reason, we suspect that receiving guidance through others diminishes the wonder of it coming directly to oneself. Or that it might suggest we have some deficiency in ourselves. We fail to appreciate a God who interrupts others and commands them to pray, seek, and use their own spiritual resources for our blessing.

> ## IN YOUR EXPERIENCE OF BEING LED, DO YOU SECRETLY COVET BEING SOME SORT OF "LONE RANGER"?

And this is not only because we need help, but simply because He likes to work through His body. This is a peculiar joy of His, earned on the cross, that having brought us together in Himself, He can give us as gifts to one another. The answers I get from the Lord through the members of our congregation do not make me feel any less special or spiritual. Nor, in your context, should it detract from your experience of being led, unless of course, you secretly covet being some sort of "Lone Ranger."

The people with whom you fellowship will understand you the best (although at times you swear they don't). They will find it easy to discern when you are not acting in accordance with who you are in Christ. If you are about to make a decision that causes a loss of spiritual equilibrium, they will notice it. Strange, dramatic plans, needlessly risky behavior, and unbiblical acting out, will alert those close to you that something is amiss, even as you claim to have the witness of the Holy Spirit in favor of it. "I have peace! I have peace!" I remember a man angrily shouting, when others were reluctant to agree with his plans. He couldn't see the irony of the moment, but everyone else did.

A close companion is only valuable if he or she is willing to tell you the truth, and perhaps hurt your feelings, maybe even crush you. "Faithful are the wounds of a friend; profuse are the kisses of an enemy" (Prov. 27:6). Politics can ruin a Spirit-led community when people begin to prize "keeping the peace" over truth, especially when that truth would have saved someone from devastation.

Maybe, though, your friend isn't the best choice for a deep discussion on spiritual direction. Some church relationships have more to do with Sunday football parties after church, assorted hobbies, or mommy play dates than deep deliberations about the inner life. We can fall into the habit of having "church pals." The maturity level of your sounding boards, therefore, should fit into your considerations.

If your spirituality is more or less on the same level as your peers, they may have some of the same blind spots as you. Rehoboam made this mistake soon after his ascent to the throne of Israel. He rejected the counsel of older men, and went with that of the fellows he'd grown up with—young friends who were graceless, with a "take no prisoners" attitude. When he heard their immature advice, which sounded uncompromising and strong, the new young ruler went with it, because it appealed to his own immaturity. The kingdom of Israel was torn apart over this poor decision, and it never healed. When you're looking for help, you might want to try shopping for maturity, rather than the comfort index.

In fact, God has supplied leaders in the community of the redeemed, and told us to listen to them (see Heb. 13:7, 17), proving that no Christian has the exhaustive sum total of spiritual knowledge. We frequently need the navigational assistance of more seasoned believers.

Still, one can be spiritually mature, but a lousy lawyer or doctor. Just because someone walks closely with the Lord doesn't make him or her an expert in every area, including the ones that are especially sensitive—like marriage. Make sure the person you are fellowshipping with is qualified to offer in-depth help. Too many well-meaning Christians are eager to step up as self-styled counselors.

I knew one woman who dispensed quite a bit of relationship "wisdom," but had been married and divorced multiple times. There might have been a lot to learn from her negative experiences, but she wanted instead to be seen as a successful relationship guru. Not only should the receiver of advice have a careful measure of humility, but the giver of it ought to as well.

All of this should remind us that our fellow Christians are as human as we are, and prone to limitations. Not all advice is good advice. We need only remember Job's friends, whom he called "miserable comforters" (Job 16:2). They so muddied his understanding of how to interpret his sufferings, that even God rebuked them at the end of the book.

At any rate, insights from other believers, as valuable as they may be, does not mean there is no need for further prayer and reflection. Nor does it mean we must take their advice without question, as though our friend were the oracle of Delphi. The practice of one person approaching another with "The Lord told me to tell you . . ." has become a rampant problem in some places, finally degrading into browbeating for financial gifts, or instructions for a person to marry a virtual stranger.

Perhaps one of the most instructive examples of all concerning the dynamics between church members and an individual occurred in Acts 21. Luke writes that Paul was on his way to Jerusalem, and stayed overnight in Tyre. "And having sought out the disciples, we stayed there for seven days. And through the Spirit they were telling Paul not to go on to Jerusalem" (21:4). Paul continued, however, and in a town farther along the way, a prophet named Agabus showed up. "And coming to us, he took Paul's belt and bound his own feet and hands and said, 'Thus says the Holy Spirit, "This is how the Jews at Jerusalem will bind the man who owns this belt and deliver him into the hands of the Gentiles"'" (21:11).

It was a moment of interception. God had designed the prophet's message as a clear "Bridge Out" sign. If there had been any doubt as to whether Paul should have altered his travel plans, Luke wrote that, "When we heard this, we and the people there urged him not to go up to Jerusalem" (21:12). Thus, a chorus grew among the believers that Paul's direction was becoming more dire, and they advised him that, at the very least, he should postpone his visit.

The fact that every one of these warnings was made through the Spirit seemed to further strengthen the case that Paul had internally missed something and God was attempting to reach his apostle through the pleas of the saints. But Paul said, "What are you doing, weeping and breaking my heart? For I am ready not only to be imprisoned but even to die in Jerusalem for the name of the Lord Jesus" (21:13).

This response indicates he had apparently not felt any misgivings himself, and thought that whatever his friends were feeling was nothing more than simple concern for his well-being. Such fears, reasoned Paul, must be overcome for the sake of the gospel. He was correct from the standpoint of his strategic calling, and an understanding that to carry out his ministry would involve suffering. However, they were also correct as to the leading of the Lord in this situation. As it turned out, Paul was indeed arrested in the city after a riot threatened his life. This led to an imprisonment that lasted for years.

Recapping what can be learned from the event, we find a few helpful principles:

1. Paul did not dismiss the words of his fellow Christians by saying, "I am the apostle Paul. I know Christ and have no need to hear from you."

2. When Paul chose not to listen, the believers did not try to force his compliance, but said, "Let the will of the Lord be done" (Acts 21:14).

3. God never charged Paul with sin for not listening, but it did create a long, difficult suffering for the apostle that could have been averted had he heeded others.

However, the Lord is Lord even over our honest mistakes, and some of Paul's deepest epistles were written in prison. Through incarceration, he brought the gospel to the heart of the Roman Empire—to Felix, to Agrippa, and maybe even to Nero himself (see 23:11; Phil. 4:22). Perhaps, as well, his life was protected from would-be assassins simply by being taken out of circulation for a while (see Acts 23:12).

All things being equal, *a* shepherd's voice clarifies *the* Shepherd's voice. It never takes the place of it, nor competes with it. Rather than believers becoming codependent on the opinions of others, rushing to them for every small matter, we should look to one another for assistance in matters of urgency, and generally cultivate an openness toward fellow saints. The members of Christ bring to one another an internal resonance. It is "deep calling to deep"—the deep place of life in me calling to the deep place of life in you.

Circumstances and Signs

Circumstances are external, not life-based like the other indicators of the Lord's leading we've already covered. However, they can suggest interesting new directions we might not have even considered. Most of the world around us is outside our control, necessitating changes of plans. I can't number the times my agenda was affected by the weather (outdoor devotions, for instance, aren't so compelling during a rainstorm) or physical illness (it's hard to attend a prayer meeting while dealing with a kidney stone attack).

These however, are reactionary in nature, in most cases calling for a simple adjustment. But circumstances can demand a more complex response when, for example, a church cannot locate a suitable facility for its regular gatherings (as was the situation for my church). Suddenly the possible solutions come in droves. Should we move into multiple homes? Merge with another church? Rent? Lease? Buy? Build? Perhaps consider entirely different models of ministry? The myriad options can quickly become bewildering. We cannot act on all of them.

Good or bad circumstances are not definite indications that "God is tryin' to tell you somethin'." Actually, much of the ministry in the New Testament involves remaining unmoved in the midst of certain situations. Paul's self-described sufferings in Second Corinthians 11, for instance, could easily look like a man cursed by God. By verse 25, when he mentions "three times I was shipwrecked," many modern Christians would advise him to go home, because, apparently, the blessing just wasn't there.

On the other hand, many folks with breathless excitement speak of a situation being a "God thing," and of divine set-ups. Such circumstances, though, might not be so simple. Paul had an open door in Troas for evangelism, which most of us would have seen as a no-brainer: *Stay there! Preach!* Yet he left that great opportunity because he had no rest in his spirit (see 2:12–13). His sense of life trumped the promising scenario.

> "OPEN DOORS" MAY COME ALONG, BUT
> WHEN DISCERNMENT SHOWS UP, THEY
> START LOOKING LIKE TRAP DOORS INSTEAD.

When the devil tempted Jesus in the wilderness, he extended the greatest offers he had ever made to a man—unlimited earthly fame and power. Instantly the possibilities would have presented themselves: *You can use this new, worldwide platform to disseminate your teachings—and all without that horrid cross!* But Jesus deftly side-stepped all of it with verses from the Bible. He brought truth to bear on the apparent glowing "opportunity" and exposed it as the worst proposal ever. Sometimes open doors come along, but when godly factors of discernment show up, they start looking like trap doors instead.

Circumstances can suggest or confirm God's mind in a certain situation, but they should not by themselves be treated as controlling factors. It might seem that an easy way around confusing circumstantial indicators would be the use of supernatural signs. Occasionally, our decisions will be time-sensitive, and we will feel pressured to choose while the clock winds down. The consequence of your decision can be so severe and life-changing, though, that it is easy to feel paralyzed with anxiety over it. At this point, many of us long for a divine tiebreaker, a sign that indicates divine favor resting upon this or that. Sometimes people in the Bible made requests of these, such as Gideon:

> Then Gideon said to God, "If you will save Israel by my hand, as you have said, behold, I am laying a fleece of wool on the threshing floor. If there is dew on the fleece alone, and it is dry on all the ground, then I shall know that you will save Israel by my hand, as you have said." And it was so. When he rose early next morning and squeezed the fleece, he wrung enough dew from the fleece to fill a bowl with water. Then Gideon said to God, "Let not your anger burn against me; let me speak just once more. Please let me test just once more with the fleece. Please let it be dry on the fleece only, and on all the ground let there be dew." And God did so that night; and it was dry on the fleece only, and on all the ground there was dew. (Judg. 6:36–40)

God went along with the odd request. But scripting such signs and requiring Him to follow them comes dangerously close to violating the command in Deuteronomy 6:16, "You shall not put the LORD your God to the test." From Gideon's fearful tone, he knew that to a certain extent, he was dangerously presumptive to request this sign. Even in the Old Testament, such behavior was not usual. How much more careful ought we to be, who already have all we need—a finished Bible in our hands, the indwelling Spirit within us, and the members of Christ all around us?

Besides, the practice of fleecing, that is, to ask God for an often random, unrelated sign to demonstrate His will, is far from inner life, even farther, in fact, than asking for reasonable circumstantial guidance. Dependence on these things seems to be an abdication of responsibility, a shortcut around thinking, prayer, and Scripture.[4] Yet such things as fleecing and casting of lots (which the early disciples practiced in Acts 1:26), are popular today among immature believers. That is, until those same believers begin to notice the failure rate of these signs increasing. M. Blaine Smith, author of *Knowing God's Will*, writes,

> Sometimes, I believe, God mercifully allows us to continue with a spiritual practice which is less than the best. He is patient with the elementary state of our faith and not willing to push us to a higher level before we are ready. Yet when he knows that we *can* handle it, psychologically and spiritually, he may allow us a hard experience with that same practice— not to break us down but to build us up. His intent is to wake us up, to quell our enthusiasm for the practice, to prod us to look for a more mature approach to spiritual insight. I strongly suspect that this explains otherwise inexplicable experiences which some Christians have with fleeces and other improper approaches to guidance.[5]

Dreams can also bring some clarity to confusing circumstances, and be useful simply because the conscious mind is not present, erecting its defensive filters. Today, in non-Christian lands where gospel witness is weak, we have heard reports of Jesus coming to the unsaved in dreams. Thank God for this. In such cases, usually the person having the dream is clear about the "who" and "what" of it. However, even with Christians, strange subconscious components can fill our dreams to the point of distraction. We end up chasing many contradictory interpretations. When it comes to believers desiring directional help, dreams should clarify, not add further levels of difficulty. Most of the dreams used in the New Testament actually surround one person, Joseph, concerning his attitudes and movements related to the birth and early childhood of Jesus. Their messages were simple and straightforward, not so fraught with imagery that they would have bedeviled the simple carpenter.

Like a lot of people, I have had a rich dream life. However, only a few of mine have had any straight line connection to spiritual themes. The rest were a bizarre mishmash of scenarios with no point, more a consequence of late night snacks than any clarifying message. I recommend an exacting attitude toward your dream life—upon reasonable consideration, if you cannot see the point of said dream, store it away in your heart, not your day planner.

Whether through dreams, signs, the Word, or life impressions, our circumstances need additional verification to discern if God is opening or closing a door. Or, if He means for us to attach any significance to the circumstance at all. Any time it becomes apparent that the divine hand is visibly at work, and controlling events for the sake of our direction, it will always be inspiring.

Wisdom Received

We navigate life much more by wisdom than we realize. While we can't say that wisdom is the same as mere knowledge and experience, it is certainly not less than those things. That is why a wisdom stream can come even from purely human advice and judgment. The father-in-law of Moses suggested to him a better way of administrating the people of Israel, even though he was not clearly a follower of Yahweh. Moses took his advice, much to his (and the people's) benefit. In other cases, like that of Abigail, who advised David, there was no evidence that she had any strong relationship with God, but her judgment was sound, nevertheless. In a similar way, non-Christian parents, and experts of various fields, can prove helpful. All such wisdom, however, must be handled carefully. Unregenerate human sources are limited, as Paul wrote, because "The natural person does not accept the things of the Spirit of God, for they are folly to him, and he is not able to understand them because they are spiritually discerned" (1 Cor. 2:14). No matter how wise, they eventually fail to reflect the nature, character, or priorities of God. We can certainly benefit from them, but cannot trust them wholesale.

James tells us, "If any of you lacks wisdom, let him ask God, who gives generously to all without reproach, and it will be given him" (1:5). This significant promise introduces us to fuller dimensions of understanding. James also says, "the wisdom from above is first pure, then peaceable, gentle, open to reason, full of mercy and good fruits, impartial and sincere" (3:17). Godly wisdom is characterized by such things as obedience to the words of Christ (see Matt. 7:24), prudence (see Prov. 8:12), humility (see 11:2), discernment (see 14:8), and fear of the Lord (see Ps. 111:10).

This kind of wisdom is indispensable when we want to make God-honoring directional decisions, and have run short of biblical information. When we consider marriage, for example, there are things not spelled out in Scripture, like what to make of differences in personality, basic temperament, family complications, practical handling of money, or whether the other person wants children. Except through extrapolation, Scripture says little directly concerning these matters. God-given wisdom will then enrich our interpretations of past experience, interpersonal learning, testing, contemplation of outcomes, consideration of possibilities, and help us see through our own self-centered agendas.

Although I highly value all the ways in which I have been led over the last almost forty years, I find myself leaning the most upon God-implanted wisdom. This has most frequently fallen into two categories of experience for me. One of them comes directly on the heels of prayer, when an instantaneous direction, or solution is made known in my mind. The other, more common experience, has to do with a gradual, dawning realization in my mind, monitored of course, by the other avenues of spiritual guidance.

The apostles exemplified such daily wisdom. When the Bible narrates their movements, it mostly does so without elaboration on how they made their decisions. A casual reader would assume Paul's missionary stops in Cyprus and then Pisidian Antioch were little more than just-so decisions. However, guys like me (especially my younger self), assume Paul and his team had an inside line on where to go, and how long to stay, at all times. But I can imagine a third way, the way of wisdom, where Paul sat down with Barnabas and Mark after being sent out in Acts 13. Maybe they had a general idea of the areas they'd want to visit with the gospel, but little else. Barnabas might have said, "Brothers, I'm from Cyprus. I know a lot of Jews there, have connections to synagogues, and lots of extended family. Plus, we'll have places to stay. Let's go there first." No one knows for sure if this discussion ever took place, or any others like it, but it's not unreasonable to think so. Paul must have taken into consideration the sizes of cities, and which of them had large synagogues, or about towns where major roads converged, and where shipping ports existed. When speaking of future ministry endeavors, he used language like, "I intend," "Perhaps," and "Wherever I go," meaning his plans could be fluid.

He, as well as other workers in the New Testament, responded to prohibitions and course changes that came directly from the Lord, yet also displayed decision-making from a combination of renewed mind, consideration of circumstances, and application of ministry vision. We cannot say that sometimes they were led by the spirit, and when they weren't, they were simply making plans. Through a life of ongoing prayer and seeking, the voice of the Shepherd was being made known to them through wise, rational means.

God is incredibly active in leading His people. This is not merely because He wants things done, but He wants us to practice inner life and its discernment through the many avenues He has provided. Perhaps in the beginning, we tend to treat these artificially, like checklists. With the increase of maturity, though, the many aids to knowing and obeying the Lord's mind will seem to organically come together. The end product will be a fuller, richer life.

However, before we can arrive at that desired place, some hurdles must be addressed.

13

Intuitive Crash and Burn

I'd rather walk in the dark with God
Than go alone in the light;
I'd rather walk by faith with Him
Than go alone by sight.

— Mary G. Brainard

IT'S EVERY PARENT'S nightmare. Little Johnny runs away from his mother toward the street. He has a good head start, and he's giggling, thinking that his mom who is chasing him and shouting his name, is playing another game of catch-and-tickle. Of course, Mom doesn't think it's funny. She yells every power word she knows, including "Stop!" and runs as hard as she can, trying to close that precious fifteen or so yards. He is squealing with delight now, and begins to maneuver between two parked cars on the curb. The sounds of engines, the swoosh of passing vehicles on the street don't faze him. He's going to keep running straight through it, because he's missed every indication of warning. And when mom catches him at the last second, jerks him up, hugs him, and then scolds him, he seems bewildered.

He did the same thing last week.

Even with the multitude of ways that God uses to restrain us, stop us, start us, adjust us, we can persist in being confused. For many the will of God seems like an enormous corn maze, full of blind alleys. Every turn looks exactly like the last one, just as full of likelihood that we'll be led nowhere.

> **IF WE THINK THERE'S SOMETHING WRONG WITH THE WAY GOD LEADS, THE PROBLEM ISN'T WITH HIM.**

During these moments, we'll assume prayer is not working, or the Bible isn't clear enough, or the surrounding circumstances are confusing. Maybe we need better mentors, or a clearer sign, or stronger feelings. At any rate, we'll think there's something wrong with the avenues through which God leads. It probably will not have dawned on us that the source of our confusion could be emanating from within ourselves. God shouts and whispers, pleads and commands. He calls you by name. He barricades the roadway. He'll even raise up circumstances that sweep you right off your feet, and away from the bus that was barreling down the street. The problem isn't with Him. Perhaps you've strayed into some sound-proof areas that all but disables your understanding of spiritual direction.

A Cocktail of Bias, Preference, and Desire

Before we begin to inquire of the Lord, we may have already made up our minds on a given matter. We're often not aware of it, though. Even while we're inclining toward our own decision, we may be going through the religious formality of seeking an answer. Why? Because we want to receive confirmation. We like the exhilaration that comes from badly wanting something, and having God agree with a resounding, *Yes!*

Over decades of time in ministry, I've heard a lot of stories about the Lord leading someone to do this or that, to move here or there. I've rarely heard anyone say that they had favored a course of action, but the Lord had said no, and they therefore had to alter their cherished plans. We want the Lord to lead us, but we also want veto power over Him, like the specially adapted student driving car that has two separate steering columns and pedals. We'll let God drive, as long as we retain the option of emergency control. This results in blurring the difference between the driver and the driving instructor. Once this subconscious attitude takes shape in us, every big decision will become a crisis moment. We will passionately want something, but at another level, disturbing reservations remain. This causes unabated seeking, as we obsessively retrace our former steps, and never find a satisfactory answer.

Most of us think our problem is related to not knowing. Actually our problem is related to our will. The will must be set right first. Jesus said, "If anyone's will is to do God's will, he will know whether the teaching is from God or whether I am speaking on my own authority" (John 7:17). At that time, some people couldn't tell whether Jesus' teaching was just the word of a man or the word of God. They teetered back and forth, hoping for conclusive proof. Insufficient evidence wasn't the problem, though. No, they lacked an adequate, up-front commitment to obey God. Because they did not "will to do God's will," as their first and primary attitude, their minds remained foggy, uncertain.

Just like them, our uncommitted will can obscure our understanding of what God is saying. Almost as soon as a matter appears on the horizon, our reasonings and desires will rush to take first place. In the absence of an established priority for the will of God, our preferences quickly harden into a fortress within. Afterwards, even if we pray, study, or approach others for clarity, it will tend to be with the hope we get the answer we naturally favor.

Bias is a difficult, thorny thing to overcome. In order to combat it, we need to settle a large life decision well in advance. That is, to obey the Lord's will first, to emphasize our relationship with Him as paramount, not ancillary. Without doing this, even if God shows us His way, it will make no difference, for our will is still not to do His will. The search for further clarity will never end.

The Scriptures may provide an answer, but guided by powerful secret desires, we may force the verses to say what we want them to say, even if our interpretation is absurd. That is why we've often seen people retrofitting verses to agree with modern agendas. Such twisting begins with an emotion already enticed, and a mind already made up. Even our prayers will not be exempt from biased mischief, as they belabor and badger the issue, hardly looking like a conversation with God. The more desperately we seek, the more fixated we become, with real answers growing more scarce by the day.

Meanwhile, a self-guided momentum is well underway, even as we seem to say and do all the right things. Take for example Balaam, a heathen prophet who was promised financial rewards if he would curse the people of Israel. He told Balak, his would-be employer, "Lodge here tonight, and I will bring back word to you, as the LORD speaks to me"

(Num. 22:8). It seemed a truly spiritual thing to say, but the prospect of money, like a hook, had been set. Balaam's alleged faithfulness to God's word was already eroding. However, God still spoke, saying to Balaam, "You shall not go with them. You shall not curse the people, for they are blessed" (22:12). It should have been settled at that point. But when a financial motive (or *any* motive, for that matter) invades a person's heart, God can never conclude a conversation with a clear and definite "No."

Balak, the man who had sought Balaam's curse-for-pay services, sweetened the deal with extra enticements:

> Once again Balak sent princes, more in number and more honorable than these. And they came to Balaam and said to him, "Thus says Balak the son of Zippor: 'Let nothing hinder you from coming to me, for I will surely do you great honor, and whatever you say to me I will do. Come, curse this people for me.'" (22:15–17)

Balaam, though, was still sticking to whatever was left of his wavering commitment to God. He answered and said to the servants of Balak, "Though Balak were to give me his house full of silver and gold, I could not go beyond the command of the LORD my God to do less or more" (22:18).

The response seemed admirable, and yet, God's previous "No" hadn't ended anything for the prophet. Balaam kept seeking. He said to the emissaries, "So you, too, please stay here tonight, that I may know what more the LORD will say to me" (22:19). Apparently, the money was simply too compelling. Though he maintained a devout sort of bearing as he talked about the Lord speaking to him, the phantom of gain was steering his heart. *Maybe God was holding out for this better offer! He might have changed His mind!*

The man then chose to seek harder and deeper for the "right answer." "And God came to Balaam at night and said to him, 'If the men have come to call you, rise, go with them; but only do what I tell you'" (Num. 22:20). With this word, at last God seemed to be directing Balaam in the direction that the prophet really wanted to go.

But this already strange situation was about to become stranger still. "God's anger was kindled because he went, and the angel of the Lord took his stand in the way as his adversary" (22:22). He had clearly given the green light for Balaam to go, yet there He was, angry with the prophet. Balaam had no idea that such was the case. On his way, he may have even mulled over the financial blessing he thought was coming, telling himself cheery things like "God is *so* good!" This puzzling situation often plays out, when someone clearly under the control of something else, cannot be restrained, when it seems that God is simply going along with their self-bound way. Indeed, the voice of the Lord and Balaam's materialistic lust had blurred together into a single impulse that even the prophet could not tell apart. It was muddy water at best, and though the Lord had certainly directed the man to go, something about Balaam remained objectionable, ugly. He seemed to move by the Lord's word, while actually moving according to money.

The narrative here in Numbers took an even more bizarre turn, when Balaam's donkey saw the angel of the Lord, and tried to avoid him, but Balaam saw nothing, and taking the animal as obstinate, beat it. It was a new low for the prophet, for the animal had demonstrated more sight and discernment than he had! Such was the blinding effect of his motives. At that point, the donkey spoke to the man, which should have stunned him, and brought him out of his obsession. But rather than come to his senses, Balaam spoke back to it, arguing and venting his anger.

> Then the LORD opened the eyes of Balaam, and he saw the angel of the LORD standing in the way, with his drawn sword in his hand. And he bowed down and fell on his face. And the angel of the LORD said to him, "Why have you struck your donkey these three times? Behold, I have come out to oppose you because your way is perverse before me. The donkey saw me and turned aside before me these three times. If she had not turned aside from me, surely just now I would have killed you and let her live. (22:31–33)

The apostle Peter spoke of the event this way: "Balaam . . . loved gain from wrongdoing, but was rebuked for his own transgression; a speechless donkey spoke with human voice and restrained the prophet's madness" (2 Pet. 2:15–16).

> **NEVER UNDERESTIMATE THE POWER OF PERSONAL DESIRE TO OBSCURE ONE'S SIGHT.**

Balaam spent his remaining days trying to find every loophole possible around the Lord's restriction against cursing Israel. He even tried to teach Balak how to lead the Israelites into idolatry, and thus provoke the Lord Himself into cursing them (see Rev. 2:14). Never underestimate the power of personal desire to obscure one's sight.

I have mostly pastored young adults over the decades, and I've noticed that the decisions they wrestle over the most are job moves and marriages. I recall one situation where a young Christian woman from another church sought out me and my wife for counsel. She had gotten serious about a young man who was a committed atheist. I immediately brought up the Bible, but she had already studied all the pertinent verses, and every alternate way of interpreting them.

Her mother, a seasoned Christian, had weighed in on the issue as well. As the young woman put it, the advice was old-fashioned and by-the-book. She had gotten input from her more contemporary Christian peers, but described it as not understanding or supportive. And now she was talking to us, and still not exactly hearing what she wanted to hear.

We reasoned with her from various standpoints of practical wisdom, doing our best to be gentle. But even things that made no sense seemed perfectly reasonable to her, such as allowing her unbelieving boyfriend to choose the church they went to, and to follow his "spiritual lead."

The one consideration that outweighed all others was the fact that she wanted this man, something the Holy Spirit did not seem happy with. "It sounds as though you've made up your mind," I told her.

"No," she replied, as though she couldn't see the obvious. "I want to follow the Lord." All the way to the altar she remained vaguely conflicted, which is what happens when our feelings are a mix of differing agendas. I hope the man she married came to Christ. I hope they're doing well. But I don't know for sure. We never saw them again.

Motives often dominate our hearts at levels of which we are hardly aware, including those of us who highly value our relationship with Christ. Our openness to the Lord and our honesty, therefore, must become as exacting as our search for answers. Once you've been made aware of a self-centered motive, bring it out before the Lord. If it involves sin, confess it.

Make it part of your ongoing conversation with Him. Don't conceal the fact that you want something. The Lord already knows you want it, anyway. Speaking openly of it to Him will be good for you. It will prevent you from praying disingenuous prayers, and deceiving yourself.

I think it's a good idea right here to balance my warning word about personal desire. At surface level, there is nothing wrong with desiring something, provided your motive in wanting it is not evil. A school of opinion exists that if we want something, or even like it, that is a proof it is of the flesh, and we should not have it at all. But such talk strongly suggests an oversimplification of spirituality, and at worse, a form of asceticism.

When this attitude gains traction in church, you'll find a lot of people mismatched with their areas of service. Talented musicians handle the church finances, but avoid leading worship because they've been told their love of music automatically signifies something fleshly. Teachers won't teach, but they'll cut grass and trim bushes on church properties, or gifted practical servants do nothing with their hands anymore, but drive themselves crazy with administrative work ot public speaking roles that they can't stand—all in the name of "taking up the cross." The illogic of this position becomes clear when we begin to shun every pleasure, every comfort, every good thing as something from the devil.

Positive predispositions toward good things are an indicator that they should be pursued, like leadership: "If anyone aspires to the office of overseer, he desires a noble task" (1 Tim. 3:1). This obviously applies to marriage, as well; both individuals must *want* to marry the other person (assuming biblical requirements are met, of course). In First Corinthians

7, Paul also makes concessions to personal wishes, as if the deciding factor in those cases was what the individual wanted. As I mentioned a few chapters ago, the leading of the Lord is not so intrusive that it must interfere with most of our normal, daily activities. We can typically expect the Lord's voice to maintain a constant, happy witness of our union with Him, even as we pursue non-offensive interests and opportunities.

The problem begins when a personal desire becomes a controlling matter, a competing god in our heart that leads us to twist the Bible, reason away inward impressions, write off others as dolts, ignore contrary circumstances, and tell wisdom, "The heart wants what it wants." Once such a deeply held motive is exposed, you must consciously exercise your commitment as a disciple, like Jesus said: "If anyone would come after me, let him deny himself and take up his cross and follow me" (Matt. 16:24).

A call to cross out these prejudices, biases, cherished dreams, and preferences can be painful. Depending on what it is, you may feel your heart is being ripped out. As a younger, more idealistic Christian, I had little sympathy for fellow believers who struggled with obedience issues. I felt they were self-indulgent and lacking in love for the Lord.

I still believe that today—except I've come to realize that *most* of us struggle with obedience, including myself. Now that I'm older, I've been in more than a few painful quandaries where I wanted to follow the Lord, but knew I was leaning hard in another direction, toward *my* preferences. Things were fine when my desire and God's were flowing in unison, but if they diverged even a foot or so, I felt it. Thus began seasons of intense struggle for me. If this describes you as well, then you should know we have something in common with Abraham,

Jacob, David, Samson, Jonah, and the twelve apostles, to name a few. All these giants of faith at some time or another were controlled by motives that got them into trouble.

Though our gold standard is obedience without delay, it doesn't always happen so fast. Due to our dense, sinful hearts, sanctification often mimics a slow drip experience. By pointing this out, I am not attempting to diminish the harm of resisting God. During the time you "struggle," Satan will be near, busily offering alternatives, shortcuts, and compromises. Frustration will be at high tide, and temptations to blaspheme God. A prolonged struggle, then, is a dangerous place to live.

Read the book of Jonah and you'll get a good idea of the unpleasantries that can befall a stubborn person. If you find yourself in this holding pattern, ask for grace to get out of it. Better yet, *plead* for grace to overcome your resistance. Tell the Lord your commitment is 100 percent obedience, with no excuses—even if, right now, you are stumbling.

Jesus told a parable about obedience and disobedience.

> "What do you think? A man had two sons. And he went to the first and said, 'Son, go and work in the vineyard today.' And he answered, 'I will not,' but afterward he changed his mind and went. And he went to the other son and said the same. And he answered, 'I go, sir,' but did not go. Which of the two did the will of his father?" They said, 'The first." (Matt. 21:28-31)

Jesus confirmed their answer was correct. Obedience promised and kept is the best course. Much to our shame, though, disobedience, then repentance and obedience, is sometimes the best we can do. Self-indulgent motives are tenacious things, with deep roots. Only the cross has a long enough reach to pluck them up.

Reckless Presumption

Good earnest hearts can sometimes be mistaken. Though we might believe strongly that the Lord has led us, the passion of that belief doesn't make it true. Sincere individuals have done a lot of damage in the religious world with mistaken convictions of all sorts. These think that healthy checks and balances are treasonous to faith. And so with the barest of evidence, they set out to do or undo, to build or tear down, to stay or go, to help or hurt, to start or stop. Since they are typically full of energy, and the boldest sort of assurance, we're apt to admire them.

But God told Saul, "Rebellion is as the sin of divination, and presumption is as iniquity and idolatry" (1 Sam. 15:23). Everyone is clear about the wrongfulness of rebellion against God. Few understand the serious nature of presumption in His name. We tend to excuse it as a "positive" sin, a mistake made in the name of zeal, or great love for God. In many respects, presumption is worse than harboring hidden agendas, because at least an agenda-driven life stands the chance of being exposed. A moment of honesty could flush it out. Presumption, however, runs on the strength of blind conviction. It often appears irrational, and if questioned, irritable.

The greatest hallmark of presumptive faith is its readiness to use any way or means to achieve its imagined end, because "God wants it." Jesus warned the disciples about such religious people when He said, "Indeed, the hour is coming when whoever kills you will think he is offering service to God" (John 16:2). Paul was one of these people—"I myself was convinced that I ought to do many things in opposing the name of Jesus of Nazareth. And I did so in Jerusalem. I not only locked up many of the saints in prison after receiving authority from the chief priests, but when they were put to death I cast my vote against them" (Acts 26:9–10). Thus in these extreme cases, courses of action allegedly for God actually managed to oppose Him.

> ## WE CAN BECOME POSSESSED OF A CERTAINTY THAT NOT ONLY PROVES WRONG, BUT EMBARRASSINGLY SO.

It is only the Lord's mercy that keeps us from traveling this far down the road of error. Still, we have often ventured just far enough to experience humiliation and disillusionment. George Whitefield was a great colonial evangelist who lived and labored with John and Charles Wesley. He was instrumental in the greatest revival America has ever seen, called the Great Awakening. During his highly effective ministry, he became certain God had told him his newborn son would also become a great evangelist. Whitefield was so convinced of this, he named the child John, after John the Baptist. He also told his congregation, and all the surrounding area about the "prophecy." However, the child died at four months old. This stung Whitefield deeply. He had cultivated a habit of trusting inward spiritual impressions with no other balancing input.[1] The disappointment crushed him for a while, but to his credit, he learned to never again lightly trust such isolated, inward feelings.

We also can become possessed of a certainty that not only proves wrong, but embarrassingly so. A man in a church I co-led, for instance, was suddenly seized with an inspiration that a particular woman would be his wife. "It just came to me," he said, "From the Lord." None of us wanted to intrude upon such personal ground, but his unquestioned certainty about it concerned us. In short order, the man followed up on what he absolutely knew to be the Lord's leading. But before long, in a bizarre reversal, the woman developed an obsession with him, complete with stalking, harassing phone calls, and when he did not propose to her quickly enough, efforts to smear his reputation. He spent a harrowing few months trying to escape her, and eventually married someone else.

I don't wish to hold anyone's mistakes up to ridicule, because I know from personal experience how easy it is to blur faith with presumption. Plenty of us with enthusiastic temperaments have taken the advice, "If you want to walk on water, you've got to get out of the boat." But before the Lord invited us, we practically had one leg already over the bow. This could mean quitting day jobs for speculative business opportunities that then failed, prophesying the outcomes of political races that then went in the opposite direction, and many other such things.

Frequently, presumption can even involve Christian ministry. This, perhaps, is the most deceitful area of presumption, for we Christians often reason that anything done for the Lord, or in His name, must be God's will. But Jesus said,

> "Not everyone who says to me, 'Lord, Lord,' will enter the kingdom of heaven, but the one who does the will of my Father who is in heaven. On that day many will say to me, 'Lord, Lord, did we not prophesy in your name, and cast out demons in your name, and do many mighty works in your name?' And then will I declare to them, 'I never knew you; depart from me, you workers of lawlessness.'" (Matt. 7:21–23)

These verses do not display false faith as much as they do presumptuous faith, work done for Jesus, without His mind, without His lordship. The religious people involved are like folks who find their master's credit card, and then go around using it to make charges. Because his name is on it, and his credit is good, the card works. Emboldened by each apparent success, they use it even more, racking up huge expenditures without his permission.

The spiritual status of the people in this passage has been hotly debated. Regardless, they were lawless workers, that is, workers without boundaries. They did whatever came into their mind to do, and the fact that it was for Jesus, did not help them.

Many of these efforts, loosely called "ministries," begin out of presumption—*For sure God wants this!* Rapid growth is taken to be confirmation of the Lord's agreement with it, but the trajectory over time becomes less and less Christ-like. When presumption is the foundation of an enterprise, it will become a continuing habit. Eventually, these workers find themselves severely overextended, having presumed their way into a corner. Financial straits pressure them into delivering endless money sermons, false promises, and even threats. They increasingly depend upon sensationalism to validate their work.

When the Lord finally confronts them, their presumption by then will have become so entrenched that they will even argue with Him! They will wave their résumé of achievements in front of Him, because this is what they have done their entire lives to anyone else who dared confront them. The Lord, however, will summarily dismiss it as lawlessness. The moment will be so shattering, so contrary to expectations, that it will be utterly terrible.

Yet, we cannot say that the Lord sprung a trap on them. More than likely these people received words, warnings, admonitions of all kinds, but they immersed themselves in the din of the religious world. The gentle, nuanced voice of the Holy Spirit was ignored in favor of ever-increasing power. The sober counsel of the Word was judged too boring, and therefore passages were gleaned for maximum flash and sizzle. The whispers of conscience were drowned out in crowd acclaim. True spirituality would have tempered these people, but the presumptuous can only hear themselves. Their certainty deafens them.

According to Jesus, the solution to this problem is to do the Father's will. However, we don't arrive at the will of the Father by latching onto an idea, and calling it God. This will require the avenues of spiritual discernment we have already discussed. It will also call for a strong measure of humility. The issue is not whether we will make a mistake, because, being sinners, that is certain. But can you be corrected? For some, that question may not yet be settled. We can be so smitten with a mission of some sort, we find it too painful to change. Having trumpeted our direction as being divine, it may be too humiliating to amend our course.

While Peter was still talking on the Mount of Transfiguration, God interrupted him and adjusted his concept. While Martha was distracted with much serving, Jesus adjusted her with a word of balance. While Apollos was carrying out his teaching ministry, Priscilla and Aquila took him aside and explained the way of God to him more accurately. All of them submitted to the necessary corrections. Can you be like them? Times will arise when we need to find out if our alleged leading is actually our own presumption. After all, who should be leading whom?

Paralyzed by Fear

The opposite error to presumption is to become so afraid of misunderstanding the Lord's mind that it leads to a paralysis of decision-making, and finally, an idle condition. This was the sin of the man in the parable of Matthew 25, who had received a talent from the Lord and did nothing with it.

> He also who had received the one talent came forward, saying, "Master, I knew you to be a hard man, reaping where you did not sow, and gathering where you scattered no seed, so I was afraid, and I went and hid your talent in the ground. Here, you have what is yours." But his master answered him, "You wicked and slothful servant! You knew that I reap where I have not sown and gather where I scattered no seed?." (25:24–26).

In this short, terse conversation, the Lord confirmed to the man that He gathers where He does not sow. Any enterprise for the kingdom of God seems to start with nothing. There is risk, discomfort, and possible loss. Faith must take over, and at some point, the Lord eventually gathers. This is the way of it. Apparently the man knew, and admitted it, catching himself in his own words.

However, Jesus would not agree that He was "hard." Such fearful mischaracterizations easily encourage slothfulness in a Christian, and failure to do what is right. This is why Jesus linked the man's fear to laziness.

Let's say I approach Howard at church and ask if he would consider a three-month commitment to a certain service area. He pauses for a moment, and then says, "Let me pray about it." At first the response sounds admirable. Maybe he wants to make sure he's truly being led by the

Lord. But several weeks later, I approach him again, and ask about his prayer. "I didn't get around to it," he says, sheepishly. Howard felt like he needed to agonize over a decision to serve in the church, but it segued into procrastination, then disappeared. Meanwhile, he joined a baseball league at work without giving it a second thought.

Why, like the slothful servant, is Howard afraid? Where does all this so-called fear come from? At the simplest level, a fellow like Howard may be afraid of saying no, and prayer is his stall tactic. In that case, maybe I should ask myself if I was too demanding. Also, perhaps, Howard needs to learn to be more assertive and honest with others.

It could be that his commitment level is already low toward the church. Or maybe he doesn't want to presumptuously wander into a service area without the Lord's mind. Meanwhile, the prospect of seeking, searching, and praying sounds so . . . well, *exhausting*. Generally though, by the time a church member is asked to do something, a number of other markers may already be in place—biblical calls to selfless service in one's devotional reading, other born-again people suggesting it, a circumstantial need for it in the church. Perhaps what one is being asked to do makes sense in certain practical, wise ways. The only questionable element may be one's personal feelings. However, with all the other considerations in place, it could hardly be called presumption if, on a minimum of feeling, one answered the call.

Fear has other reasons, though. Sometimes we're afraid of new horizons, steep learning curves, and the possibility of failure. As a person prone to anxiety, I can testify that nearly everything I've ever done for the Lord was in the beginning sandbagged with my fear of a humiliating, if not disastrous, outcome. A lot of us delay, waiting for indications of success before we're willing to move a muscle. Maybe we've heard too many stories of failure—or worse yet, too many success stories from the religious crowd, and now the bar has been set so artificially high we're intimidated. Our chief concern turns from faithful obedience to the possible outcome. How big will it be? How dramatic? Will it at least be peaceful, comfortable? These considerations can eclipse everything else.

One night in a group fellowship, a woman was boasting about how she had not prayed or received any leading about an important decision she'd made, and "Everything turned out fine." Apparently she was telling the story to justify her lack of spirituality in the matter, and how we needn't trouble ourselves with all the silly rigmarole of being led by the Spirit. After all, it had ended on a good note for her.

In contrast, the apostle Paul walked in Spirit, traveled by revelation, and prayed as a lifestyle, yet ended up imprisoned several times, and was executed. Rather than becoming religious celebrities, he wrote, "We have become, and are still, like the scum of the world" (1 Cor. 4:13).

> ## WE MUST NOT ALLOW FEAR TO INTIMIDATE US INTO IDLENESS.

Therefore, does every short-term, visible outcome really reflect the inherent value of discerning the Lord's mind? Not if we follow the rest of Paul's story, the part that continues beyond his death. We'll note that his public and private correspondences have nourished the Christian church for twenty centuries. His voice still speaks beyond the grave, empowered of course, by the Holy Spirit, and has brought countless millions to Christ. Even that massive fruitfulness is still not the last word though—not until Paul receives the crown of glory, a full and public vindication of his faithfulness.

We must not allow fear to intimidate us into idleness. Learn to trust God with outcomes. Like Abraham, who "went out, not knowing where he was going" (Heb. 11:8), we also may venture into situations that require a postponement of comfort. Our forerunners endured long seasons of sacrifice before God led them into fulfillments that astonished their hearts. If the history of the church had been full of saints wanting assurances of safety and success before they followed the Lord, we would have no role models today—certainly no train of martyred souls, no reformers, no missionaries. While trying to play it safe, the church would have been another self-centered, stalled-out organization.

In my own life, I've caught myself sunk down in short-sightedness. I'm thinking of the time my wife and I were led to relocate across town. As a young couple just starting off in ministry, we couldn't afford the rent in that more expensive area of the city, so a single older woman volunteered to move in with us and help with the expense. Almost immediately, some of the ugliest personality clashes occurred right there in our newly rented home. It was my introduction to the dark brew of pettiness, selfishness, and surly remarks that even Christians can experience while trying to cohabitate. God had disclosed none of this to me in advance, and if He had, I might have thought twice about signing up for it.

Maybe that's the reason we're not given a blow-by-blow preview of the way things will transpire in the short term—because we'd try to avoid the discomfort, and lose the Spirit's long-term work in our lives. In the name of fear, we'd give up before we obtained the fullness of blessing we had hoped for. In my case, I had wanted to move closer to the campus in order to help strengthen the student ministry of our church. With the fermenting situation in the new house, and seeing only lackluster results of ministry after months of work, I began to wonder if the whole thing had been worth it.

Meanwhile, the man across the street (who was *not* a student) was about to experience an eternal change in his life. In yet another experience of being led (which I didn't want to obey at first), I knocked on his door, introduced myself, and asked if he would like to read the Bible with me. In short, he did. He and his wife met Christ. And through them, some of his colleagues, as well. After more than thirty years, I'm sure the ripples of that event have not stopped spreading, though they are currently hidden from my sight.

In the initial phase, God leads us as much by the details He withholds from us as by those He provides.[2] Perhaps we will not live long enough to see all the unfolded consequences of the particular direction in which we were led. The downstream portion of God's work, like a river, often turns a bend, concealing itself from us. God may guide us to start, stop, stay, or rest, but He may not always reveal the reasons why.

Ultimately, the best possible thing for us is to follow Christ, even when currents of His leading become rough. We should not let this generate dread in our hearts; we need to reject that unfortunate caricature of a God who simply can't wait to sabotage our lives, and lead gullible souls into things that aren't good for them.

"All of God's glory is good for us," Randy Alcorn assures us. "What is in God's best interests is also in ours and others' (not immediately, perhaps, but ultimately). God has not created a universe where you must choose between your joy and His glory."[3]

In our foolishness, we implicitly believe we know better than He, and indeed, we are good at identifying and choosing short-term happiness. But Jesus warned of this when He said, "Enter by the narrow gate. For the gate is wide and the way is easy that leads to destruction, and those who enter by it are many. For the gate is narrow and the way is hard that leads to life, and those who find it are few" (Matt. 7:13–14). What really counts is where one ends up, not how much comfort one feels along the way. In fact, the pleasures along the easy way always prove to be nothing more than wallpaper, something to distract and entertain the traveler, while he or she heads toward eternal loss. Meanwhile, the narrow way is "hard," but ends up in life—where joy is substantial and permanent. Remember this the next time fear begins to paralyze you.

The Lord has no intention of shaping us into indecisive, noncommittal people. But what if, while loving Him and seeking His glory, we still make wrong decisions? The most sincere Christians can fail to correctly interpret spiritual intuition. Honest mistakes, though, do not change the fact that we are in the hands of a gracious God who knows all. If, in the long record of redemptive history, He has turned deliberate evils to the fulfillment of His plan, He can certainly use our godly mistakes even more. No heart that seeks His kingdom first, could ever fail to be blessed.

Jesus said, "No longer do I call you servants, for the servant does not know what his master is doing; but I have called you friends, for all that I have heard from my Father I have made known to you" (John 15:15). For a while among them, what He said and did seemed cryptic to their minds.

However, at this late point in their relationship with Him, they began to *know*.

And at some point in your developing inner life relationship with Him, you also come to know this Friend. He has a way of thinking. He feels a certain way about things, and does them a certain way. You will progressively understand this, not because you cracked a code, or mastered a formula. The fact is, through new birth you've been enabled to know Him in the deepest possible way. He gave His life so we could share it with Him. Truly, that is the most intimate friendship of all. In this union, He corrects us through our conscience, glorifies God through our worship, and leads us through intuitive perception.

It couldn't seem to get any richer, until you start adding other people who have the same thing going on within them.

14

The Church—
A Matrix of Life

One hundred religious persons knit into a unity
by careful organization do not constitute a
church any more than eleven dead men make a
football team. The first requisite is life, always.

— A.W. Tozer

The church is so subnormal that if it ever got back to the New
Testament normal it would seem to people to be abnormal.

— Vance Havner

YOU CAN HARDLY make it through elementary school science without being introduced to the famous lima bean experiment. It's simple. Sandwich a lima bean between two moist paper towels, place it in direct sunlight, and a few days later, it sprouts. Many kids have been wowed by this tiny miracle, but none of them come to the conclusion that since they were able to make it happen on a window sill, we can do away with farms. Why have an agricultural collective when you can manage growth individually, right at home? Obviously that conclusion would be silly, even for an eight-year-old.

But reasoning of this kind is common for a burgeoning number of contemporary Christians. Why have church, they ask, when we can individually duplicate some semblance of spiritual life? *I can listen to my audio Bible on the way to work. If I want further study, I can join a parachurch ministry that specializes in it. I can pray anytime. If I run into challenges, I can call an old mentor. There are thousands of sermon podcasts and YouTube videos online. If I'm in the mood for worship, I have tons of Christian music downloads I can sing along with.*

> **YOU NEED THE CHURCH—A GROUP**
> **OF PEOPLE WHO DO THEIR BEST**
> **TO CONFESS AND HOLD THE FAITH.**

When people make this kind of case, they're actually minimizing how difficult it is to cultivate spiritual life—as though all you need is an internet connection and some personal religious inclinations. It's actually dangerous for inner life to even flirt with this idea. Brett McCraken, author of the book *Uncomfortable: The Awkward and Essential Challenge of Christian Community*, writes, "I've heard too many of my millennial friends say they no longer attend church because they experience God more by hiking in Big Sur or by roasting exceptional coffee beans. But that is the first step to abandoning faith altogether."[1]

Yes, we need the church. And no, I'm not talking about cults, abusive organizations, or progressive groups that reinterpret Jesus and diminish the authority of the Bible. By "church," I refer to those that do their best to confess and hold the faith. Not a perfect church (because there isn't one), but one complete with eccentricities, weaknesses, quirkiness, extremes, and mistakes. Even with those associated headaches, you need that church, for it is specifically how God intends to preserve and stimulate spiritual life.

In fact, once we dispense with church involvement, much of the life described in the Bible will no longer make sense to us. We'll have to shoehorn a lot of what we read there into a self-centered context. The spiritual blessings of Ephesians 1 that issue in the church, the body of Christ, now become something for personal or family gratification. They enable my child to become a sports star, or my spouse to get over the stomach flu. They help me become a better dad, or husband. And of course, the most massive blessing of all—finding our dream home at a good price.

Without the church, the very idea of "one another" used so much in the New Testament, will simply leave us stumped. Maybe it refers to interactions at home, or the random encounters we have with people in the workplace. Through an individualistic lens, we fail to detect the Bible's use of the word "you" (often plural in Greek) as meaning the faith community, and will always interpret it to mean "you" the individual. This gives us the mistaken impression that we are the primary recipients of the Word, standing by ourselves, apart from others. Doubtless "you" (singular) is contained within the collective "you" (plural) of the church, so of course these plural "you" verses apply to you personally. But without a larger, group mindset to govern our understanding, we will end up a self-contradiction—a flock of one, a school of one, a pack of one, a group of one.

However, even the attitude that we need the church to augment our private spirituality falls short. Taken as a whole, as Will Walker says, "Community is not a part of spiritual life, but spiritual life itself."[2]

Members—Joined at the Life Level

Are we over-promoting the church when we make it so central to spiritual life? Not likely. Jesus began framing the idea of the centrality of the church when He spoke of the disciples as branches and Himself as the vine. In so doing, He portrayed a life union not only between Himself and the branches, but the branches with one another (see John 15). He defined the coming church as a reality that would only be known through healthy attachment.

Jesus continued to reinforce this thought so that it would carry forward and develop throughout the New Testament. He appeared to Paul, a man who had mounted an ongoing harassment of the early Christians. Jesus asked him, "Why are you persecuting me?" (Acts 9:4). He could just as easily have asked, "Why are you persecuting my people?" but selected the more direct sense, portraying all the believers as being one with Him.

This view provided an important foundational understanding for Paul's lifelong ministry, which he later presented in a grand metaphor: "For just as the body is one and has many members, and all the members of the body, though many, are one body, so it is with Christ" (1 Cor. 12:12). This, Paul would say, is Christ in the complete sense of the word. He is not a disembodied head floating above us, nor is He attached separately to each member. He is distinctly the Head in glory and office, joined to a redeemed body composed of distinct members, yet possessing a union of life that circulates throughout the whole.

This imagery, perhaps more than any other, demonstrates how dangerous isolation is for a Christian. When in a state of spiritual detachment, he or she becomes like a severed limb, bleeding out, slowly dying. It has only so long to be stitched back on before the worst sort of effects set in.

Most of us would agree that we must therefore abide in Christ. But Paul specifies in Romans 12:5 that we are "members one of another," not members each exclusively attached to the head. Paul had every intention of presenting a relationship where Christians move and work together in coordinated fashion. We often discover our gifts by being placed next to another person with entirely different ones. This is why none of us can ever say, "I have no need of you" (1 Cor. 12:21). We *do* need others, because self-imposed isolation never brings the blessed experience of services and gifts operating in harmony.

The word "member" has valuable theological significance, but it's also a common term used by many organizations, in a way that has nothing whatsoever to do with spiritual life. "Member" usually pertains to anyone who has some level of commitment to an event, activity, or entity.

A surprising number of Christians use the term exactly the same way when describing their relationship to the church. However, nothing short of receiving the life of Christ can make a person a member of His body. Without eternal life, even attending membership classes, signing covenants, and undergoing baptism ceremonies cannot make a person a member in the eyes of God. We may be able to call these people guests, visitors, or friends, but not members. In the absence of new birth, a man can never be more than a prosthetic limb.

However, the moment you receive the Spirit of life, you become a fruit-bearing branch in the universal Vine, a gifted member in the body of Christ, animated with a life supply from the Head. You become part of something larger than yourself, filled with hundreds of millions of others, both past and present. That is the proper setting for an enlivened person. After all, the best place for an arm is attached to a shoulder on one end, and a hand at the other, not drifting through life, disembodied, and trying to be healthy in spite of it.

This is why, immediately following your second birth, you sense a need to join other Christians. Something about it seems right. A few days after my salvation, I began to have my first-ever experience of a newly enlivened intuition, an understanding of the Lord leading me. I still remember that moment thirty-seven years ago, as I was walking along a sidewalk, deep in contemplation about how my new life would develop. I had been leaning heavily toward keeping it all to myself. Then for a split second I thought about a small group of Christians that met in my Army barracks for prayer and to discuss Scripture. Instantly, I received an inward impression: *Go find them.* I did a U-turn on the spot, and went to tell them I had been born again and wanted to be with them.

Though I had been led to join the fellowship of the guys in my barracks, and later, more visible structures of church, I found it rewarding in a completely different way than I ever expected. People don't "pay off" like amusement park rides. It took time. As an introvert in the midst of folks, I had to learn the many lessons of community—not only maxims such as "It's not about you," but being tempered by the differences in others. This helped me to get out of foolish fantasies about myself, and learn how I was supposed to give and receive life. I found that fellowship runs between the members through a living network, not from organizational trickle-down.

I realize this is difficult for a Christian generation that has been taught to think of self first—*my* fulfillment, *my* own private Jesus, *my* ministry. Even some Christians have adopted the mantra, "We like Jesus, but not the church." I understand. What could be more romantic than the life of a lonely prophet, his Bible under one arm, and prayer by a wooded stream? A life like that one won't be disturbed by human drama. Yet such a peaceful individual existence is not where inner life thrives, and if we think it does, we have only experienced life in the shallowest sense of the word.

We need the church. This is not a well-understood concept, nor is it even well-respected. We misunderstand needing people as being "needy." I'm doing fine on my own, we tell ourselves. But no matter how fulfilled we are, an eyeball was never intended to float in a tank of saline solution. The life in it only makes sense when it is situated in an eye socket. Christ uses His body in the same fashion, providing the context for us to bless and be blessed.

Stones—Built and Fitted in Life

We find other apostles enhancing the concept of church to the extent that we can never again think of it in ghetto terms. The apostle Peter reminds those who have already come to Christ, to make a habit of doing so. "As you come to him," we are told, you will find the Lord to be not a provider of milk, nor a shepherd, but "a living stone rejected by men but in the sight of God chosen and precious" (1 Pet. 2:4).

This stone represents the chief building material for God's house, an eternal, spiritual dwelling place for His glory. When we encounter Christ this way, we begin to realize He is not simply for us and our needs—our hunger, thirst, guidance, comfort—but He is for God. In fact, He is so much for God that men find it impossible to recruit Him for their selfish fallen purposes, and they therefore reject Him as worthless. But His very identity as a stone serves to satisfy the deepest purpose of God's heart. Therefore, He is eternally chosen, and precious.

> **INNER LIFE AND ITS TRANSFORMATIVE PROPERTIES, MORE THAN ANYTHING ELSE, MAKE US ABLE TO BE WITH OTHER PEOPLE.**

As we come to this living stone, Peter says, "You yourselves like living stones are being built up as a spiritual house, to be a holy priesthood, to offer spiritual sacrifices acceptable to God through Jesus Christ" (1 Pet. 2:5). Here in this verse, Peter no longer refers to us as living infants, as he did in verses 2 and 3, but as living *stones*. We have approached the original living stone to the extent that we have become like Him. This, you might say, is the radiating, transformative influence of Christ. The point, however, does not stop with our being transformed, but that in the process of being transformed, we are being built up together. We are more than a gem collection, individual stones in a display drawer. Our purpose lies in becoming a spiritual *house*.

Inner life and its transformative properties, more than anything else, make us able to be with other people. Sometimes inner life has been mistaken as private spiritual pursuits, and at worst, self-centered spirituality. Believers caught in this trap are prone to devalue the church, the spiritual house, treating it as a nuisance that gets in the way of personal development. Where this unfortunate attitude takes root, consumerism rules. We pick and choose whatever gratifies us the most and challenges us the least.

This kind of comfort does nothing to enhance inner life, and in almost every case causes us to be *ill-fitted* to God's plan for a spiritual house. Some of the most unpleasant, eccentric Christians I have ever met lie enthralled with their own spirituality. They tend to be small-hearted people who have a difficult time tolerating, much less investing in, other believers. Building is out of the question. But God uses our inner life—conscience, worship, and intuition—to enrich the believers who stand next to us. And typically this leads to our own enrichment as well, as we become more multifaceted and flexible in close proximity to them.

The longer we persist in our closeness to fellow Christians, the more it goes somewhere. Peter tells us the spiritual house takes on further shape as a "holy priesthood," a joint service of rich dimensions.

Probably at no time are we more aware of how inwardly impoverished we are than when we move to serve with others. Small ministry efforts and service groups quickly manifest the attitudes we have toward those beside us. Something as mundane as a few saints planning a potluck dinner can expose despising judgments against one another. A community outreach can be torn with dissension before the first bottled water is handed out. A small group formed for fellowship can display preferential attitudes by which church members it does or does not include.

Such failures to be Christ-like rarely happen during a latte-laced morning devotional time. They emerge between people as they seek to serve God.

At times of friction between "priests," nothing is more important than the concept of inner life. I recall an early church planting experience with other ministry interns. The members of the team couldn't have been more different. We had gotten along well enough at a distance from one another in the same large church, but suddenly sent out on mission to the same place, we found ourselves crammed together in one living room.

Until that time, I had never needed to have so many "robust" conversations with God—all of which had to do with things I had said and attitudes I had harbored against others. There was no place to hide; I was forced to find a richer, better, worship than the kind that had floated me along in larger church settings. Now, with less than twenty of us present on any given Sunday, it meant everyone had to listen and contribute, setting aside moods and paying attention to the flow of life. I could no longer allow myself to drift in and out of the moment. At every dinner table and prayer time, I had to go deep.

The sum total of these experiences upon this "stone" was to shave me down, smooth me out, build me up with others, and make me far more able than I had ever been to blend into priestly service.

That doesn't mean I lost my individuality. Some are afraid that such experiences will suck all the positive distinctions out of them, reducing them to what Pink Floyd called "Just another brick in the wall." If anything, the uniqueness of our identities comes out in harmonious relation to other people.

We tend to think our individuality is established by getting our way, or rebelling against the perceived status quo, but it's amazing how easily blue hair and ripped jeans can become a passé form of individualism. By the same token, so can the super-talented Christian who knows how to entertain a crowd, but not peaceably serve God in a group of garden-variety believers. In my case, the only thing I lost during that time were combative traits that would not allow me to fit in with fellow saints.

The complaint of "not fitting in" is perhaps the most common that I hear from Christians who seek church fellowship. Most of the blame for this hardship typically gets projected onto the church. But at the end of the day, when a congregation has worked on greeting newcomers properly, offering open doors, and purposely adjusting potentially offensive features of its culture for the sake of visitors, it still takes effort on the part of the individual to enter that fellowship. "I'm not comfortable in this group," could easily mean "I am not willing to learn anything, and I'd rather look for a low-cost, low-gain group to join."

As for my wife and myself, most of our church experience has consistently been one of not fitting in—at least not for a while. If we hadn't learned to identify spiritual life and pay almost complete attention to it, we wouldn't have been able to last in any church we've approached in the last decades.

As a newly married couple transferred by the military to Texas, my wife and I met with a Mexican church, where we didn't feel that we fit, either racially, culturally, or linguistically. After many meals in homes, and sustained personal contact, though, we began to experience a joint edification there. It was so good that I tried to resist our next move. But nobody fights Army reassignments and wins, so we were transferred to Ohio, where we met with a congregation that had a sizable Asian membership and older white suburban types who were mostly educated, and well . . . *northern.*

Once again, we didn't quite fit. It took a year or so before we began to feel built in, but that was with heavy involvement. The experience of staying there for many years significantly enriched us, though it did cost my wife her southern accent, and I was exposed to more ethnic food than my small soul found comfortable.

Skipping a long way into the future, and over a lot of ministry war stories, we planted a church in the Columbus, Ohio metro area. This time we were the eldest couple, the most experienced. And once again, we didn't fit. We found ourselves surrounded with a youthful crowd, some young enough to be our kids.

But by then we knew the church must be a spiritual house, a priesthood, not a lounge. The only way to get there was by the power of life. Had we not paid attention to it, and instead stressed background, age, race, personality, hobbies, education, income, politics, and a host of opinions too numerous to count, nothing could have been built up.

For those of us stuck on living room sofas because of concerns about generally imperfect people at church, we will never touch the important biblical command to "Let all things be done for building up" (1 Cor. 14:26). At an initial phase, building up means "Joining your imperfect self to many other imperfect selves to form an imperfect community that, through Jesus, embarks on a journey toward a better future."[3] No doubt the bringing together of "selves" is bound to provoke trouble. It is far more preferable to counsel believers to only bring their share of Christ together. But holding out for perfection is delusional, if not a lie. The very idea of building up means traveling through phases of serious imperfection. The life in the stones is not afraid of such challenges.

Siblings—Loving those of the Same Life

The apostle John specializes in a theology of family when he talks about the church, appealing to our innate desire to be with one another. We commonly find people on social media holding up placards asking for help to find their parents or siblings. Why do they do this? Why don't they simply live out their lives and forget about it? Because they are haunted by the idea that someone out there shares their life, their genes, their flesh and blood. Their winsome desire to meet these people therefore becomes a driving search.

In similar fashion, the Bible refers to all people who have been born of God and received His life as "children of God" (1 John 3:1). The automatic response felt between these people for each other proves we are born of the same Father: "We know that we have passed out of death into life, because we love the brothers. Whoever does not love abides in death" (3:14).[4] This family orientation also surfaces throughout the New Testament with its emphasis upon mutual care, greetings of affection, the closest personal ties, and unprecedented forms of loyalty, such as in John's first letter, where he says, "By this we know love, that he [Christ] laid down his life for us, and we ought to lay down our lives for the brothers" (3:16).

Joseph Hellerman, author of *The Ancient Church as Family*, has identified this sibling kinship as the earliest and most prominent concept that governed the Christian individual.

> From first-century Palestine to third-century Carthage, the social matrix most central to early Christian conceptions

of community was the surrogate kinship group of siblings who understood themselves to be the sons and daughters of God. For the early Christians, the church was a family.[5]

This relational affection and longing is a natural outcome of eternal life. That explains why Christians experiencing the new birth normally seek out church fellowship as soon as possible. We do not feel a magnetism toward organizational systems, but want to find our siblings. It is a desire so compelling within us that John says if we squelch it or ignore it, that means we're abiding in spiritual death (see 1 John 3:14).

> ## RELATIONAL AFFECTION AND WARMTH PROVIDES THE FRAMEWORK FOR BIBLICAL CHURCH LIFE.

A world of broken relationships has made human beings hungry for family. The church, therefore, is something of a gracious bequest for those of us who come to Christ. Indeed, the New Testament directs through a large number of passages how members of the faith family ought (and ought not) to treat one another. The command to "Love one another" leads the pack, being mentioned at least sixteen times (John 13:34). That emphasis demonstrates how relational affection and warmth provides the framework for biblical church life.

The Bible contains many relational commands for us:

- Be devoted to one another in love. Honor one another above yourselves. (Rom. 12:10, NIV)
- Live in harmony with one another. (12:16)
- Encourage one another and build one another up. (1 Thess. 5:11)
- Be likeminded one toward another. (Rom. 15:5, KJV)

- Accept one another. (Rom. 15:7, NASB)
- Admonish one another. (15:14, NASB; Col. 3:16)
- Greet one another. (Rom. 16:16)
- Care for one another (1 Cor. 12:25)
- Serve one another (Gal. 5:13)
- Bear one another's burdens (6:2; Eph. 4:2)
- Forgive one another (Eph. 4:32; Col. 3:13)
- Be patient with one another (Eph. 4:2, NIV)
- Speak the truth in love (4:15, 25)
- Be kind and compassionate to one another (4:32, NIV)
- Speak to one another with . . . songs. (5:19, NIV)
- Submit to one another (5:21, NIV)
- Consider others better than yourselves (Phil. 2:3, NIV)
- Look . . . to the interests of one another (2:4, NIV)
- [Bear] with one another (Col. 3:13)
- [Teach] one another (3:16)
- Comfort one another (1 Thess. 4:18, NASB)
- Encourage one another (5:11)
- Exhort one another (Heb. 3:13)
- Stir up one another to love and good works (10:24)
- Show hospitality to one another (1 Pet. 4:9)
- As each has received . . . to serve one another (4:10)
- Clothe yourselves with humility toward one another (5:5, NASB)
- Pray for one another (James 5:16)
- Confess your sins to one another (5:16)

Once you begin to experience these things, however imperfectly, you will at the same time be experiencing the familial life of the children of God—eternal life in the horizontal.

It should go without saying that such a level of interaction requires sustained contact with others. And yet, for all its blessings, contemporary Christians relentlessly try to sidestep the people component of church. We've often unconsciously traded in fellowship for substitutes like social media. This kind of connectedness is easier, especially when your plate is simply too crowded for real people. And so we climb onto a digital stage, where we can be seen, pitied, commented upon, or "liked," all from a safe distance. Some people I know complain about friends and relatives who will bare the most sensitive details of their lives to strangers online, but refuse to answer telephone calls from their own family. They manage to live a life through carefully crafted posts. Others opt for anonymity within cavernous Christian groups, wishing not to know or be known by anyone else. They never experience the grace of "one anothering." Instead, their only connection is with the lone preacher who stands two hundred feet away on an elevated platform once a week, and who does not know their name. It is a life of "crowded loneliness."[6]

Our culture admires the rugged individual who goes it alone, but the truth is, the life we've received in Christ isn't oriented that way. God addressed this concern at the beginning of the world with Adam: "It is not good for the man to be alone" (Gen. 2:18, NASB). *Not good.* Although Adam had a talking relationship with God, and had been placed in the center of paradise, something was still off-kilter. Nor could animal companionship help it. God had marched all the creatures in front of the man, but with every name Adam gave them, it became clearer that none had life that matched his. Even if he had surrounded himself with Labrador Retriever puppies, an unbridgeable gap would have remained between animal and human.

Until "woman," the bone of his bones and flesh of his flesh, he would never be content. This dissatisfaction should become just as marked with believers when we've surrounded ourselves with people and events that do not have eternal life at their core.

Still, loneliness is weirdly convenient. It allows you to do everything on your own terms, and erects a privacy fence to prevent unwanted intrusions and disclosures. At one point about eight years ago, I had the worst kidney stone of my life. I managed the disabling pain of it with copious amounts of water, herbal supplements, and ibuprofen. During that time I continued meeting with the elders, giving sermons, and attending seminary classes—all with a foreign body inflicting upon me an incredible amount of discomfort.

When I heard that my wife and another woman in the church were praying the stone would pass, I distinctly remember feeling embarrassed. I wasn't keen on the idea of people thinking about what went on in my bathroom. Besides, I thought it was weak to ask for help. Men of God were supposed to shrug off pain and keep going. In the meantime, I couldn't deny that my morale was beginning to wane, as there was no change in my disorder from day to day.

One morning. while my wife was in the other room whispering prayers for me over the phone with her prayer partner, I went to the bathroom and passed that stone. It had been a miserable three months.

Pride gets us all in trouble when we hide behind carefully cultivated appearances. Such inhibition can be utterly unChristlike. Jesus revealed His condition to His disciples the night he prayed in the garden, saying to them, "My soul is very sorrowful, even to death." He not only petitioned the Father, but also attempted to recruit their support, telling them,

"Remain here and watch [pray]" (Mark 14:34). They failed Him; let's not repeat the same mistake toward one another. Nor should we close ourselves off to the kindness of God's family. Sometimes the Father reserves the most effective grace for that which comes through brothers and sisters in the faith.

A person who hangs around the church with little or no interest in this kind of gracious fellowship easily becomes a problem to the congregation. He or she lurks on the periphery, bringing gossip, or furnishing hostile opinions about whatever they think is wrong with the church.

But even those of us who love our faith siblings frequently end up in interpersonal conflict with them. If this were not the case, there would not be so many reminders to love and forgive one another throughout the New Testament. Euodius and Syntyche, fellow workers with the apostle Paul, had gotten into a severe disagreement, and were engaged in a cold war of sorts with one another (see Phil. 4:2–3). And most of the Corinthian church had descended into a state of division.

Contemporary believers try to avoid these problems by fleeing churches, but they only end up looking for the next church they will eventually need to leave. Wherever there are people, there are difficulties. And some of those difficulties are within the very person who is leaving. A large part of what made the previous church "bad" was his or her own poor spiritual condition. However, "messes are incubators for miracles."[7] Major life transformation often occurs in the midst of trying circumstances. Unless the church is overrun with heresy or abusiveness, don't immediately look for the fire escape.

Instead, engage in unstopping wells, and releasing a fresh supply of life. We should practice confessing our faults to one another (see James 5:16) and, on the positive end, strive to develop an inner life that practices the "one anothering" commands of Scripture.

Like dunking a nerf basketball into one of those kiddie-size hoops, it's too easy to bash the church. John Ortberg wrote a book called *Everybody's Normal Till You Get to Know Them*, in which he compared people to porcupines. From a comfortable distance they all look ordinary. Get close to them, though, and you will start bumping into quills.

Marriage, roommates, best friends, and office environments all count as places of painful contact—any situation, in fact, that brings folks together in sustained proximity. You'll discover the person you initially connected with so well seems intolerable later. The one guy in the office you picked to be your buddy is so frugal it's impossible to choose a place for lunch unless he has a coupon. At first you were bemused. As his close friend though, you've become irritated.

> **WHEN PAUL TOLD US TO BEAR ONE ANOTHER IN LOVE, HE DIDN'T MEAN TO TOLERATE THEM, BUT CARRY THEM.**

The church especially counts as one of those places where the quills come out. Believers have an entire range of control issues, hot tempers, social handicaps, secret weaknesses, depressions, dark backgrounds, lusts for more than what we need, tragic mistakes, legalism in the name of God, identity crises, sexual shame, disappointments, eating disorders, procrastination, laziness, and addictions to everything from tobacco to chocolate. People with problems cause problems.

Still, these are your brothers and sisters, people who have eternal life abiding in them. When Paul told us to bear one another in love (see Eph. 4:2), he didn't mean to tolerate them, but carry them. Seek to understand them, but in the meantime, while you don't "get" them, forgo your judgment. In this family dynamic, eventually either they will grow, or you will, or both.

Ultimately, we are not cheerleaders for some kind of church subculture, complete with associated tokens. We are enthusiasts for the brothers and sisters and the flow of life between them. They are not part of a package; they *are* the package. They are not the means to reach a goal; they *are* the goal.

Gatherings—Coming Together in the Living Christ

If you're a fan of simple church philosophy,[8] you will probably find it easy to agree with many of the points we've already covered in this chapter. There's something charmingly idealistic about church community as experienced in daily scenarios. We like eternal life flowing through our backyard barbeques, zoo trips, kids' play dates, celebrations, and hang time. But to emphasize it as being powerfully present in our scheduled meetings, is another thing. Corporate church gatherings call for things we balk at, like structure and planning, especially if a congregation has too many people to meet in a single home.

Of all the most frequently criticized features of the church, regular gatherings must rank at the top. The enduring question is whether an hour and a half, plus travel time, is worth it. We go to work every day of the week, and run kids around to various activities. On Saturday we try to do neglected chores. Then on Sunday we're getting dressed, and rousting sometimes uncooperative children while putting on the Christian gameface. The sheer ongoing discipline of being at the same place at the same time every week can feel like a needless drain. And if you have been tapped as a volunteer, you will feel it even more acutely because of the extra hours for preparation or practice.

In the face of this less-than-inspiring view, evangelicals have coined a rallying cry: "We don't *go to* church, we *are* the church." I believe in the inherent truth of that statement, but many use it to justify distancing themselves from the visible church. They redefine the nature of our gatherings as being haphazard, on the fly, or incidental to other activities. This abstract sort of church life sounds appealing. However, I've followed the literature of those who recommend quitting church, and their alternative approaches never quite lead to the revivals they promise. Besides, those sometimes unwieldy Sunday services that seem to require such exorbitant amounts of time and energy, can have a premium effect upon us, not to mention as a public witness to the world.

Gatherings of all configurations and styles continue to put us in touch with Christ in a much larger way than we could manage on our own. For instance, Jesus promised, "where two or three are gathered in my name, there am I among them" (Matt. 18:20). The idea here is that *even if* a number so small were to come together, He would indeed be present in a palpable way. This does not mean two or three are a suitable replacement for the church at large, but that even in such a small gathering, the living Christ would validate their prayer, making them aware of it.

An amplification of this smaller setting is shown in First Corinthians 14, where the entire church comes together for the sake of mutual building up. Paul specifies inner life as the dynamic going on in it. He wrote,

> I will pray with my spirit, but I will pray with my mind also; I will sing praise with my spirit, but I will sing with my mind also. Otherwise, if you give thanks with your spirit, how can anyone in the position of an outsider say 'Amen' to your thanksgiving when he does not know what you are saying? For you may be giving thanks well enough, but the other person is not being built up. (1 Cor. 14:15–17)

The use of our mind ensures understanding in the other meeting participants, while our enlivened spirit offers a fellowship of life. This cooperation of spirit-mind-spirit-mind in the midst of our meetings, causes building up, which is the chief intention of the gathering (see 14:26).

Not only so, but evangelism is often the result: "But if all prophesy, and an unbeliever or outsider enters, he is convicted by all, he is called to account by all, the secrets of his heart are disclosed, and so, falling on his face, he will worship God and declare that God is really among you" (14:24–25).

And indeed, He is. Christ speaks prophetically in Psalm 22:22, "I will tell of your name to my brothers; in the midst of the congregation I will praise you." The writer of Hebrews picked up this Psalm and applied it to Christian meetings. He saw the assembly singing hymns, worshiping God through mind and spirit, and Christ being there in the midst, singing in their singing with one voice, praising in their praises. Their meeting would therefore bring them into the larger reality of the resurrected Man, Jesus Christ. Assembling together boosts the odds of meeting Jesus, even if you've had a difficult time finding Him. We will come away feeling we have rediscovered His glory, and not that we've wasted an hour and a half.

This is the reason Satanic warfare often surrounds the meeting hour, when a sudden quarrel breaks out, or we come in contact with some issue that creates anxiety. We feel unnaturally fatigued, or suddenly ill. Why? Because the powers of darkness know that the largest Christ you will meet all week is with gathered Christians. His power will be there when you are assembled with others (see 1 Cor. 5:4). If you respond too easily to stimuli that keep you at home and away from the congregation, the same problematic things will always seem to happen on Sundays, except with a smaller dosage each time. One week you have a cold and decide to stay home. Another week you stay home because you think you *feel* a cold coming on. Then you stay in because you're worried you'll catch a cold from someone at church. Before you know it, you're waking up on Sunday and taking a road trip to a local corn dog festival. How did you get so far away? Satan has weaned you from the rich life shared in the congregation.

Preachers like to quote Hebrews 10:25 as scriptural proof that we should regularly attend church—"not neglecting to meet together, as is the habit of some, but encouraging one another, and all the more as you see the Day drawing near." But that is not a standalone thought. Verse 25 occurs in the middle of a sentence, meaning there are thoughts ahead of it already in motion. Note the italicized terms:

> Since we have a great priest over the house of God, let us draw near with a *true heart* in *full assurance* of faith, with our *hearts sprinkled clean from an evil conscience* and our bodies washed with pure water. Let us hold fast the confession of our *hope* without wavering, for he who promised is faithful. And let us consider how to stir up one another to *love* and

good works, not neglecting to meet together, as is the habit
of some, but *encouraging* one another, and all the more as
you see the Day drawing near. (Heb. 10:21–25)

All of these points form a composite, describing the
healthy inward state of a Christian. But notice how right
along with it, the idea of church is interspersed throughout—"the house of God" in verse 21, "one another" in verse
24, "one another" in verse 25, and "meet together," also in
verse 25. The church and positive aspects of Christian spirituality have a symbiotic relationship. They're supposed to
benefit and support each other.

What happens when believers neglect the gathered
church? Some of us would say, "Nothing." But both experience and observation say that's not true. Without the church,
the inner life described in Hebrews 10 will lose its fizz,
like a can of flat soda. Go back through the list of positive
features in verses 21 to 25, and replace each of them with
their antonyms. That's where faith goes when our gatherings
disappear, and along with them, our accountability and commitment toward one another.

ATTEMPTING TO FOLLOW CHRIST MINUS THE BODY OF CHRIST YIELDS POOR RESULTS.

Scripture commands us not to neglect meeting together,
and mentions that some have made a habit of this. My strong
suggestion is that you stop making a decision every week to
attend gatherings, and make that decision *once*. I decided
thirty-seven years ago that barring sickness and travel I could
not avoid, I knew where I would be on Sunday morning.
Otherwise, trying to make that determination every week

would emotionally drain me. A one-time decision meant that if I felt like it, I would attend, and if I didn't feel like it, I would attend.

Did it sometimes feel like duty? Yes, but there are a lot of things in our lives that we do habitually, and out of duty—work, household chores, and various commitments. None of these are more important than giving and receiving life, being built up together, reuniting with those who share eternal life with us, and encountering the living Christ. We made one decision for the exalted head, Jesus, and we need to make one for His body, the church.

Most of my serious backsliding episodes occurred while I was distant from other believers. This included stubborn bouts of depression (I was single and lonely), susceptibility to temptations (I had a wild streak), and breaking the law several times (I had a stupid streak, too). Trial and error has shown me that attempting to follow Christ minus the body of Christ yields poor results. Not only so, but I've noticed that many others who tried the same solo act got similar results—a diluted version of the Christian life.

Often though, people drop out of a fellowship after years of stalwart attendance. There are many reasons for this happening, but one of them is that the church doesn't function very well as life support for passive Christians. An hour's worth of IV drips and respirator tubes once a week on Sunday couldn't possibly be fulfilling for long. This, unfortunately, is the main experience in some congregations that promote passivity. Church fellowship is supposed to be a river flowing between believers, not stage performances, GQ preachers, and perpetually immature people who show up to watch all of it.

And, no doubt, toxic groups dot the church landscape, doing more harm than good. Ex-church folk roam about like wounded warriors, decrying the failures of these "churches." If you pull up a chair they'll tell you plenty. And they are not alone; I have some tales of woe myself. But McCracken reminds us,

> No one should stay in an abusive relationship, and sometimes the line between a highly uncomfortable environment and an unhealthy or unsafe environment can be blurry. We need to be willing to leave if things are constantly toxic and not getting better, but we shouldn't confuse discomfort and dysfunction.[9]

The Bible often describes churches in less-than-ideal ways, like the ones we find in Revelation 2 and 3. Regardless, these problematic assemblies were still called lampstands. The Holy Spirit instructed the believers in those places to overcome the sins and shortcomings there, but never to discard the church at large. You cannot find any scriptural rationale that justifies announcing yourself an assembly of one. As a born-again person, you have a New Covenant right to church fellowship, and you are expected not to give up until you drill down into it and measurably possess it. Yes, it is a cultivated discipline unto spiritual life, as basic as reading your Bible and praying.

At a certain level, deeper than facilities and programs, the gathered church is supposed to grant a foretaste of what eternity will be like. New Testament fellowship is not a lame placeholder. When the great multitude of the redeemed appears at last with Jesus in glory (see Rev. 7:9–12), no one in that scene would rather be doing anything else.

15

A Life Practical, Normal, and Working

INNER LIFE IS NEVER a problem because of there being too much of it. No, difficulties only emerge when there is too much of this good thing imperfectly understood, and therefore improperly applied. For some, unfortunately, "life" has become a spiritual code word that allows a way around rigorous reflection, and even righteousness— "I'm feeling uncomfortable addressing this; let's get back to *life*," or, "Forget the poor; let's pay attention to *life*," or, "I know this behavior was illegal and unjust; let *life* take care of it." These statements all appear to have a commitment to something called life, but a life so truncated it seems vaguely unchristian—aloof, virtueless, and punctuated with spiritual-speak. The following reads as though it might have come straight out of one of their playbooks:

> He saw people love each other, and he saw that love made strenuous demands on the lovers. He saw that love required sacrifice and self-denial. He saw that love produced arguments, jealousy, and sorrow. He decided that love cost too much. He decided not to diminish his life with love.
>
> He saw people strive for distant and hazy goals. He saw men strive for success and women strive for high ideals. He

saw that the striving was often mixed with disappointment. He saw strong and committed men fail, and he saw weak, undeserving men succeed. He saw that striving sometimes forced people into pettiness and greed. He decided that it cost too much. He decided not to soil his life with striving.

He saw people serving others. He saw men give money to the poor and helpless. He saw that the more they served, the faster the need grew. He saw ungrateful receivers turn on their serving friends. He decided not to soil his life with serving.

When he died, he walked up to God and presented his life to him—undiminished, unmarred, unsoiled. The man was clean and untouched by the filth of the world, and he presented himself to God, proudly saying, "Here is my life!"

And God said, "Life? *What* life?"[1]

SPIRITUAL LIFE THAT NEVER TRANSLATES INTO VISIBLE ACTION IS SPIRITUAL POVERTY.

We can easily see in this anecdote an application to believers who get the wrong idea about inner life. They may understand life as a substance to possess, to use selectively for their own enjoyment—spiritual candy. But Peter saw Jesus as something more than a mystic occupied with private feelings. "He went about doing good" (Acts 10:38), Peter said of Him, and we would expect nothing less of the Lord's life today, wherever it authentically appears on this earth.

Spiritual life that never translates into such visible action is spiritual poverty. Jesus said that life is ultimately known by the fruit it produces—"every healthy tree bears good fruit" (Matt. 7:17). This is the most fitting note to strike as we close this book. For after so much has been said of feelings and interior experiences, only visible outcomes *prove* the life within. The Lord Himself modeled this principle. He said, "He who sent me is with me. He has not left me alone, for I always do the things that are pleasing to him" (John 8:29). When Jesus spoke of how the Father was with Him, He could have appealed to some hidden recess of His being, telling us about how He had an eternal life relationship with the Father. Instead, He chose to cite the things He did. True inner life evidences itself in tangible ways.

An Embodied Spirituality

Any time the visible or tangible is brought up, there will be some measure of bias against it, especially from those of us who tend toward deeper forms of spirituality. We love the hidden and inward (rightly so), but to exclude the outward dimension of the Christian life is not a good idea.

We throw containers away when the content has been used up, whether it's milk, soda, or ketchup. They go right into the trash or the recycle bin. Most of us have probably been raised believing it works that way with the human body. There's a common form of theology that teaches when a person dies, their soul goes off to be with God and their body gets buried. That's it, for eternity. This incomplete concept typically treats the body and its many practicalities as little more than a disposable container.

There are serious side effects to this type of assumption. For instance, various schools of ancient Gnosticism saw the body as an inherently low, evil thing. Though Gnosticism did not appear in developed form until the second century, the apostles often confronted and condemned its early strands of error. Paul anticipated this heresy as the focal point of a gathering storm:

> Now the Spirit expressly says that in later times some will depart from the faith by devoting themselves to deceitful spirits and teachings of demons, through the insincerity of liars whose consciences are seared,who forbid marriage and require abstinence from foods that God created to be received with thanksgiving by those who believe and know the truth. For everything created by God is good, and nothing is to be rejected if it is received with thanksgiving, for it is made holy by the word of God and prayer. (1 Tim. 4:1-5)

Note in these verses the negative emphasis upon marriage (in which legitimate sexual relations occur), and foods. Erroneous teachings frequently get around to framing physical items as though they are somehow toxic to true spirituality. Some of these bad attitudes have penetrated Christian thought because, among other reasons, we fail to discern the difference between the sinful tendencies of our flesh, and the legitimate features of our God-created human bodies. Do spiritual people get married, and enjoy having sex with their spouses? We cringe to think of it. Perhaps they do it in order to have children, but certainly, we assure ourselves, not because it is enjoyable. Do spiritual people eat pork rinds, crawfish, or bacon sandwiches? It would be easier for us to think they only consume communion bread.

Our aversions to the body are deeply etched. Author Rodney Clapp writes,

> We do not often consider Jesus of Nazareth with a digestive system and working bowels. Indeed, the church father Clement of Alexandria followed the Gnostic Valentinus on just this point. Clement endorsed Valentinus's opinion

that "Jesus endured all things and was continent; it was his endeavour to earn a divine nature; he ate and drank in a manner peculiar to himself, and the food did not pass out of his body. Such was the power of His continence that food was not corrupted within him; for he himself was not subject to the process of corruption."[2]

No one denies that in a glorified state, and in full possession of our new creation identity, such functions will be needless. However, the spiritual man or woman who reads this book, I trust, has not yet been fully glorified. Nor would it do them any good to pretend otherwise. Spiritual people (such as Jesus!) spoke of bathroom breaks as though He possessed a firsthand experience of them (see Matt. 15:17). And why not? God sent His own Son in the "likeness of sinful flesh" (Rom. 8:3), and "The Word became flesh and dwelt among us" (John 1:14). This was not a special flesh, but an exact replica, without sin (see Heb. 4:15).

The human body does not contradict spirituality. Without a profound respect for it, we will fall into asceticism, that is, extremes of living. We will consider the body a loathsome mule whose legitimate needs should be ignored and resisted at every turn. Under this supposition, we will live as though we are not human.

And yet a dismissal of the body and its practicalities makes way for another fundamental heresy—that the body simply doesn't matter. The Corinthian believers adopted a saying that "'Food is meant for the stomach and the stomach for food'—and God will destroy both one and the other" (1 Cor. 6:13). They were correct about the relation between stomach and food, but not about God's destruction of the body. Our bodies are not meant for discard in a landfill, as though they were inconsequential. But once we accept this thought into our belief grid, worse ideas follow. For if the body ultimately counts for nothing, it makes little difference what we do with it in the here and now. Why not simply gratify illicit sexual lusts if the body will be destroyed anyway? What difference does it make? Surely only the spirit counts? Only the life within?

The Corinthians had begun to reason in just that way, thinking that if the stomach was for use in eating whatever one desired, then sexual organs were also for sexual use in whatever way one desired. These believers inadvertently placed eating shellfish on the same level as having sex with prostitutes. Paul then corrected them by saying, "The body is not meant for sexual immorality, but for the Lord, and the Lord for the body" (1 Cor. 6:13).

In an almost startling move, he added, "Do you not know that your bodies are members of Christ? Shall I then take the members of Christ and make them members of a prostitute? Never!" (6:15). We are joined to the Lord in spirit, according to First Corinthians 6:17, but our bodily members in some sense have also become His members. This should remind us that we are not an assemblage of independent parts (as was pointed out in chapter 4).

That line of thinking would lead us to create separate rules of conduct for the outside and the inside of our being. In certain select areas of life, then, a person could be spiritual, even *hyper*-spiritual, and yet manage to live completely contrary to Christ in certain outward ways, having no compunctions of conscience, no sense of contradiction. They would simply tell themselves that only the spirit counts. All the rest is simply physical equipment to be used until it finally breaks down.

However, our current body, derelict as it might seem, is a precursor to something far more glorious: "If the Spirit of him who raised Jesus from the dead dwells in you, he who raised Christ Jesus from the dead will also give life to your mortal bodies through his Spirit who dwells in you" (Rom. 8:11). Inner life, then, is supposed to affect the body, to spread its influence, until finally at the resurrection, the body is changed.

> So is it with the resurrection of the dead. What is sown is perishable; what is raised is imperishable. It is sown in dishonor; it is raised in glory. It is sown in weakness; it is raised in power. It is sown a natural body; it is raised a spiritual body. If there is a natural body, there is also a spiritual body. (1 Cor. 15:42–44)

"Spiritual body" denotes the final victory of resurrection life, the completeness of God's work, having reached not only spirit, but soul and body as well (see 1 Thess. 5:23). Before that time, while we now live in an imperfect but ongoing state of growth, spiritual life must practically manifest itself through eyes and mouth, arms and legs, hands and feet. It appears in a bodily way.

The Normal among the Abnormal

Not only do poor definitions of spiritual life warp how we view the body, but how we perceive what is generally normal. Inner life people often have the unfortunate habit of conceptually separating Christ from His life. Once we do this, life turns into a cosmic experience void of personality and the whole range of virtues related to personhood. Life becomes a feeling, a power, an influencer, which makes it not very much different from electricity. When we use the term "life," rather than Christ or the Spirit, we ought to be describing the thought of comprehensive inward interaction with God.

During my tenure as a minister and church leader, people have from time to time enthusiastically recommended I listen to certain preachers. They believed this one or that one had some sort of special anointing. "His messages are so life-giving!" they assured me. When following up on these endorsements, I often found little more than stage performances with exaggerated emotions, inflections, and eloquence.[3] It is as though the Christian public assumes "life" is the same as adrenaline. And while separated from Christ, it might as well be. In fact, it could be almost anything you want it to be.

> **THE INNER LIFE DOES NOT TURN US INTO SOME TYPE OF ANGELIC VARIANT THAT TOLERATES THE MORTALS AROUND US.**

Hopefully by this stage in our study, we know that biblical inner life has to do with conscience, worship, and intuition. Still, how is this definition of life ultimately proven? How can we gauge it? Does it show up in austerity? Is it demonstrated through religious eccentricities? Some think so. They seem more absorbed in things they don't do, or can't do, than anything else (*we don't celebrate Christmas, we don't do birthdays, we don't go to movie theaters, we don't go to restaurants, we don't laugh*, etc.). Meanwhile, such people are almost unable to carry on a conversation with another human being because they hardly even inhabit this planet.

Life does not mean we are odd, nor does it turn us into some type of angelic variant that barely tolerates the mortals around us. Personally, I have many interests. In addition to the things you would think are predictable, like long prayer walks, and nineteenth-century theology books, I also like fine art, historical documentaries, photography, bass fishing, drawing cartoons, cooking, fossil collecting, target shooting, indie movies, model railroad magazines, fiction writing, classical music, bookcase war games, vintage trucks, 70's comics, and Ohio State football (when they're championship bound). Some of those latter things don't seem to gel with each other, and they certainly don't fit any deep spiritual stereotype. I suppose it demonstrates that I, like you, tend to be an interesting composition of colors. It also shows that spiritual life does not wipe out our personalities. Rather, it enriches and uplifts them.

We are people who live "Jesusly Normal" lives, although admittedly, we often appear repressed and overly conservative to the world.

> For the time that is past suffices for doing what the Gentiles want to do, living in sensuality, passions, drunkenness, orgies, drinking parties, and lawless idolatry. With respect to this they are surprised when you do not join them in the same flood of debauchery, and they malign you. (1 Pet. 4:3–4)

The surprise registered here indicates that the Gentiles (the non-people of God) have their definition of normal, and they are shocked when we fail to match it. Today, unfortunately, Christian outreach philosophy has sometimes gone in the direction of trying to soften their bewilderment. It tries to prove that Christians can be cool, and that we swear, drink, and indulge in prurient forms of pop culture just like everyone else. But the normal that God establishes does not lie in synchronizing us to the standards of the world. It consists of bringing us into intimate contact with the Holy Spirit, and causes us to become wonderfully human, the way God intended. This is why passages like Galatians 5:22–23 play such a strategic part in our understanding of what healthy Christian life looks like: "But the fruit of the Spirit is love, joy, peace, patience, kindness, goodness, faithfulness, gentleness, self-control; against such things there is no law."

Alexander MacLaren says these virtues are simply "the results of communion with God—the certain manifestations of the better life of the Spirit."[4] Not one item among the fruits of the Spirit is esoteric, or mysterious. It is perceptible, and comes from divinity meeting humanity, producing an outcome that is familiar to other human beings. MacLaren adds, "All the results of the life of the Spirit in the human spirit are to be regarded as a whole that has a natural growth."[5] In other words, the natural, or normal outcome of spiritual life lies in producing this virtuous fruit.

Inner life makes us normal. And in a world so full of abnormality, this indeed stands out. The last phrase of verse 23—"against such things there is no law"—means no one can find fault with the character sketch given here. Its normalcy must be recognized and affirmed by any fair-minded observer.

First, the life of the Spirit produces love. As John said, "We know that we have passed out of death into life because we love the brothers" (1 John 3:14). It is hard to find a more definitive connection between life and love than this one. Love is the fruit of the Spirit, proof that we walk in Him, proof that we abide in life, for "whoever does not love abides in death" (3:14). With such a chief virtue commanded throughout Scripture, and the fact that "God is love" (4:8), it is amazing how spiritual people could fail this test in so many undetected ways—indifference, for instance, or hatred camouflaged with fair-sounding words.

In response to the way moderns turn love into licentiousness, we often go in the other direction, and stress truth, instead. Our reason for doing this lies in wanting to guard the sanctity of God, and not allow standards to be lowered. Unfortunately while doing this, we often come across as self-appointed scolds. A closer reading of First Corinthians 13 will show that we do not need an alternative to love. Love has no valid "other side" for a Christian—nor would we need one. Within love is a limitless commitment to moral boundaries, righteousness and truth:

> Love is patient and kind; love does not envy or boast; it is not arrogant or rude. It does not insist on its own way; it is not irritable or resentful; it does not rejoice at wrongdoing, but rejoices with the truth. Love bears all things, believes all things, hopes all things, endures all things. (1 Cor. 13:4–7)

Love is the expression of inner life, and what others ought to feel from us when they are around us.

Life is joyful. The misguided saint believes otherwise, that a somber, morose attitude shows depth of spirituality. I've known a few of these well-meaning believers, and they seem to drag down the mood in every setting they enter, whether it is a prayer meeting or a meal. They want to demonstrate their weightiness. Instead, they display a certain joylessness. This is not to say joy means goofiness, either. It is an elevated, positive state, a living fruit that occurs as a result of the Spirit's indwelling.

Life is peaceful. Again, superior spirituality is often thought of as being in a conscious state of war against everything we judge as sub-spiritual. We end up stewing over behavior, or over people with whom we disagree. I remember how a church leader once described someone who always seemed to be involved in controversies with others. He said with a sigh, "Everyone bothers her, and she bothers everyone." Imagining ourselves as spiritual powerhouses will only cause us to be like oil on water, never able to blend with others. These attitudes are not a description of life, or maturity of life. It's a ticket to be disinvited from every event, excluded, shunned. Peace comes from the Spirit and is a characteristic of life.

Life is patient. "The patience of God is that excellency which causes Him to sustain great injuries without immediately avenging himself."[6] We know that "God's patience waited in the days of Noah, while the ark was being prepared" (1 Pet. 3:20); later, He waited four hundred years until the sins of the Amorites were complete (see Gen. 15:16). God's timing is impeccable.

I think of myself as a spiritual man, but I'm ashamed to say you wouldn't be able to tell while I'm driving. I am never more aware of my lack of life than when someone takes too long hitting the accelerator after the light turns green. So-called spiritual people excuse a great many of these "inconsequential" weaknesses. Rather, we pay a lot of attention to how we appear in regards to high profile matters, especially if others are watching. Patience, even in small things, is a perfection of trust in God. It is native to divine life, and therefore should show up in us.

Life is kind. We've recast kindness as a sort of grandfatherly weakness. Yet, without it, we would all be doomed. It is the kindness of God that leads us to repentance (Rom. 2:4). Also, "when the goodness and loving kindness of God our Savior appeared, he saved us" (Titus 3:4–5). As this divine trait trickles down to us in the life of the Spirit, it creates a multitude of small deeds. Most of these require no long term plans, or budgets. They tend to be low risk gestures powered by inner life. And they could number in the thousands: A smile. A compliment. An offer to help. An unexpected gift. A word of encouragement. An embrace. A treat. Service. A visit. Such graciousness causes other people to thrive, especially those who feel they don't deserve it, or who are suffering. The very character of the Spirit resonates with doing things this way. His life is a kind life, and when it emerges from us, kindness proliferates.

> **FOR A SPIRITUAL PERSON NOT TO BE PERCEIVED AS GOOD WOULD BE A CONTRADICTION IN TERMS.**

Life is good. I've actually heard from some allegedly spiritual people that goodness is a low virtue. A few of them even demonize goodness by setting it at variance with life. This rationale seems to come from our reaction to the problem of independent goodness, that is, goodness humanly manufactured apart from God. The Bible tells us, "all our righteous deeds are like a polluted garment" (Isa. 64:6). Perhaps from that standpoint, those poor appraisals of "good" are correct. However, to stop with such an unbalanced view is to do a grave disservice to the virtue itself. An immense number of times in the Bible God is called good, as well as His gospel (the word gospel actually means "good message"), and we are encouraged to do good works out of the goodness of the Spirit. Goodness conveys the idea of all-around benevolence, a summation of virtue. In fact, for a spiritual person not to be perceived as good would be a contradiction in terms, and in the eyes of most people, rank hypocrisy.

Life is faithful. The words and promises of men are brittle, frail things easily broken. When spiritual life is prominent in a person, it makes them trustworthy. Paul found this important in his dealings with the Corinthians when they accused him of being fickle. He asked them, "Do I make my plans according to the flesh, ready to say 'Yes, yes' and 'No, no' at the same time? As surely as God is faithful, our word to you has not been Yes and No" (2 Cor. 1:17–18).

People who talk a lot about being led by the Lord often wrestle with the problem of faithfulness. They "feel" led to get involved in many things, then later they abruptly quit. This is what happens when inner life devolves into mere subjectivity. We will find saints declaring that God has brought them to a church or a mission field, or a service. Then, in an evidently premature way, "God" changes His mind. Life does not make us flighty. It causes us to become promise keepers, being where we promised to be, doing what we promised to do.

Life is meek. Though the English Standard Version translates the Greek word *prantes* as "gentleness," it could also be translated "meekness," a word closely related to humility. Even when faced with the problematic Corinthians, Paul entreated them "by the meekness and gentleness of Christ" (10:1). Too many Christian leaders take on an "alpha dog" role that relies on rebuke and rough treatment, as though it were a badge of honor. No one would ever consider them meek—or spiritual.

Again, one of the chief characteristics of the Messiah as prophesied in Zechariah, was that of humility: "Rejoice greatly, O daughter of Zion! Shout aloud, O daughter of

Jerusalem! Behold, your king is coming to you; righteous and having salvation is he, humble and mounted on a donkey, on a colt, the foal of a donkey" (Zech. 9:9).

Humility is a notoriously difficult virtue to nurture, especially for those believers who pay scrupulous attention to inner life. Pride easily grows in places where we don't recognize it, even while we're looking directly at it. Church atmospheres that promote spiritual depth, for instance, might unknowingly foster a great deal of pride, not surrounding one's education, clothing styles, car, or home, but surrounding one's poverty, austerity, suffering, and (most ironic) one's *humility*! Real humility is not a facade we practice. Nor does it mean self-abasement, or thinking less of oneself. Instead, it means not being occupied with oneself at all. Tim Keller has spoken of it as "self-forgetfulness." Life in the Spirit has a habit of being occupied with the loveliness of Christ and the virtues of those around us.

Life is self-controlled. The more spiritual among us want to correct and refashion that statement to read "Spirit-controlled." But Paul got it right the first time. Life means I can say no to myself. Life means I stop overeating. I take steps to control addictions. I stop my mouth from saying those words. I decide to curb the temper tantrum. I don't click the internet link that promises some dark forbidden sexual adventure. I put a stop to online shopping. The more full of life I am, the more I can say no to myself. A person out of control of himself or herself has little handle on spiritual life. "Life needs to do it," they say, in an attempt to escape responsibility. But passivity never accomplishes anything. We are to "Reign in life" (Rom. 5:17), and the first thing we reign over is our own selves.

In other words, without a robust inner life, we are ugly, unpleasant people. Those who assume they are full of the Spirit but exhibit little of the Spirit's fruit are actually full of religion. That is probably why religious folks have garnered such a bad reputation with their neighbors. The power and beauty of life is missing.

It is also why ethical relationships can so quickly deteriorate. For instance, husbands should love their wives (see Eph. 5:25). This may sound obvious, but it is disturbing how a so-called spiritual man can consider himself above love, and even above affection. Nor does the thought of self-sacrifice for her cross his mind. Or the hyper-spiritual wife who feels she does not need to listen to her husband. Why should she, when she is smarter, and more spiritual than he? (Or so she thinks.)

We also sometimes hear about "spiritual" children despising, rather than honoring, their parents. Or the "spiritual" dad who, rather than providing a godly upbringing, falls into physical, sexual, or verbal abuse against his own children. Or "spiritual" employees who, rather than submit to workplace authority, actively undermine those in charge. Or the "spiritual" supervisor who doesn't think he or she owes any respect to underlings, turning the workplace into a bullying environment.

All of these can happen even while the people doing them consider themselves spiritually strong. They assume their inner life is mainly for display at church functions. Though so many grievous and disappointing failures have occurred in these close relationships, probably no greater proving ground for spiritual life exists than in familial or employment circles. Perhaps this is why the apostle Paul spoke with such certainty about household salvation (see Acts

16:31). He assumed newly born-again people would begin living their faith in front of those they knew best. Through this close, sustained contact, new life would be witnessed firsthand—all the virtues and relational uplifts we have already talked about. The hoped-for result would be a domino effect throughout the entire family. Jesus warned that these intra-household relationships could (at least temporarily) become places of conflict (see Matt. 10:35–36), as relatives at first responded adversely to the new Christian among them. But there has never been a more effective evangelistic staging area for His life than among our closest friends and kinsfolk.

The fruit of the Spirit gives that life definition, tethering it to recognizable virtues. Our conscience works to convict any attitudes within us that oppose those virtues. Our worship of God causes us to resonate with those virtues. And our intuition leads us into those virtues. Thus we appear "Jesusly" normal, not strange, erratic, nebulous, or mannequin-like. True inner life has a discernible outward form that reasonable onlookers must at least affirm, even if they continue to resist the verbal preaching of our gospel.

Life that Works

In his era, the apostle James saw among his Christian brethren cases of hidden, stunted faith—precisely the problem we've been discussing. While Paul's list of virtues concern who we are, James especially concerned himself with what we *do*.

> What good is it, my brothers, if someone says he has faith but does not have works? Can that faith save him? If a brother or sister is poorly clothed and lacking in daily food, and one of you says to them, 'Go in peace, be warmed and filled,' without giving them the things needed for the body, what

good is that? So also faith by itself, if it does not have works, is dead. (James 2:14–17)

The very word "works" brings to mind the unfortunate image of a religious slave bearing burdens. It raises the hackles of believers who delight in the doctrines of grace and inner life, and see work as fundamentally hostile to an otherwise happy Christian life. However, James does not seek to invalidate faith, but to assess its health. The example he provided in the verse above is that of someone, probably a believer in the faith community, who is in need. Rather than help him, an alleged man of faith tells that person to go in peace, be warmed and filled. James diagnoses such faith as "dead."

The apostle John provides the same example, and arrives at a similar conclusion: "But if anyone has the world's goods and sees his brother in need, yet closes his heart against him, how does God's love abide in him? Little children, let us not love in word or talk but in deed and in truth" (1 John 3:17–18).

According to John, who exercised the most eminent ministry of life among the apostles, there was altogether too much talking, and not enough true doing.

Both James and John believed the inward dimension of faith should spill over into very practical, outward dimensions like financial generosity. James figured that if your faith could not overcome your closed wallet, then that faith probably shouldn't be considered alive at all. I don't believe the point here has to do with feeding the world, answering the call of every charity that asks for money, nor every panhandler who approaches you. Both apostles use the terminology of "brother" or "sister" which more than likely refers to people in the faith community. I do not wish to suggest we must know someone in order to help them. The Bible provides examples of our ministering to strangers. The point here is that sometimes the opportunities to test the power of inner life are right at our elbows—in the pew or the chair next to us.

James mentions the flowery, but impotent well-wishes to "Go in peace, be warmed and filled" as a religious slogan—an attempt to sweeten the fact that we intend to do nothing.

An additional assumption of this flawed spirituality seems to suggest that physical needs are largely unimportant. It wouldn't be hard to imagine someone under this influence counseling the needy man to "Just enjoy the Lord." James would have opposed that counsel though, by calling it nonsense. "Your faith does not work," he would have told the would-be counselor. Then he would say, "Show me your faith apart from your works, and I will show you my faith by my works" (2:18). Again, this statement demonstrates the concern for a living faith that can be *seen*. "Show me," James says. "Don't just tell me."

> **A FAITH NOT SEEN, NOT BROUGHT INTO ANY INCARNATIONAL REALITY, IS HYPOCRISY.**

Some of us are wary of this kind of exhortation, as if works occupy too central a role in the Christian life. Yet, we have often felt the scandal of a man who talks, feels, and believes all manner of advanced Christian teaching, while neglecting responsibilities at home. He is not appreciated among coworkers, because of his poor office ethic. He is not known for commitment at church. But he claims a deeply felt experience of life. We typically call this hypocrisy, but to put it in more specific terms, it means a faith not seen, not brought into any incarnational reality.

James strengthens his thesis by insisting, "For as the body apart from the spirit is dead, so also faith apart from works is dead" (2:26). With this point we circle back to the idea that living faith needs an embodiment. It cannot dwell in a vague void, or in a cloud of eloquence. Inner life does things, and it ultimately seeks to make itself known.

Nor do we need an inordinate amount of time to figure out what to do. If works are little more than our invention, the burning bush will always be in danger of becoming the *burned-out* bush. It is evident that James does not intend to promote such dead works, but works of faith, as Paul also highly commended— "Remembering before our God and Father your work of faith and labor of love and steadfastness of hope in our Lord Jesus Christ" (1 Thess. 1:3).

We do not need to force ourselves into servile works of human imagination, for inner life has its own resolutions, molded by the guidance of Scripture, and adapted to the needs of others. "To this end we always pray for you, that our God may make you worthy of his calling and may fulfill every resolve for good and every work of faith by his power" (2 Thess. 1:11). "Every resolve" and "every work" tells us that spiritual life is ready not only for grand initiatives, but a far greater multitude of small kindnesses, generosity, personal service, and ministry that requires commitments of time, long or short.

Indeed, premature involvement in high level, complex ministry ideas can become distracting for a saint. As a general suggestion, be more abundantly liberal in personal works, but more discerning in works that need organization, budgets, and volunteers.

Even the most immature spiritual life seems willing to spring into some form of action, though the work itself might appear juvenile. I recall the earliest days of my new and living faith, and the eagerness I felt to preach the gospel to everyone I could, and to do something, anything, that might help someone else. Some of my efforts fizzled, and in retrospect, were awkward, if not silly. But even those prepared me for a future when more daring work would be needed, and I had gotten accustomed to an exercise of self-sacrifice.

In any case, life hardly needs coaxing. It not only works, but it wants to work through any child of God. "We are here as men and women, not as half-fledged angels," Oswald Chambers admonishes us, "to do the work of the world, and to do it with an infinitely greater power to stand the turmoil because we have been born from above."[7]

A Final Word

IN APPROXIMATELY 957 BC, the glory of God filled the temple of Solomon. That day did not make headlines in other nations. It went largely unnoticed by the world. There are no ancient Egyptian wall carvings, nor any other records from the other nations of the Middle East, to celebrate God's gracious condescension to live among men. It may as well have been just another day. And yet, instantly, that temple became the most glorious place on Earth, because it was the chosen dwelling of the living God.

Slowly, as the news spread, people from far away began coming to see. They found that the reports they had heard were true. There was a house peculiarly built in three parts, with a fully functioning priesthood, blood sacrifice, and in the deepest room, hidden from direct view, the God of the universe. Attached to all of it was the fabulous kingdom of Solomon, and the joyful people of Israel. The queen of Sheba said that after seeing the sight, it took her breath away.

According to the latest stats, a similar but greater scene takes place a few thousand times a day, as people all over the world come to Christ. The glory of God enters human beings. Television news never talks about it. No government announces a celebration to mark His gracious indwelling.

And yet, instantly, each deadened spirit comes to life through the risen Lord Jesus Christ, and is born all over again. Now the most living place on earth is the spirit of these saints, the abode of the unique Spirit of Life.

From a distance, no one can see the interactions that take place within us—the power of an enlivened conscience washed in the blood of Christ, worship inspired by encountering God, and intuition that comes from being attached to One whose wisdom is far greater than Solomon. They do not see or know any of this until we open our mouths to "speak all the words of this life," or allow some precious deed of the Savior to reach them through us. Only then does it begin to become clear.

This, my friends, is our story. And every day, like that queen of long ago, it should take our breath away.

Notes

Chapter 1: The Christian Dilemma of Inward Decay

1. Eric Sandras, *Buck Naked Faith* (Colorado Springs: Navpress, 2004), 13.

2. Eric Sandras, 13.

3. Tom Davis & Tammy Maltby, *Confessions of a Good Christan Guy* (Nashville: Thomas Nelson, 2007), 7.

Chapter 2: The New Life—Real, or Religious Delusion?

1. Dallas Willard, *Hearing God* (Downer's Grove, IL: InterVarsity Press, 2012), 283–284.

2. Luke Timothy Johnson, *Religious Experience in Earliest Christianity* (Minneapolis: Augsburg Fortress, 1998), 5.

3. Luke Timothy Johnson, 6–7.

4. Luke Timothy Johnson, 8.

5. Barry L. Callen, *Authentic Spirituality* (Grand Rapids: Baker, 2001), 81.

6. Quoted by William C. Frend, in "Persecution in the Early Church," *Christian History* magazine, Issue 27, Vol. IX, No. 3, 8.

7. Herbert Musurillo, transl., *The Acts of the Christian Martyrs*, quoted in "Perpetua & Polycarp: Two Heroic Martyrs," *Christian History* magazine, (Issue 27, Vol. IX, No. 3), 13.

8. Quoted by John O. Good, in "Martyrs and Confessors," *Christian History* magazine, Issue 27, Volume IX, No. 3, 32.

9. James & Marti Hefley, *By Their Blood* (Grand Rapids: Baker, 1988), 589.

10. DC Talk & The Voice of the Martyrs, *Jesus Freaks* (Tulsa: Albury Publishing, 1999), 124.

11. Voice of the Martyrs, *Extreme Devotion* (Nashville: Thomas Nelson, 2001), 128.

12. Voice of the Martyrs, *Extreme Devotion*, 121.

13. Alexander Roberts and James Donaldson, transl., *The Apologies of Justin Martyr* (Greenwood, WI: Suzeto Enterprises, 2012), Kindle ed.: loc. 367 of 2237.

14. Tertullian, *The Apology*, transl. T. Herbert Bindley (London: Parker and Co., 1890), 114.

15. Julian the Apostate, quoted in James Spencer Northcote, *Epitaphs of the Catacombs* (London: Longmans, Gren, 1878), 149.

16. D.L. Moody, quoted in James Gilchrist Lawson, *Deeper Experiences of Famous Christians* (Bristol: White Tree Publishing, 2018), Kindle Loc. 2544.

17. Charles Spurgeon, *How to Have Real Joy* (New Kensington, PA: Whitaker, 1998), 16.

18. David L. Goetz, *Death by Suburb* (San Francisco: Harper, 2006), 12–13.

Chapter 3: The Miracle Within

1. Victor Kuligin, *The Language of Salvation* (Wooster, OH: Weaver Book Company, 2015), Kindle ed., loc. 484.

2. John Bickford Heard, *The Tripartite Nature of Man* (Edinburgh: T. & T. Clark, 1875), 203.

3. C.S. Lewis, *Surprised by Joy* (New York: Harvest, 1955), 227.

4. Clifford Williams, *Existential Reasons for Belief in God* (Downers Grove, IL: InterVarsity, 2011), 119.

5. Clifford Williams, 79.

6. Timothy Keller, *Counterfeit Gods* (New York: Penguin, 2009), xxv.

7. Elliott Almond, "A Headfirst Dive," *Los Angeles Times*, Aug. 20, 1995. Online ed.

8. Corinne Heller, "Michael Phelps Recalls Depression Battle: 'I Just Didn't Want to Be Alive,'" www.NBCPhiladelphia.com, Oct. 25, 2018.

9. "Water" has been variously understood as: 1) baptismal water, 2) the breaking water of pregnancy in the first birth, or 3) a word synonymous with the effect of the Spirit, drawing Nicodemus' attention back to Ezekiel 36:25–27. My interpretational sympathy lies with the latter thought. However, this is certainly not to imply that baptism is unimportant. All true believers and would-be disciples of Jesus should be baptized, based on His example (see Matt. 3:13–17) and His command (see 28:19).

10. Patrick Kingsley, "The Jihadi Who Turned to Jesus," *The New York Times*, Mar. 24, 2017 (online ed.).

11. Rosaria Butterfield, *The Secret Thoughts of an Unlikely Convert* (Pittsburgh: Crown & Covenant, 2012).

Chapter 4: The Fully Functional You

1. Human physical features are often attributed to God in the Bible—hands, feet, eyes, etc. (a term called "anthropomorphism"). They are used to communicate features recognizable to human beings, but are not meant to suggest that God, who is a Spirit, literally has them or needs them. God is not an absolute unknowable entity, nor is He the same as we are in the vulgar fashion that the Greeks stylized their gods. The incarnation of Christ demonstrated the high respect God has for the human body, however, and His desire to be seen in it. As to our physical creation, our bodies have been formed not only for maximum survival in this world, but appear to follow our inward moral/spiritual/soulish faculties that in a higher way "see," "hear," "taste," "smell," and "touch."

2. Lewis Chafer, as quoted by John B. Woodward, *Man as Spirit, Soul, and Body: A Study of Biblical Psychology* (Pigeon Forge, TN: Grace Fellowship International, 2007), 17.

3. John B. Woodward, 102.

4. William James, *The Varieties of Religious Experience* (New York: Longmans, Green and Company, 1903), 58.

5. Clifford Williams, 32.

6. For those who may not remember, this classic, long-running television show from the 1970s, about a rural family during the Great Depression, featured a lot of home-spun wisdom.

7. C.S. Lewis, as indirectly quoted by Clifford Williams, 113.

8. John Bickford Heard, 112.

9. For a thorough explanation of eternal security, see my book, *Solid: An Indestructible Foundation for New Christians* (Columbus, OH: Gospel Outfitters, 2006).

10. John Bickford Heard, 109, 111.

Chapter 5: Conscience—the Truth-Teller

1. Paul Strohm, *Conscience: A Very Short Introduction* (Oxford: Oxford University Press, 2011), 1.

2. Martin Van Creveld, *Conscience: A Biography* (London: Reaktion Books, Ltd., 2015), 153.

3. Thomas Baird, *Conscience* (New York: Charles C. Cook, 1914), 30–31.

4. Christopher Ash, *Discovering the Joy of a Clear Conscience* (Phillipsburg, NJ: P&R Publishing, 2012), Kindle ed.: loc. 116 **of 3262.**

5. Thomas Guthrie, ed. *The Sunday Magazine for 1867* (London: Strahan & Co. Magazine Publishers, 1867), 472–473.

6. Martin Van Creveld, 210.

7. Martin Van Creveld, 236.

8. Thomas Baird, Kindle ed.: loc. 972 of 1066.

9. Paul Strohm, 71.

10. John F. MacArthur, *The Vanishing Conscience* (Dallas: Word Publishing, 1994), 63.

11. Martha Stout, *The Sociopath Next Door* (New York: Harmony, 2006), 185, 188.

12. Tom Allen, *With No Remorse* (Camp Hill, PA: Horizon Books, 1999), 4–5, 85–86.

13. Martin Van Creveld, 42.

14. Martin Van Creveld, 193.

15. John Bickford Heard, 205.

16. Bonaventure, as quoted by Christopher Ash, loc. 2856 **of 3262.**

17. Thomas Baird, 82.

18. Leon Morris, *The Gospel According to John* (Grand Rapids: Eerd-mans, 1995), 618–19.

19. John Bickford Heard, 206.

20. John Bickford Heard, 213 (quoting Wordsworth's poem, "Ode").

21. John F. MacArthur, 91.

22. John Bickford Heard, 206.

Chapter 6:
Conscience—A Guide to Care and Maintenance

1. Thomas Baird, *Conscience*, Kindle ed.: loc. 943 of 1066.

2. Thomas Baird, 26.

3. Christopher Ash, Kindle ed.: loc. 111 **of 3262.**

4. Watchman Nee, *The Spiritual Man* (New York: Christian Fellow-ship Publishers, 1968), Part 2, 121.

5. Watchman Nee, 121.

6. Christopher Ash, Kindle ed.: loc. 1749-1760 of 3262.

7. Thomas Baird, Kindle ed.: loc. 774 of 3262.

8. Paul Strohm, 45.

9. Thomas Baird, Kindle ed.: loc. 937 of 3262.

10. Christopher Ash, Kindle ed.: loc. 2252 of 3262.

11. Martin Luther, *Book of Concord--Small Catechism* (Online: www.bookofconcord.org, 2001), Preface 02.

12. Paul Strohm, 21–22.

13. Christopher Ash, Kindle ed.: loc. 2061 of 3262.

14. Thomas Baird, 66.

15. Christopher Ash, Kindle ed.: loc. 2141 of 3262.

Chapter 7: The Conscience Gone Haywire

1. Warren Wiersbe, *The Strategy of Satan: How to Detect and Defeat Him* (Wheaton, IL: Tyndale, 1979), 86.

Chapter 8: Worship—Enjoying God Forever

1. Samaritans, a mixed race of Jewish/Assyrian descent, developed a powerful enmity against the Jews after being rebuffed from aiding in the rebuilding of the Jerusalem temple. A rival temple was therefore built on Mount Gerizim for Samaritan worship in the fifth century BC, but John Hyrcanus destroyed it in 109 BC. Herod built another temple for the Samaritans in 25 BC, but they rejected it and continued to worship on Mount Gerizim, the original site of their temple.

2. George Wade Robinson, "Loved with Everlasting Love" (hymn), 1838-1877.

3. John Owen, *Communion With God*, abridged ed. (Edinburgh: Banner of Truth Trust, 1991), 59.

4. Jonathan Edwards, *The Experience that Counts!* (London: Evangelical Press, 1991), 85.

5. Justin Buzzard, "Never Stop Exploring" (blog post, April 11, 2016), online at https://www.justinbuzzard.net/2016/04/11/never-stop-exploring.

Chapter 9: Worship—Cultivating Enjoyment

1. Francis A Schaeffer, *True Spirituality* (Carol Stream, IL: Tyndale, 2001), 5.

2. Charles C. Ryrie, *Balancing the Christian Life* (Chicago: Moody, 1994), 66.

3. Jared C. Wilson, *Supernatural Power for Everyday People* (Nashville: Nelson, 2018), 61.

4. Kevin DeYoung, *Taking God at His Word* (Wheaton, IL: Crossway, 2014), 36.

5. Kevin DeYoung, 39.

6. Timothy Ward, *Words of Life* (Downers Grove, IL: InterVarsity, 2009), 27.

7. Timothy Keller, *Prayer: Experiencing Awe and Intimacy with God* (New York: Penguin, 2014), 56–57.

8. S.D. Gordon, *Quiet Talks on Prayer* (New York: Grosett and Dunlap, 1941), 107.

9. Andrew Murray, *The Inner Chamber and the Inner Life* (New York: Fleming H. Revell, 1905), 72–73.

10. This practical exercise seems to have been first introduced by Hannah Whitall Smith in her book, *The Christian's Secret of a Happy Life* (Bristol: White Tree Publishing, 2017 [from 1899 British ed.]), Kindle ed., 41–42.

11. Donald S. Whitney, *Spiritual Disciplines for the Christian Life* (Colorado Springs: Navpress, 2014), 57.

12. Sereno E. Dwight, "Memoirs of Jonathan Edwards," in Edward Hickman, ed., *The Works of Jonathan Edwards* (Edinburgh: Banner of Truth, 1974), 1:xiii.

13. Andrew Murray, 18–19.

14. Philip Yancey, *Prayer: Does It Make Any Difference?* (Grand Rapids: Zondervan, 2006), 154.

Chapter 10: Worship Falling Flat

1. Watchman Nee, *The Spiritual Man*, Part 2, 226.

2. Bob Rognlien, *Experiential Worship* (Colorado Springs: NavPress. 2005), 117.

3. Brian Steven Borgman, *Feelings and Faith* (Wheaton, IL: Crossway, 2009), 45.

4. J.I. Packer, *Knowing God* (Downers Grove, IL: InterVaristy Press, 1993), 223.

5. Archibald Alexander, *Thoughts on Religious Experience* (Carlisle, PA: Banner of Truth, 1998), 158.

6. D. Martyn Lloyd-Jones, *Spiritual Depression: Its Causes and Cures* (Grand Rapids: Eerdmans, 2001), 109.

7. Brian Steven Borgman, 141.

8. Brian Steven Borgman, 67.

9. Brian Steven Borgman, 206.

Chapter 11: Enlivened Intuition

1. The Bible uses several Greek words for knowledge; *ginosko* and *oida* are often said to mean "knowing about" versus "knowing by experience." However, there is significant overlap between these two; neither word can be said to strictly mean one or the other. Both are necessary to arrive at a knowledge of God.

2. Dallas Willard, 33.

3. M. Blaine Smith, *Knowing God's Will* (Downers Grove, IL: Inter-Varsity Press. 1991), 71.

4. Henry Blackaby and Richard Blackaby, *Hearing God's Voice* (Nashville: Broadman & Holman, 2002), 41.

5. Dallas Willard, 77.

Chapter 12: Intuition Becomes Leading

1. Phillip D. Jenson and Tony Payne, *Guidance and the Voice of God* (Kingsford, NSW: Matthias Media, 2012) Kindle ed. loc. 888–894 of 1929.

2. J.D. Greear, *Jesus, Continued: Why the Spirit Inside You Is Better Than Jesus Beside You* (Grand Rapids: Zondervan, 2014), 22.

3. J.I. Packer and Carolyn Nystrom, *God's Will: Finding Guidance for Everyday Decisions* (Grand Rapids: Baker, 2008), 140.

4. M. Blaine Smith, 158.

5. M. Blaine Smith, 161–162.

Chapter 13: Intuitive Crash and Burn

1. Related both by Arnold A. Dallimore in his biography, *George Whitefield: God's Anointed Servant in the Great Revival of the Eighteenth Century* (Wheaton, IL: Crossway, 1990), 114–115, and Timothy Keller in *Prayer: Experiencing Awe and Intimacy with God* (New York: Penguin, 2014), 62.

2. M. Blaine Smith, 60.

3. Randy Alcorn, *Seeing the Unseen* (Carol Stream, IL: Tyndale, 2007), Kindle edition: loc. 951 of 1719.

Chapter 14: The Church—A Matrix of Life

1. Brett McCracken, *Uncomfortable* (Wheaton, IL: Crossway, 2017), 147.

2. Will Walker, *The Kingdom of Couches* (Orlando, FL: Cru Press, 2005), 20.

3. Brett McCracken, 125.

4. The word "brothers" is a representative term that subsumes both genders, and is therefore not meant to be exclusive. The Bible also frequently speaks of "sisters" as well in other passages.

5. Joseph H. Hellerman, *The Ancient Church as Family* (Minneapolis: Fortress Press, 2001), 225.

6. Randy Frazee, *Making Room for Life* (Grand Rapids: Zondervan, 2003), 33.

7. Heather Zempel, *Community Is Messy* (Downers Grove, IL: InterVarsity, 2012), 40.

8. Although "simple church" is a coined term used in various books and fellowship networks, I use it in a broader, more generic sense. My use of the term means an approach to church that deliberately involves low cost, low tech, and low organizational complexity. Typically that means deprioritizing professional staff, facilities, congregation size, and programming in favor of a more nimble, people-oriented, and truth/life-centered church experience.

9. Brett McCracken, 176.

Chapter 15: A Life Practical, Normal, and Working

1. Wayne Rice, *Hot Illustrations for Youth Talks* (El Cajon, CA: Youth Specialties, 1994), 221.

2. Rodney Clapp, *Tortured Wonders: Christian Spirituality for People, Not Angels* (Grand Rapids: Brazos Press, 2004), 178.

3. I realize that such judgments could easily be called unfair, because they seem only to rest upon the subjectivity of the listener. But even non-spiritual people can discern rehearsed or forced behavior.

4. Alexander MacLaren, *Expositions of Holy Scripture* (New York: George H. Doran and Co., n.d. [digital ed., 2008 on gutenberg.org]), sec. 164.

5. Alexander MacLaren, sec. 167.

6. Arthur W. Pink, *The Attributes of God* (Alexandria, LA: Lamplighter Publications, n.d.), 71–72.

7. Oswald Chambers, *My Utmost for His Highest*, updated edition (Grand Rapids: Our Daily Bread, 1992), 132.

Fort Washington, PA 19034

This book is published by CLC Publications, an outreach of CLC Ministries International. The purpose of CLC is to make evangelical Christian literature available to all nations so that people may come to faith and maturity in the Lord Jesus Christ. We hope this book has been life changing and has enriched your walk with God through the work of the Holy Spirit. If you would like to know more about CLC, we invite you to visit our website:

www.clcusa.org

To know more about the remarkable story of the founding
of CLC International, we encourage you to read

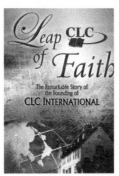

LEAP OF FAITH

Norman Grubb

Paperback
Size 5¹/₄ x 8, Pages 248
ISBN: 978-0-87508-650-7
ISBN (*e-book*): 978-1-61958-055-8